The Vietnam War

Uncovering the Past: Documentary Readers in American History
Series Editors: Steven Lawson and Nancy Hewitt

The books in this series introduce students in American history courses to two impor-tant dimensions of historical analysis. They enable students to engage actively in historical interpretation, and they further students' understanding of the interplay between social and political forces in historical developments.

Consisting of primary sources and an introductory essay, these readers are aimed at the major courses in the American history curriculum, as outlined further below. Each book in the series will be approximately 225–50 pages, including a 25–30 page intro-duction addressing key issues and questions about the subject under consideration, a discussion of sources and methodology, and a bibliography of suggested secondary readings.

Published

Paul G. E. Clemens
The Colonial Era: A Documentary Reader

Sean Patrick Adams
The Early American Republic: A Documentary Reader

Stanley Harrold
The Civil War and Reconstruction: A Documentary Reader

Steven Mintz
African American Voices: A Documentary Reader, 1619-1877

Robert P. Ingalls and David K. Johnson
The United States Since 1945: A Documentary Reader

Camilla Townsend
American Indian History: A Documentary Reader

Steven Mintz
Mexican American Voices: A Documentary Reader

Brian Ward
The 1960s: A Documentary Reader

Nancy Rosenbloom
Women in American History Since 1880: A Documentary Reader

Jeremi Suri
American Foreign Relations Since 1898: A Documentary Reader

Carol Faulkner
Women in American History to 1880: A Documentary Reader

David Welky
America Between the Wars, 1919-1941: A Documentary Reader

William A. Link and Susannah J. Link
The Gilded Age and Progressive Era: A Documentary Reader

G. Kurt Piehler
The United States in World War II: A Documentary Reader

Leslie Brown
African American Voices: A Documentary Reader, 1863-Present

David Freund
The Modern American Metropolis: A Documentary Reader

Edward Miller
The Vietnam War: A Documentary Reader

The Vietnam War

A Documentary Reader

Edited by Edward Miller

WILEY Blackwell

Registered Office
John Wiley & Sons Ltd, The Atrium, Southern Gate, Chichester, West Sussex, PO19 8SQ, UK

Editorial Offices
350 Main Street, Malden, MA 02148-5020, USA
9600 Garsington Road, Oxford, OX4 2DQ, UK
The Atrium, Southern Gate, Chichester, West Sussex, PO19 8SQ, UK

For details of our global editorial offices, for customer services, and for information about how to apply for permission to reuse the copyright material in this book please see our website at www.wiley.com/wiley-blackwell.

The right of Edward Miller to be identified as the author of the editorial material in this work has been asserted in accordance with the UK Copyright, Designs and Patents Act 1988.

Library of Congress Cataloging-in-Publication Data

The Vietnam War : a documentary reader / edited by Edward Miller.
   pages cm. – (Uncovering the past: documentary readers in American history)
   Includes index.
   ISBN 978-1-4051-9677-2 (cloth) – ISBN 978-1-4051-9678-9 (pbk.)   1. Vietnam War, 1961-1975–Sources.   I. Miller, Edward Garvey, editor.
   DS557.4.V573 2015
   959.704'3–dc23   2015019089

A catalogue record for this book is available from the British Library.

Cover image: US Marines wade through a marsh, Vietnam, November 1965. Photo © Paul Schutzer/Time Life Pictures/Getty Images
Set in 10/12.5pt Sabon by Aptara Inc., New Delhi, India
Printed and bound in Malaysia by Vivar Printing Sdn Bhd

1 2016

Contents

Series Editors' Preface

Primary sources have become an essential component in the teaching of history to undergraduates. They engage students in the process of historical interpretation and analysis and help them understand that facts do not speak for themselves. Rather, students see how historians construct narratives that recreate the past. Most students assume that the pursuit of knowledge is a solitary endeavor; yet historians constantly interact with their peers, building upon previous research and arguing among themselves over the interpretation of documents and their larger meaning. The documentary readers in this series highlight the value of this collaborative creative process and encourage students to participate in it.

Each book in the series introduces students in American history courses to two important dimensions of historical analysis. They enable students to engage actively in historical interpretation, and they further students' understanding of the interplay among social, cultural, economic, and political forces in historical developments. In pursuit of these goals, the documents in each text embrace a broad range of sources, including such items as illustrations of material artifacts, letters and diaries, sermons, maps, photographs, song lyrics, selections from fiction and memoirs, legal statutes, court decisions, presidential orders, speeches, and political cartoons.

Each volume in the series is edited by a specialist in the field who is concerned with undergraduate teaching. The goal is not to offer a comprehensive selection of material but to provide items that reflect major themes and debates; that illustrate significant social, cultural, political, and economic dimensions of an era or subject; and that inform, intrigue, and inspire undergraduate students. The editor of each volume has written an introduction that discusses the central questions that have occupied historians in this field and the ways historians have used primary sources to answer them. In addition, each introductory essay contains an explanation of the kinds of materials available to investigate a particular subject, the methods by which scholars analyze them, and the considerations that go into interpreting them. Each source selection is introduced by a short head note that gives students the necessary information and a context for understanding the document. Also, each section of the volume includes questions to guide student reading and stimulate classroom discussion.

Edward Miller's *The Vietnam War: A Documentary Reader* makes a substantial contribution through primary sources to understanding the long history of the Vietnam War or what was really a succession of conflicts. Unlike many other books, this volume ranges beyond the American experience to include the viewpoints of the Vietnamese on both sides of the struggle. It provides American-authored documents such as photographs, memoirs, songs, and speeches as well as selections offered by Vietnamese and people of other nationalities. By combining both American and Vietnamese primary sources, Miller opens up new possibilities for interpreting the origins and consequences of the war. Rather than focusing on the morality of the war, Miller succeeds in helping readers understand why the legacy of the Vietnam War remains so powerful today and an issue that is still hotly debated among Vietnamese and Americans.

The Vietnam War furnishes an assortment of rich documents with head notes and questions in each chapter that will encourage students to create history and show that facts do not speak for themselves. Students can analyze the views of politicians, diplomats, journalists, military leaders, soldiers, protesters, and peasants as they grapple with the experiences and memories of the Vietnam War. In addition, Professor Miller furnishes an incomparable introduction that places this long and costly war in its broad historical context and provides a framework for understanding its evolution.

Steven F. Lawson and Nancy A. Hewitt
Series Editors

Acknowledgements

The study of the Vietnam War poses special challenges for historians. In addition to being a deeply controversial war – not only in the United States and Vietnam, but around the world – the Vietnam War was a very long and complex event, which involved multiple nations and governments, and which profoundly affected the lives of millions across the globe. Documenting such a war in a single volume has proved much more difficult than I anticipated. Yet my work on this book has been made immensely easier by the help and advice I have received from fellow scholars and colleagues. Thanks are due first of all to *Uncovering the Past* editors Nancy A. Hewitt and Steven F. Lawson, who invited me to contribute to their fine series and who provided sage counsel and direction along the way. In my efforts to identify particular primary sources or to track down especially elusive documents, I drew heavily on the expertise of other historians who specialize in the history of the Vietnam War and Modern Vietnamese History; I am indebted to Larry Berman, David Biggs, Haydon Cherry, Kelly Crager, Gregory Daddis, David Elliott, Christina Firpo, Stuart Finkel, Chris Goscha, Tuan Hoang, David Hunt, Matt Masur, Lien-Hang T. Nguyen, Hue-Tam Ho Tai, and Tuong Vu. Special gratitude is due to Merle Pribbenow, who generously permitted me to use his translations of some of the Vietnamese documents contained in these pages, and whose knowledge of Vietnam War history is unsurpassed. I must also acknowledge the aid rendered by the late Vinh Sinh, a model scholar and a pioneer in the field of Vietnamese studies. At my home institution of Dartmouth College, Gail Patten and Bruch Lehman furnished excellent technical and administrative support, while Fran Oscadal and John Cocklin delivered invaluable guidance on library and archival matters. Finally, I thank the outstanding team at Wiley, including Julia Kirk, Carolyn Hensman, Georgina Coleby, and especially Peter Coveney for their dedication, advice, and patience. Their work is apparent on every page.

Introduction

In a city full of monuments, the Vietnam Veterans Memorial in Washington, DC stands apart. Compared with the majestic structures around it, this memorial appears simple and understated. Its central feature is a long, low wall of black granite that is set into the earth and stands only ten feet high at its apex. However, the simplicity of "the wall" belies its extraordinary emotional power. Its reflective panels display the names of more than 58,000 American military personnel who died or went missing while serving in Indochina (the countries of Vietnam, Cambodia, or Laos) between 1959 and 1975. Every year, around three million people visit the memorial. Many of them come to find a particular name, or to remember a friend, loved one, or fallen comrade-in-arms. Others come to reflect on questions about war, peace, and America's place in the world.

On the other side of the world from Washington, another memorial stands in the city of Hanoi, the capital of Vietnam. The Tomb of the Unknown Soldier is located on the edge of Ba Dinh Square, part of an elaborate collection of monuments built by the Vietnamese state and its ruling Vietnamese Communist Party (VCP). Although the tomb is less visually dramatic than the nearby mausoleum of VCP founder and hero Ho Chi Minh, it features a strikingly beautiful archway, similar in some respects to the Arc de Triomphe in Paris. Unlike many other monuments to unknown soldiers, this one does not contain any human remains. This is because it is dedicated to the uncounted "nameless" (*vô danh*) Vietnamese soldiers who died in the fight against the United States, and whose final resting places remain unknown even today. In Hanoi and throughout Vietnam, these soldiers are remembered as "martyrs" who sacrificed themselves on behalf of Vietnam's national struggle against American imperialism.

Back across the Pacific Ocean, in the city of Westminster in southern California, stands a third monument to fallen soldiers. Known simply as the Vietnam War Memorial, it was constructed mostly with funds donated by Vietnamese Americans and dedicated in 2003. In contrast to its counterparts in Washington and Hanoi, this memorial explicitly honors the wartime service of both Americans and Vietnamese. Its central element is a statue that depicts a US soldier standing back-to-back with a soldier of the Army of the Republic of Vietnam (ARVN), the main military force of the anti-communist state of South Vietnam.

Although separated by thousands of miles, the three memorials in Washington, Hanoi, and Westminster are all part of the complex historical legacy of the conflict known as the Vietnam War. Even in comparison to other twentieth-century wars, the Vietnam War was bloody and costly. Over nearly two decades, it claimed perhaps as many as three million lives and consumed billions of dollars. But mere statistics alone cannot reveal the larger historical forces that gave rise to the war, or capture the diverse human experiences that it produced.

For people in Vietnam and the adjacent countries of Cambodia and Laos, the Vietnam War was part of the ongoing process of decolonization in Indochina. As they saw it, the war was a continuation of the political and military conflicts that began in Indochina during the century-long period of French colonial rule. Following the dismantling of the colonial state in 1954, the most obvious axis of conflict within Indochina was the rivalry between communist North Vietnam and anticommunist South Vietnam. However, the communist–anticommunist divide was not the only fault line running through Vietnamese society. Other points of friction had to do with region, religion, social class, and ethnic identity, as well as deep disagreements over what kind of postcolonial nation Vietnam ought to be. Vietnamese therefore perceived the Vietnam War as a civil war, despite the massive involvement of the United States and other foreign powers in the conflict.

For most Americans, the Vietnam War was something rather different. Americans initially perceived the conflict not as a war of decolonization but as an episode in the larger geopolitical clash known as the Cold War. Then, over the course of the 1960s, the war evolved into a bitter struggle on the US home front – indeed, it divided Americans as no issue had since the US Civil War a century earlier. For both supporters and opponents, the war in Vietnam became a touchstone issue not only in debates about US foreign policy, but also in clashes over politics, culture, and morality at home. By the late 1960s, the controversy over the war had provoked acrimonious arguments over whether or not the United States was a "sick" society that had lost its moral bearings.

This documentary reader uses primary sources to explore the history of the Vietnam War from diverse perspectives. Unlike many other books on the war, this volume does not focus only or even primarily on American experiences and viewpoints. Instead, it uses American-authored materials (including government documents, photographs, memoirs, songs, and speeches) in conjunction with other sources authored by Vietnamese and people of other nationalities. My decision to include these non-American sources is not intended to promote a particular interpretation of the war; nor do I seek to provide definitive, unambiguous answers to the enduring questions about the wisdom and morality of the war. Instead, the main objective of this book is to furnish students with the means to craft their own interpretations and to formulate their own answers to these important historical questions. By incorporating both American and Vietnamese primary sources into the study of the war, we can gain new insight into the origins, evolution, and consequences of the conflict. We can also begin to understand why the memory of the war remains so controversial and so fiercely contested today, among Vietnamese and Americans alike.

From Dai Viet to Vietnam

Since the early twentieth century, it has been common for Vietnamese nationalists – both communists and non-communists – to refer to Vietnam as an "ancient nation." Many nationalist writers have traced the origins of this national identity to the period of the Hung Kings (*Hùng Vương*) who are said to have ruled a kingdom based in the Red River Delta of northern Vietnam for more than 2000 years. This kingdom fell to an invading army from Southern China in 207 BCE, inaugurating a millennium-long era of Chinese "domination" of Vietnam. However, despite this lengthy period of subordination, Vietnamese nationalists insist, the residents of the Red River Delta maintained their identity as a separate nation and people. This identity was said to have manifested itself in local rebellions against their Chinese overlords, leading eventually to the re-establishment of independence and the founding of a new Vietnamese monarchy in 939 CE. For the next nine centuries, a succession of dynasties ruled a kingdom known as Dai Viet from its capital at Thanh Long (present-day Hanoi). Meanwhile, Vietnamese settlers and administrators were gradually expanding southward, toward the fertile lands of the lower Mekong river delta. In the early nineteenth century, this "southern advance" culminated in the establishment of the Nguyen dynasty, the first royal house to rule over all of Vietnam's present territory. According to Vietnamese nationalists, this centuries-long process of territorial defense and state consolidation made Vietnamese determined to resist any future foreign invaders—no matter if they were Chinese, French, or American.

In recent years, historians have questioned some aspects of this nationalist historical narrative. One problem has to do with the narrative's anachronistic qualities – that is, its projection of modern-day notions of nationhood backwards onto earlier times. It is doubtful that the ordinary farmers and merchants of Dai Viet ever thought of themselves as members of a Vietnamese nation; they felt much more loyalty to local communities and patrons than to any emerging sense of nationhood. Indeed, the name "Viet Nam" was itself coined only in the early nineteenth century, during a diplomatic exchange between Nguyen officials and the Chinese imperial court in Beijing.

Another problem with the nationalist version of Vietnamese history has to do with its overemphasis on military conflict. Although Dai Viet endured occasional Chinese invasions after becoming an independent polity in the tenth century CE, these attacks were relatively few and far between. Moreover, in the long intervals between wars, Vietnamese engaged in extensive diplomatic, economic, and cultural exchanges with China. Vietnamese politics were therefore defined less by any external rivalry with China than by the fierce internal competitions among Vietnamese elites. During the seventeenth and eighteenth centuries, for example, the territory of Dai Viet was split in two, with one noble house in control of Hanoi and the Red River Delta and another faction ensconced in the provinces around the city of Hue on the central coast.

The nationalist narrative is further undermined by the inconvenient fact that Vietnamese were not always the victims of foreign aggression. Indeed, as the historical record demonstrates, Vietnamese could also play the role of invaders and overlords. This is particularly apparent in the history of the "southern advance," which required the conquest and subordination of non-Vietnamese states and populations. By the early nineteenth century, Vietnam had become an imperial power in its own right, as the Nguyen kings seized control over parts of Cambodia. However, nationalist sentiment was still not yet widespread among ordinary Vietnamese. The emergence of nationalism as a mass phenomenon in Vietnam would come only in the wake of a new conquest of the country – one carried out not by Chinese armies, but by French colonialists.

Colonialism, Nationalism, and the Making of French Indochina

In 1858, a French naval armada appeared off the coast of Central Vietnam. Over the next few decades, French military forces carried out a gradual conquest of Vietnam and the neighboring territories of Cambodia and Laos. In the process, they created a patchwork of colonies and protectorates that collectively became known as "French Indochina." This colonial federation would endure for nearly a century and profoundly shaped the lives of the millions of people who lived within its borders.

The first parts of Vietnam to be ceded to the invaders were its southern provinces, including the city of Saigon and the lower Mekong Delta. In this region, which the French called Cochinchina, a tiny elite of French settlers and wealthy Vietnamese built large rice and rubber plantations that produced crops for export to world markets. The bulk of the southern population consisted of poor farmers and laborers, many of whom either rented land at unfavorable rates or earned subsistence wages on the big plantations.

By the 1880s, the French had also seized control of northern and central Vietnam (known as Tonkin and Annam, respectively). While landowning patterns were relatively more equitable in the northern and central provinces than in the south, most residents of those regions were still poor farmers engaged in subsistence agriculture. In all three regions, ordinary Vietnamese struggled to cope not only with poverty and economic exploitation but also with the onerous policies of the colonial state. These policies included a much-hated "head tax" as well as other levies on commodities such as salt and opium. Rural residents particularly resented the practice of *corvée* labor, in which men were forced to perform backbreaking work on roads, canals, and other public works projects, often for little or no pay.

The emergence of Vietnamese nationalism during the colonial era can be understood as a product of the interplay between two seemingly opposite impulses: resistance and collaboration. From the first stages of the French conquest, many Vietnamese struggled and fought against the colonial state. The most obvious examples of this resistance involved armed uprisings, such as those organized by former Nguyen court officials during the 1870s and 1880s. Vietnamese also engaged in more everyday forms of resistance, such as refusing to show deference to a European, or simply invoking the forbidden term "Vietnam" when they spoke. Paradoxically, however, such acts of resistance were most frequently undertaken by those Vietnamese who were most familiar with – and most admiring of – colonial institutions, ideas, and practices.

The tensions produced by these contradictory impulses can be glimpsed in the activism of Vietnam's first cohort of self-proclaimed "revolutionaries" during the 1900s and 1910s. Phan Boi Chau (1867–1940), the pre-eminent member of this cohort, tried to undermine the French colonial state through various acts of violence, including rebellion and assassination. Yet he also argued that Vietnam needed to appropriate and assimilate European knowledge and culture in order to become a modern nation. The generation of nationalist leaders who followed Phan – those who came of age in the 1920s and 1930s – were even more steeped in the language and culture of colonialism, due to their education in French schools in Indochina and in Europe.

The linkages between colonialism and nationalism are apparent in the life and early career of Vietnam's most famous revolutionary: Ho Chi Minh (1890?–1969). Born in Central Vietnam, Ho harbored patriotic sentiments from an early age. However, he also studied at a school with a French curriculum, and as a young man he applied to be trained as a colonial administrator. After leaving Vietnam in 1911, Ho lived for several years in France, where he first learned about socialism and communism. In the 1920s, Ho became a devoted follower of Vladimir Lenin and moved to the Soviet Union, where he received training in theory and strategy from the Comintern, the Soviet agency set up to promote communist revolutions around the world. In 1930, he founded the Vietnamese Communist Party while living in southern China.

Although Ho would subsequently be criticized by some of his fellow communists for being too focused on Vietnam's national liberation from colonial rule, he insisted that there was no contradiction between his nationalist and socialist convictions. When he finally returned to Vietnam in 1941, he resolved to focus first and foremost on expelling the French from the country. Once the "national question" had been resolved, he reasoned, the communist party could turn its attention to the "social question" and the realization of its socialist goals.

Ho's strategy during World War II was embodied in his 1941 decision to create a new organization known as the Vietnamese League for Independence, or "Viet Minh" for short. The league was a front organization dedicated to fighting the French colonial regime and the Imperial Japanese occupation forces that had just arrived in Indochina. Although ostensibly non-communist, the Viet Minh was in fact secretly controlled by the communist party (which by this time had been renamed the Indochinese Communist Party, or ICP). Over the next four years, Ho and his ICP comrades built the Viet Minh into a formidable organization with substantial popular support. The party also established the first elements of what would eventually become a formidable fighting force, the People's Army of Vietnam (PAVN).

In August 1945, when Japan surrendered to the Allies, the Viet Minh suddenly found itself in prime position to seize power. In a series of events known as the August Revolution – a term selected in conscious imitation of Russia's October Revolution of 1917 – Viet Minh forces took control of Hanoi and many other cities and towns across Indochina. On September 2, 1945, Ho Chi Minh stood before a huge crowd of his compatriots in Hanoi's Ba Dinh square and proclaimed Vietnam independent. He also announced the formation of a new Viet Minh-sponsored state, the Democratic Republic of Vietnam (DRV). In this moment of triumph, Ho spoke only of national liberation, and said nothing about socialist revolution or communism. He also quoted from the American Declaration of Independence – a calculated move designed to impress a small group of US military officers who were present. Vietnam's independence had not yet been secured, but it was clear that the country would never be the same.

War, Decolonization, and the Two Vietnams

The August Revolution of 1945 marked the beginning of the end of French colonial rule in Indochina. Yet it also marked the point at which the United States first emerged as a key actor in Indochinese affairs. Over the next 30 years, the lives of Americans and Vietnamese became intertwined in ways that no one could have foreseen. During this period, Vietnam and the neighboring countries of Laos and Cambodia endured not one but two massively destructive wars: the First Indochina War of 1945–1954 and the Second Indochina War of 1959–1975. While the second of these was the conflict that Americans would come to know as "the Vietnam War," Vietnamese knew that the roots of that later struggle could be traced directly to the earlier one.

The First Indochina War pitted France, which was determined to restore its colonial dominion in Indochina, against Ho and the Viet Minh movement. Although both antagonists appealed to the United States for assistance – Ho asked US President Harry Truman in 1946 to "interfere urgently in support of our independence" – Washington initially opted to remain neutral. However, by the late 1940s US strategists had come to view Indochina as a key front in the global Cold War against the Soviet Union. Following the 1949 victory of Mao Zedong's communist movement in the Chinese civil war, many American leaders began to worry about a "domino effect" in which Asian nations would fall to communism one by one. Truman's calculations were also affected by an emerging "red scare" within the United States, and especially by allegations of communist subversion within his administration.

In early 1950, Truman endorsed a State Department proposal to militarize the Cold War through massive increases in defense spending. Shortly afterwards, he announced the dispatch of military and economic aid to French forces in Indochina. By 1954, American assistance covered more than three-fourths of the cost of France's war effort.

The massive influx of American aid to the French after 1950 was matched by the Soviet Union and the People's Republic of China, both of which began supplying the Viet Minh with weapons, supplies, and strategic advice. This outside aid greatly increased the firepower wielded by both sides in the war, but did not allow either to gain a decisive edge on the battlefield. After years of stalemate, the Viet Minh finally scored a dramatic victory in 1954, when they besieged and captured a French base in a remote northern valley known as Dien Bien Phu. In the midst of the siege, desperate French officials asked Truman's successor, Dwight D. Eisenhower, to use American airpower to save the garrison. Eisenhower initially seemed in favor of meeting the French request – and may even have toyed with the possible use of a tactical nuclear strike – before deciding against intervention.

The Viet Minh victory at Dien Bien Phu held enormous symbolic value, and it convinced French leaders to make peace. However, the ensuing negotiations, held at an international conference at Geneva during the summer of 1954, resulted in a compromise settlement. The agreement, known as the Geneva Accords, stipulated that Vietnam was independent, but that the country would be temporarily split in two. All territory north of the 17th parallel was to be administered by Ho's DRV government from its capital at Hanoi. The land to the south of that line was placed under the jurisdiction of the Saigon-based State of Vietnam, soon to be renamed the Republic of Vietnam (RVN). The Accords specified that this arrangement would last for no more than two years, and would end with nationwide reunification elections to select a single, all-Vietnam government. These terms were considerably less than the complete victory that Ho and his communist comrades had hoped to claim. However, they decided to accept the accords, with the expectation that the prestige they had gained in the war against France would translate into popularity at the ballot box.

The reunification elections were never held. The primary reason was the opposition of Ngo Dinh Diem, a devout Catholic and staunch anticommunist who became the leader of the Saigon regime in mid-1954. After outmaneuvering his rivals and consolidating his grip on power in the south, Diem announced that he would not be bound by the terms of the Geneva agreements (which his government had not endorsed) and that he had no intention of consulting with DRV leaders about the elections. Hanoi protested bitterly, but to no avail. After some initial hesitation, American leaders backed Diem strongly and the US media hailed him as the "miracle man" of Southeast Asia. By 1955, Washington had displaced the French as the primary provider of military, economic, and diplomatic support to Diem's RVN government. The divide between North Vietnam and South Vietnam (as the DRV and RVN states were now unofficially called) seemed to be hardening into a permanent separation.

Diem proceeded to implement an elaborate array of nation-building programs in South Vietnam. These included various schemes to relocate large numbers of rural residents to newly created communities, many of them in remote parts of the Mekong Delta and Central Highlands. Diem also launched the "Denounce Communists" campaign, which used propaganda and surveillance to root out the covert network of communist operatives who had remained in the south after Geneva. The regime's methods were brutally effective, at least in the short term. By the late 1950s, more than 80% of these stay-behind cadres – whom RVN officials disparagingly referred to as "Viet Cong" – had been detained or killed. Diem's ruthless efficiency in the south seemed a sharp contrast with the situation in North Vietnam, where the DRV government's harsh land reform program resulted in the executions of thousands of people, including many who had previously supported the revolution. In 1956, Ho Chi Minh felt obliged to issue a public apology for the "errors." By the end of the decade, it seemed to many observers that South Vietnam had begun to pull ahead of the North in the competition between the two states.

It was at this seemingly inauspicious moment that insurgents in South Vietnam launched the rebellion that would eventually become the Vietnam War. Small-scale attacks on isolated government targets during 1959 gave way to a series of "concerted uprisings" in the Mekong Delta in 1960. By the following year, the rebels had seized the initiative and controlled large swaths of territory and population. In its initial stages, the insurrection was fueled by popular anger with official corruption and Diem's indiscriminate security measures. The latter included his draconian 10/59 law, which permitted summary executions by guillotine. However, the insurgency was also driven by the actions of communist party cadres, who played a critical role in organizing the resistance and in mobilizing popular participation in it – by persuasion if possible, but also by manipulation and coercion when necessary. In December 1960, the rebels announced the formation of the National Liberation Front for South Vietnam (NLF). Although it was ostensibly a noncommunist organization open to anyone who was willing to fight the South Vietnamese government, the NLF was in fact controlled from the outset by communist operatives, who took their orders from the senior party leadership in Hanoi.

The rapid expansion of the insurgency was cause for concern in both Saigon and Washington. In 1961, the newly inaugurated US President John F. Kennedy rejected his advisors' recommendations to send American combat units to South Vietnam. However, he sharply increased economic and military aid to Diem's government, and also greatly expanded the number of American military advisors working with the South Vietnamese army, the Army of the Republic of Vietnam (ARVN). At first, this new approach seemed to work. During 1962, the ARVN's battlefield performance against the NLF improved dramatically, thanks in part to the increased mobility conferred by US-supplied helicopters and armored vehicles. Meanwhile, the Diem government launched an ambitious counterinsurgency initiative known as the Strategic Hamlet Program, which aimed to fortify every rural settlement in South Vietnam to protect the population from the "Viet Cong." However, the insurgents soon devised new tactics to counter these threats. At the Battle of Ap Bac in January 1963, an NLF unit mauled a much larger ARVN force and shot down five helicopters before escaping. The revolutionaries also discovered that many of the Strategic Hamlets had been built too quickly and were inadequately defended.

In the end, Diem's fate was sealed not by his communist enemies, but by his former supporters and allies. In spring 1963, South Vietnam was plunged into crisis by anti-Diem protests led by Buddhist monks. Although many of the protest leaders had previously enjoyed good relations with the government, they now accused Diem of religious favoritism and persecution. The movement garnered worldwide attention due to the self-immolation of the monk Thich Quang Duc, who was photographed as he burned himself to death on a Saigon street. As the political crisis in Saigon escalated, Diem disregarded US warnings not to use force against the Buddhists. In August, RVN security forces crushed the movement with a series of midnight raids against the pagodas that served as the movement's headquarters. Shortly after the crackdown, Kennedy gave his approval – albeit in a highly qualified and ambivalent manner – to a plan to encourage the ARVN's senior generals to overthrow Diem.

The ARVN coup against Diem was launched on November 1, 1963, and Diem and his brother Ngo Dinh Nhu were detained and killed the next day. Kennedy himself would be assassinated in Dallas just three weeks later. This historical coincidence meant that the president did not have to face the consequences of the regime change he had authorized. It would also spark a retrospective debate about what further choices Kennedy would have made in Vietnam if he had lived. A few weeks before his death, Kennedy approved a plan to begin withdrawing US military advisors from the country, a decision that some commentators would later cite as evidence of his determination to get out of the war. However, others note that the withdrawal seemed to be based on the mistaken assumption that the ARVN was marching toward victory over the NLF – a belief that events would soon disprove. Because the question of what Kennedy *might* have done is a counterfactual one, it will never be settled definitively. There is no doubt, however, that the events of November 1963 would have far-reaching and devastating effects for the United States and Vietnam. For the citizens of both countries, the war's destruction and turmoil was about to begin in earnest.

Lyndon Johnson's War

The coup against Diem helped to set the stage for a massive escalation of the Vietnam War over the next two years. A few weeks after the coup, the communist party's central committee in Hanoi endorsed a plan to bring down the South Vietnamese government quickly, by stepping up the rate at which PAVN soldiers were infiltrating South Vietnam from the North. This shift in strategy was the work of Le Duan, the party's First Secretary and a longtime advocate of a more aggressive strategy in the south. During the first months of 1964, it appeared that Le Duan's objectives might be within reach. Saigon endured a series of short-lived governments, each seemingly less competent than the previous one. Meanwhile, NLF forces made rapid gains in the countryside. In May, the US Central Intelligence Agency warned that the "tide of deterioration" could result in the collapse of the RVN state by the end of the year.

Unfortunately for Le Duan, the new US president had escalatory plans of his own. Lyndon Johnson brought a unique mix of ambition and insecurity to the White House. Although he dreamed of ending poverty in America and promoting development in Third World nations, Johnson was also anxious not to become "the first American president to lose a war," as he put it. In August 1964, the president seized on reports that PAVN torpedo boats had twice fired upon US destroyers operating in international waters in the Gulf of Tonkin, off the coast of North Vietnam. At Johnson's behest, Congress quickly passed a resolution that denounced the DRV's "deliberate and systematic campaign of aggression" and authorized the president to take "all necessary measures" in response. The White House did not disclose that the US ships had been supporting a covert mission to infiltrate South Vietnamese commandos into North Vietnam; nor did it acknowledge that the reports of the second of the alleged torpedo attacks turned out to be erroneous. The resolution was endorsed unanimously in the House of Representatives, and with only two dissenting votes in the Senate.

In his initial moves after the Tonkin Gulf incident, Johnson was careful to display restraint, insisting that the US sought "no wider war" in Vietnam. However, following his landslide victory in the November 1964 presidential election, he moved quickly both to expand the war and to transform it into an American conflict. In February 1965, Johnson ordered the US Air Force and Navy to launch Operation Rolling Thunder, a strategic bombing campaign against North Vietnam that was intended to force Hanoi to cease its support for the insurgency in the south. For the next three-and-a-half years, American bombs fell on North Vietnam on an almost daily basis.

The start of the air war led in short order to the deployment of US ground forces to South Vietnam. In June 1965, in response to a request from General William Westmoreland, the top US Army commander in Vietnam, Johnson ordered the dispatch of tens of thousands of troops and promised to send additional units as necessary. In doing so, he disregarded the advice of Undersecretary of State George Ball, who presciently warned the president that victory in Vietnam might prove impossible. By the end of the year, there were 184,000 US military personnel in South Vietnam, with more on the way.

Le Duan's and Johnson's decisions paved the way for a massively more violent and destructive war. Between 1965 and 1968, General Westmoreland pursued a strategy that combined "pacification" operations in South Vietnamese villages with large-scale "search and destroy" missions against enemy main force units. In this way, he aimed to isolate the NLF from the rural population that sustained it, while also waging a war of attrition against the PAVN. Such a strategy seemed sensible, insofar as it was designed to exploit the substantial firepower advantages enjoyed by US forces.

However, Westmoreland's strategic objectives led him to adopt controversial tactics: the forced relocation of civilians and the deliberate destruction of their homes and farms; the establishment of "free fire zones" in which US and RVN units were allowed to treat any human being they encountered as a hostile combatant; the heavy reliance on post-battle "body counts" of dead Vietnamese as an indicator of progress in the war. Such tactics, critics charged, were counterproductive, since they often alienated the Vietnamese hearts and minds that US officials claimed to want to win. Even worse, these tactics were blamed for creating a permissive environment in which US soldiers, sailors, airmen, and marines could violate the laws of war with impunity. As the war ground on, journalists, veterans, and others alleged that American forces routinely committed torture, rape, mutilation, and murder in Vietnam. For many Americans back home, these charges were powerfully substantiated by revelations about the My Lai massacre, a 1968 incident in which a US Army company slaughtered hundreds of defenseless civilians in a village in Central Vietnam.

While media attention in the United States and around the world focused mainly on the fighting in South Vietnam and the bombing of the North, a more hidden – but no less violent – struggle was taking place across the border in landlocked Laos. Laos had been in upheaval since 1960, following the collapse of a power-sharing agreement among the country's communist, anticommunist, and neutralist factions. North Vietnamese forces exploited the turmoil by using Lao territory to smuggle soldiers and supplies into South Vietnam via a network of paths and roads known as the "Ho Chi Minh trail." In late 1964, in a bid to interdict the traffic along the trail, Lyndon Johnson launched what would become a nearly decade-long bombing campaign in Laos. By 1973, US warplanes had dropped more than 2.1 million tons of explosives on Laos, making it the most bombed country on a per capita basis in world history. Meanwhile, CIA operatives funneled weapons and money to anticommunist forces, including a guerrilla army made up mostly of members of the Hmong ethnic group. To finance these activities, the agency became involved in the Lao opium trade. All of these measures were conducted illegally and secretly, to preserve the fiction that the US was supporting the neutrality of Laos. However, they mostly failed to disrupt traffic along the trail, which actually expanded during the late 1960s and early 1970s.

The Tet Offensive and the Quest for "Peace with Honor"

The infiltration of men and supplies via the Ho Chi Minh trail was merely one component of the larger strategy for victory that the PAVN and the NLF were pursuing. Although the communists claimed to be following Mao Zedong's model of "people's war," Le Duan was not content to rely only on guerrilla tactics. Instead, he instructed his commanders in the south to fight and win "decisive victories" against US and ARVN units. According to Le Duan, such victories would pave the way for a "general offensive, general uprising" – an all-out military attack on South Vietnam's cities and towns, followed by a general uprising of the population against the RVN state. Although the revolutionaries mostly failed to win the "decisive victories" on the scale that Le Duan envisioned, by mid-1967 he was convinced that the time had come to move to the next stage of the plan.

NLF and PAVN units scheduled the Tet Offensive for the first day of Vietnam's lunar new year holiday in late January 1968. In keeping with the "general offensive" component of the plan, the attackers struck high-profile targets inside all of South Vietnam's major cities and towns. In Saigon, NLF fighters took over part of the US embassy compound for several hours.

However, despite having achieved tactical surprise, the revolutionaries were quickly thrown back in most areas following counterattacks by American and South Vietnamese troops. Although US forces sustained their heaviest losses of the war during the offensive, the casualties on the communist side were far higher, especially among NLF units. Even worse for the revolutionaries, the expected "general uprising" of the urban population did not materialize. In these respects, Tet '68 was clearly a defeat for the insurgents.

However, in many other ways, the Tet Offensive would redound to the communists' benefit. In the first days of the offensive, the extent of the insurgents' losses was far from clear. What *was* clear to most Americans was that the victory that Johnson and Westmoreland had promised was nowhere in sight, even after three years of fighting. It was also apparent that the toll of American dead and wounded was rising, overall support for the war among the US public was waning, and the deficit spending that Johnson had used to fund the war to that point had become unsustainable. Americans were shocked by some of the media coverage of the offensive, especially an Associated Press photograph that depicted the RVN National Police Chief shooting a captured "Viet Cong" suspect to death on a Saigon street. Among those who realized that Tet marked a turning point in the war was Lyndon Johnson. On March 31, he announced that the US was curtailing the bombing campaign against North Vietnam and offered to begin peace talks with Hanoi. He then stunned the country by withdrawing from the 1968 presidential race.

In January 1969, Johnson handed over the White House to Richard Nixon, who had eked out a narrow win in the election two months earlier. Nixon, who ran on a promise to get America out of the war, realized that outright military triumph in Vietnam was infeasible. However, he was still determined to secure what he called "peace with honor." He would spend the next four years in pursuit of this ill-defined goal. Along with his National Security Advisor, Henry Kissinger, Nixon envisioned a negotiated settlement with Hanoi that would preserve South Vietnam's status as an independent and non-communist state – if not indefinitely, then at least for a period of time. In the meantime, he planned to unilaterally withdraw American troops from the war – US force levels peaked in 1969 and declined steadily thereafter – and to systematically strengthen the ARVN in a process dubbed "Vietnamization." Unfortunately for Nixon, this scheme did not produce the diplomatic breakthrough he wanted. Although DRV representatives agreed to hold secret talks with Kissinger beginning in 1969, they did so mainly to buy time in which to rebuild their forces and recover from the losses sustained during Tet. As his frustration grew, Nixon tried to increase the pressure on Hanoi by launching "incursions" against PAVN units operating inside Cambodia (1970) and Laos (1971).

Like Johnson before him, Nixon had to contend with one of the strongest domestic antiwar movements in American history. From its origins in 1965, the movement was diverse and diffuse. It began as a "movement of movements," a coalition of peace groups, civil rights activists, and leftist student organizations. Its participants initially concentrated on legal forms of antidraft activism, protest marches and demonstrations, and educational "teach-ins" on college campuses. By the late 1960s, the antiwar cause had gained significant support among politically moderate Americans, including several members of Congress. However, it also attracted more radical adherents, including some who embraced the use of violence as a form of protest. At the same time, movement supporters were increasingly subjected to violence, including attacks perpetrated by US government agencies and police forces. In Chicago during August of 1968, antiwar demonstrators who had gathered in a park outside the Democratic Party's National Convention were brutally assaulted by city police officers. In the spring of 1970, National Guardsmen shot and killed four students during an antiwar protest at Kent State University in Ohio; a few days later, two more demonstrators were gunned down by police at Jackson State University in Mississippi.

While many Americans deplored the use of violence against peaceful antiwar demonstrators, such sentiments did not always translate into sympathy for the movement or its goals. For all of its considerable strength, the American movement to end the Vietnam War failed to gain majoritarian support. Media coverage of the movement tended to focus disproportionately on the violent forms of protest embraced by radical groups such as the Weather Underground, a Marxist–Leninist organization that advocated the overthrow of the US government. Meanwhile, conservative critics of the movement associated it with hippies, drugs, and other elements of the 1960s counterculture; they also exploited growing racial tensions in US society, and the resulting white backlash against the African American freedom struggle. Nixon proved especially adept at appealing to what he described as the "silent majority" of Americans who found the antiwar movement distasteful. In the 1972 presidential election, despite having failed to deliver on his 1968 campaign promise to get the United States out of Vietnam, Nixon trounced the antiwar candidate George McGovern, winning more than 60% of the popular vote. By that point, both the war and the antiwar movement were deeply unpopular in the United States – an ironic turn of events that would have enduring implications for postwar battles over the meaning and memory of the war.

Victories, Defeats, Legacies, and Lessons

Nixon finally reached a negotiated settlement with North Vietnamese leaders – albeit one that seemed to fall short of "peace with honor" in the eyes of many. In March 1972, PAVN forces launched a massive new offensive designed to smash the retooled ARVN. However, after making strong initial gains, the attackers were forced back by stiffer-than-expected South Vietnamese resistance and by Nixon's massive deployment of US tactical airpower. In the wake of this latest setback, DRV leaders signaled they were finally ready to make a deal. The Paris Peace Accords of January 1973 obliged North Vietnam to return several hundred US prisoners of war and also permitted South Vietnamese President Nguyen Van Thieu to remain in power. However, in a critical concession to Hanoi, the Accords made no mention of the hundreds of thousands of PAVN soldiers who had been infiltrated into South Vietnam and who continued to pose a mortal threat to the RVN regime.

In the end, the Paris Accords did little to promote the cause of peace in Vietnam. Fighting between North and South Vietnamese forces had resumed even before the last US combat units had departed in March 1973. The war between the two Vietnams continued for two more years, and for a time it seemed as if the RVN regime might survive indefinitely. However, in early 1975, PAVN probes in the Central Highlands discovered that ARVN defenses there appeared to be crumbling. Communist leaders in Hanoi approved the launch of yet another offensive, with the expectation that it would last two years. However, this assessment proved far too pessimistic. Within weeks, North Vietnamese forces had seized control of the northern half of South Vietnam and were closing in on Saigon. In the South Vietnamese capital, US officials delayed ordering an evacuation to avoid triggering a general panic. However, this served only to make the actual evacuation more chaotic and resulted in thousands of Vietnamese being left behind, despite promises to the contrary. The last helicopters took off from the roof of the US embassy shortly after dawn on April 30, 1975. A few hours later, a PAVN tank crashed through the main gate of the South Vietnamese presidential palace.

In the United States, some Americans responded to the end of the Vietnam War by declaring that the conflict could and should be forgotten as quickly as possible. US President Gerald Ford urged his fellow citizens to "stop refighting the battles and recriminations of the past" and instead look to the future. But the war proved difficult to put aside. Beginning in the late 1970s and early 1980s and continuing in the decades since, Americans have explored the history, memory, and meaning of the war via books, Hollywood films, college courses, memorials, and museum exhibits. The war has also figured prominently in political campaigns, academic conferences, courtrooms, and media commentaries. Many of these ways of thinking and talking about the war have revolved around the experiences of US veterans – both their battlefield service and the cold and hostile treatment that many of them received upon their return home. Americans have also grappled with some of the war's most painful emotional and physical legacies, such as the widespread incidence of post-traumatic stress disorder (PTSD) among former soldiers. Many veterans continue to struggle with devastating health impacts of Agent Orange, a toxic chemical defoliant, which US forces used to destroy vegetation and ground cover in South Vietnam, but which was later shown to be dangerous to humans.

Not surprisingly, memories and legacies of the war have also featured prominently in the politics and culture of Vietnam since 1975. For the victorious VCP, the outcome of the war was the triumphant culmination of the country's long struggle for national liberation. However, the early postwar period was a time neither of peace nor of prosperity for Vietnam, due both to a disastrous effort to collectivize the economy and to a new series of military clashes with China and the Khmer Rouge regime in Cambodia. Beginning in the mid-1980s, Vietnam's economic prospects began to improve with the adoption of market-style reforms, and the 1990s was an era of growth and optimism, underlined by the normalization of diplomatic ties with the United States in 1995. Throughout this period and down to today, VCP historians have faithfully tended to the official narrative of "the war of resistance against the Americans," as the conflict is officially known. However, even as the communist party has retained its monopoly on political power in Vietnam, alternative ways of remembering the war and its legacies have appeared and proliferated. In novels, short stories, newspaper articles, public speeches, and private acts of commemoration, Vietnamese have found ways to remember the war and the often devastating impact it had on their communities and families, as well as on their nation. In Vietnam, no less than in the United States, the Vietnam War is remembered in multiple and often divergent ways, even as the governments of both nations continue to promote official forms of commemoration.

Reading the Documents: Key Questions

The documents presented in this volume have been selected to provide readers with multiple perspectives on the complex history of the Vietnam War. While the documents raise many important issues and problems in this history, the following questions may prove particularly useful when reading and discussing them.

What was the nature and role of Vietnamese nationalism in the history of the Vietnam War?

References to national liberation and resistance to foreign domination figure prominently in many of the documents. However, the documents also suggest that Vietnamese nationalism was far from uniform or monolithic – in other words, there were many different ways of being a Vietnamese nationalist during the Vietnam War, and no one group or party had a monopoly on nationalist sentiments. By examining the different expressions of nationalist identity contained in these documents, readers can acquire a more nuanced understanding of how nationalism shaped the actions and ambitions of various Vietnamese groups and individuals.

How and why did US leaders decide to invest massive amounts of blood, treasure, and prestige in Vietnam during the period between 1950 and 1975?

Historians have long stressed the importance of Cold War geopolitical considerations and specifically the belief in the "domino theory" as key causal factors behind the US intervention. However, some authors have perceived other motives – economic interests, electoral considerations, racism, ideas about modernization and development – lying underneath the Cold War rhetoric. Many of the documents shed light on these diverse motives and provide clues about the concerns that loomed largest in the minds of US leaders.

What were the key turning points in the history of the Vietnam War, and what explains the eventual outcome of the conflict?

Most scholars agree that the Tet Offensive of 1968 was a watershed, but there are sharply different views of how and why Tet contributed to the eventual victory of the Vietnamese Communist movement and the defeat of the United States and South Vietnam. Some maintain that the US could have prevailed if it had prosecuted the war differently (either before or after Tet). Others hold that the defeat of South Vietnam was inevitable, no matter what strategies or tactics the US might have pursued.

What were the domestic political, cultural, and social effects of the Vietnam War in both the United States and Vietnam?

The Vietnam War was profoundly important to both nations – and not solely because of the deaths and injuries that it inflicted. In different ways, the war became the defining issue of the day both in the US and in Vietnam. Military veterans and the civilian victims of combat were among those most obviously affected by the war, but the conflict also impacted millions of Americans and Vietnamese who never set foot on a battlefield. Significant antiwar movements appeared in both countries, and the controversy engendered by the war created or exacerbated numerous political, cultural, and social fissures, many of which endured long after the war had ended (and some of which still endure today).

Chapter 1   Colonialism, Nationalism, and Communism

Tam Lang, I Pulled a Rickshaw (1932)[1]

*The 1920s and 1930s were a time of great political, social, and cultural
upheaval in French Indochina. As some young Vietnamese embraced
revolutionary causes, others became advocates for various kinds of social and
cultural reform. While these reformers often criticized the colonial state and
its policies, they maintained that national liberation required Vietnamese to
abandon traditional practices in favor of "modern" notions about family life,
gender roles, labor, education, and social relations. The reform impulse could
be glimpsed in the work of Vietnamese novelists, memoirists, and journalists,
many of whom styled themselves social realists, in imitation of their
counterparts in France and other European countries.*

*One prominent Vietnamese social critic of the interwar period was Vu
Dinh Chi, who wrote under the pen name of Tam Lang. A native of Hanoi,
Tam Lang began working as a journalist in the 1920s and earned a
reputation for attacking social injustice. In 1932, he garnered wide attention
for his investigative report entitled "I pulled a Rickshaw" (Tôi kéo xe). The*

[1] *The Light of the Capital: Three Modern Vietnamese Classics.* Greg Lockhart and Monique
Lockhart, trans. (New York: Oxford University Press, 1996), 70–74, 112–114.

Original publication details: 1.1 Lockhard & Lockhart, 1995. Reproduced with permission
from G. Lockhart & M. Lockhart. 1.2 Phan Boi Chau, 1950. 1.3 Problemy vostokovedeniia,
1960. Translation: Ho Chi Minh: Selected Works, 1962. 1.4 Ho Chi Minh: Selected Writings,
19201969, 1973. 1.5 Declaration of Independence of the Democratic Republic of Vietnam, 2
September 1945. www.chinhphu.vn/portal/page/portal/English/

report detailed the hard lives and brutal exploitation of Hanoi rickshaw drivers, who transported well-to-do customers (both French and Vietnamese) around the city by pulling them in two-wheeled carriages. Tam Lang explained to readers that he had disguised himself as a coolie (a poor laborer) and took a job as a driver, which allowed him to experience the humiliation and degrading conditions of the trade. In the excerpts of the report presented here, Tam Lang describes spending the night with a fellow driver in an opium den in after a hard day of work on the streets. He also offers his assessment of responsibility for the suffering that he witnessed.

A rickshaw lamp swung beneath my friend's hand like a flickering firefly. Passing a dike a little over 2 meters high, we descended into a deep depression that was as dark as a grave.

No longer could we see the row of electric lights along the Don Thuy Road. Obscured by the long dike, they gave off a dull glow above our heads. What a sad scene.

I followed my friend's footsteps. There were no stars in the sky. A pulsating chorus of croaking frogs and toads and crickets resounded all around me.

That's the area of the southern slums!

The home of a group of poor, wretched people. A torn basket full of rubbish at the foot of a row of imposing villas!

There was no ray of light. Not one tire mark. Here, the light of civilization is blocked by a wall of dirt; the wheel of progress is stopped by a long stretch of dike.

And yet something has managed to cross it!

This is the Opium Spirit with tortoiseshell red wings attached to its back. This is Miss Phu Dung, the spirit with the beautiful name that people know well how to call.[2]

That night, I saw Miss Phu Dung lie there, in the compartment of a leaf-covered dwelling that was slanted on a twisted house post and in which ten people were packed as though in a jar.

I bent down and slipped through a doorway that was no higher than a meter. My friend pointed out Tu, who was lying beside an opium tray. Then, taking off his blue outer shirt, my friend said: 'This person wants to sleep here for a while.'

I nodded a greeting and handed over 2 sous I had just taken out of my pocket.

The person lying beside the opium tray lifted his head, raised his arm to take the money without uttering a word.

[2] Miss Phu Dung: a Vietnamese slang term for opium.

He was about forty, pale, and with sunken cheeks. His eyes were also deeply sunk into his head. His arms were as thin as reeds. His pants were rolled up above his knees, showing two legs that were no stouter than his arms.

Without being invited, I sat down on the bed beside our friend, who was lying there, smoking opium.

After exhaling a long trail of smoke, he sat up, drew his knees up, undid his flask on the opium pipe, bared his chest, rolled his sleeves up to his shoulders, and scraped the residue out of the flask.

In one corner, a number of others, all men, some wearing shirts, others bare-chested, were sitting on a piece of sleeping mat with their heads converging around a smoky lamp on a tray. They made noisy cries as they gathered around playing a kind of card game called 'Bat': 'Pull', 'Turn it over', 'Bat', 'Damn your mother', 'Damn your father'.

Rickshaw coolies robbing rickshaw coolies; crippled chickens scratching around the grinding stone to peck at empty husks!

A woman holding a child lay on a hammock that was hidden in the darkness. She popped her head out from time to time, opened her mouth and asked: 'Did the "wooden fish" win, or who?'

My friend who brought me here, joined the group playing cards. I was left with Tu, and, having the opportunity, I coaxed him with a question: 'Each day, how many pipes do you smoke?'

After putting the top back on the flask, he looked up at me: 'Did you say this is the first time you've been here?'

'Yes. The other man has just brought me here today.'

'You look as though you're from Hanoi.'

'No, I just came down from the highlands a few days ago.'

With the opium pipe standing at the foot of the bed, Tu took a long draw on it. Without giving him the time to judge me, I asked again: 'Each day, how many pipes do you smoke?'

Lying down slowly, Tu invited me to join him.

Inserting the point of the opium pick into the ball of residue and holding it up to the lamp, Tu said as he prepared the opium: 'Twenty sous a day, as I have only one session at night. Mixed opium can be smoked many times and the residue lasts.'

'So, in that case, how many pipes?'

'Three pipes, sometimes four, but no more, because the residue gets too strong and damaging, and I haven't got the strength to draw on it.'

'At 20 sous, you must spend 6 or 7 piastres a month.'

'No, not that much. I cook the residue again, so that I save a bit each month.'

'Smoking like that, surely you can't work at night?'

'No, I only hire a rickshaw and pull it at night. During the day, it's extremely hot and very hard work.'

'So if you work at night, when are you able to find the time to smoke opium?'

'At 2 a.m. I return the rickshaw. I get back here a little before you just arrived. I smoke 'till morning. After eating, I sleep until five in the afternoon, get up, eat again, and go to work.'

'Money for hiring the rickshaw, for opium, and also for food; how can you make enough to afford it working only seven or eight hours?'

I asked him his story, and he smoked as he responded. By now, his cold attitude had completely disappeared. Hearing me ask the last question, he just laughed and did not answer…

The group playing cards had broken up. It was almost morning.

On a few flimsy bamboo beds, over ten coolies, who had just been fighting to fleece each other at cards, now lay rolling around exhausted, offering a sweaty banquet to the mosquitoes that swarmed above them.

Lying beside the miserable opium tray and preparing the opium for Tu to smoke, I had become his close friend.

Through the sounds of children crying, the heavy snoring of the half-dead gamblers, we continued to exchange confidences.

I didn't sleep throughout the whole night….

Now let me say to you here that perhaps there were times when you, Dear Readers, said to your friends: 'That's enough! Why bother arguing with those rickshaw coolies!'

I must also confess that there have been times when I said to my friends: 'Those coolies, why waste energy quarrelling with them!'

Dear Readers, I have been of the same mind as you: we have despised the class of people who pull other people.

But do they really deserve such contempt? Today, let us rethink this question.

Now, let's imagine that someone asked: 'Who is to blame for the class of people in our society that works like animals pulling other people?'

What would you say?

If you think carefully, I dare say you would answer honestly as follows: 'Society is to blame.'

According to its strict meaning, 'society' is all of the people who come from the same origins and who all live together under the same system, and that includes you and me.

Yes, you and me, all of us are equally at fault.

To lower a powerless person from his status as a human being to that of a horse, to give him two wooden shafts and say 'I will sit up here while you pull me' is the same as saying 'You are not a human being.'

Having been unjustly denied membership in the human race, why do rickshaw coolies need self-respect?

We take away their dignity without knowing it. Why do we scorn them for supposedly doing undignified things?

The Trial Testimony of Phan Boi Chau (1925)[3]

During the first two decades of the twentieth century, Phan Boi Chau was Vietnam's best-known anticolonial revolutionary. Phan grew up in the central Vietnamese province of Nghe An – the province in which Ho Chi Minh was born – during the early stages of the French conquest of Indochina. Although he spent years studying Confucian thought and classical Chinese texts, Phan opted not to pursue a career as a mandarin, on the grounds that the Vietnamese imperial bureaucracy had become the corrupt instrument of the French colonial state. In 1903, he founded a patriotic movement that recruited Vietnamese boys to go to Japan to be trained as revolutionaries. After he and his students were expelled from Japan in 1909, Phan continued his anti-French activism in southern China, where he and his followers tried to organize armed attacks on colonial officials inside Vietnam. Most of these operations missed their targets, but they strongly reinforced Phan's reputation as a national hero.

In 1925, an informer in Phan's group betrayed him to the French, who arrested him and took him back to Vietnam for trial on charges of murder and treason. A panel of French judges convicted Phan and gave him a life sentence of hard labor. However, Phan successfully used the proceedings to portray himself as an advocate of democracy, independence, and modernization; he also called on the French colonial state to fulfill the "civilizing mission" that it claimed to be pursuing in Indochina. Many Vietnamese were especially moved by Phan's final statement to the court. Thanks to widespread coverage of the trial in Vietnamese newspapers, Phan's conviction produced a popular outcry and demands for lenience, leading eventually to a French decision to commute his sentence to a form of house arrest. The main effect of the trial was thus to underscore the depth of

---

[3] "Phan Bội Châu trước Hội-Đồng Đề-hình" ["Phan Boi Chau appears before the Council of Judges"], in Thế Nguyễn, *Phan Bội Châu, 1867–1940* (Saigon: Nhà Xuất Bản Tân Việt Phát Hành, 1950), 47–49. Translated by Edward Miller.

Vietnamese dissatisfaction with French rule, and the growing strength of nationalist sentiment.

The country of the south[4] is a country that has long languished under tyranny, and its people have suffered greatly. The kings and mandarins have for too long lived apart from the people and oppressed them, leaving them with no means to gain prosperity. Since the French protectorate is a civilized government—that is, one that aims to enlighten and uplift its subjects—I am sure that the people of Vietnam are happy to be associated with it. Surely the government's rule over the past 20 years has brought many beneficial changes...

I am a man of the country of the South, and I want to wake up the Vietnamese nation. I have witnessed the birth of the idea of political opposition. If my side had a few hundred thousand sailors, a few tens of thousands of soldiers, armed with many guns, warships and airplanes, then I would submit my declaration of war and righteously resist the colonial government. But I am merely a student, my pockets are empty of money, I have no weapons, I cannot engage in armed resistance. Thus I have only sought to use culture—which is to say that I tried to mobilize the people to demand political reforms. No doubt the government distrusted and arrested me because I was hiding in a foreign country for the purpose of pursuing my goals.

I called upon my friends and compatriots to contribute money to send students to school and to provide the people with books [for the purpose of learning]. My work is merely to use my tongue and my pen, and my goal is political reform; the movement I lead is simple and righteous.

If I have done wrong, my only sins are the following:

1. Even though no one else opposed the colonial government, I alone resisted, because I wanted the country to be independent;
2. The country formerly had an absolute monarchy, but I wanted it to become a republic;
3. The colonial state banned people from travelling overseas for study, but I fled and recruited students to go to foreign countries to study;
4. I tried to mobilize and awaken the people of the country of the south, to demand that the government institute political reforms to complete its mandate to bring enlightenment [to the country].

---

[4] "The country of the South": a traditional way of referring to Vietnam, which implicitly locates it by reference to its northern neighbor, China.

Ho Chi Minh, The Path which Led Me to Leninism (1960)[5]

Between 1945 and his death in 1969, Ho Chi Minh was the pre-eminent leader of the Vietnamese Revolution and one of the world's most famous communists. However, his political career had begun decades before 1945, under a different name. In 1911, a young man named Nguyen Tat Thanh left Vietnam for Europe. After failing to gain admission to the Colonial School, an institution that trained officials to assume civil service positions in the French colonies, Thanh spent several years working and travelling in various parts of Europe, North Africa, and North America (including the United States). During this time, Thanh became increasingly critical of French colonial rule in Indochina, even though he was not yet a communist. After returning to France in 1917, he became active in anticolonial and socialist political circles and began using the alias "Nguyen Ai Quoc," which can be translated as "Nguyen the patriot." In 1919, he signed this name to a petition that called on US President Woodrow Wilson to support autonomy and political freedom for the Vietnamese. The following year, Nguyen Ai Quoc became a founding member of the French Communist Party.

Decades later, in April 1960, Ho Chi Minh published the following essay, in which he recalled his first encounters with socialist thought as a young man in France. Like most of the other autobiographical accounts that Ho wrote during his later years, this one was colored by hindsight and by contemporary political events. At the time this essay appeared in a Russian magazine, relations between Communist China and the Soviet Union were under severe strain, as leaders in both governments accusing the other of abandoning communist principles. Since Ho hoped to remain on good terms with both communist powers, his portrayal of himself as a Leninist should be read in light of this emerging rivalry. Yet the essay still provides some valuable clues about the early evolution of Ho's thinking, and especially about the reasons for his enthusiastic embrace of Lenin's ideas.

After World War I, I made my living in Paris, now as a retoucher at a photographer's, now as painter of "Chinese antiquities" (made in France!). I would distribute leaflets denouncing the crimes committed by the French colonialists in Viet Nam. At that time, I supported the October Revolution only instinctively, not yet grasping all its historic importance. I loved and admired Lenin because he was a great patriot who liberated his compatriots; until then, I had read none of his books. . . .

[5] First published in Russian in the Soviet magazine *Problems of the East*, April 1960. English translation in *Ho Chi Minh: Selected Works* (Hanoi: Foreign Language Publishing House, 1962), 448–450.

Heated discussions were then taking place in the branches of the Socialist Party, about the question whether the Socialist Party should remain in the Second International, should a Second and a half International be founded or should the Socialist Party join Lenin's Third International? I attended the meetings regularly, twice or thrice a week and attentively listened to the discussion. First, I could not understand thoroughly. Why were the discussions so heated? Either with the Second, Second and a half or Third International, the revolution could be waged. What was the use of arguing then? As for the First International, what had become of it?

What I wanted most to know—and this precisely was not debated in the meetings—was: which International sides with the peoples of colonial countries? I raised this question—the most important in my opinion—in a meeting. Some comrades answered: It is the Third, not the Second International. And a comrade gave me Lenin's "Thesis on the national and colonial questions" published by *l'Humanité*[6] to read.

There were political terms difficult to understand in this thesis. But by dint of reading it again and again, finally I could grasp the main part of it... Though sitting alone in my room, I shouted out aloud as if addressing large crowds: "Dear martyrs, compatriots! This is what we need, this is the path to our liberation!"

After then, I had entire confidence in Lenin, in the Third International. Formerly, during the meetings of the Party branch, I only listened to the discussion; I had a vague belief that all were logical, and could not differentiate as to who were right and who were wrong. But from then on, I also plunged into the debates and discussed with fervor. Though I was still lacking French words to express all my thoughts, I smashed the allegations attacking Lenin and the Third International with no less vigor. My only argument was: "If you do not condemn colonialism, if you do not side with the colonial people, what kind of revolution are you waging? ... "

At first, patriotism, not yet communism, led me to have confidence in Lenin, in the Third International. Step by step, through the struggle, by studying Marxism-Leninism parallel with participation in practical activities, I gradually came upon the fact that only socialism and communism can liberate the oppressed nations and the working people throughout the world from slavery.

There is a legend, in our country as well as in China, on the miraculous "Book of the Wise". When facing great difficulties, one opens it and finds a way out. Leninism is not only a miraculous "book of the wise," a

---

[6] *L'Humanité*: a leftist French daily newspaper launched in 1904.

compass for us Vietnamese revolutionaries and people; it is also the radiant sun illuminating our path to final victory, to socialism and communism.

Nguyen Ai Quoc (Ho Chi Minh), Appeal Made on the Occasion of the Founding of the Vietnamese Communist Party (1930)[7]

In 1924, Nguyen Ai Quoc left France for the Soviet Union. Upon his arrival in Moscow, he was recruited to work as an operative for the Comintern, the Soviet-sponsored organization dedicated to the promotion of Marxist revolution around the world. After a year of training, Quoc was dispatched to southern China, where he established a new organization known as the Vietnam Revolutionary Youth League. By the late 1920s, the Youth League had hundreds of members, most of them inside Indochina; however, a schism had developed within the League over the issue of revolutionary strategy. Some members argued that the League ought to focus first and foremost on the issue of national liberation from French colonial rule (the "national question"). But others disagreed, arguing that an emphasis on class struggle and social transformation (the "social question") was the only way to ensure the success of the revolution in the long run.

In the fall of 1930, Quoc made a bid to heal the rift in the league by inviting the leaders of the rival factions to attend a "Unity Conference" in Hong Kong. At the conference, Quoc persuaded the participants to join him in creating a new organization: the Vietnamese Communist Party (VCP). His program advocated national liberation followed by social revolution – a formula that appeared to give precedence to "the national question." However, as the public appeal that he issued after the conference suggests, Quoc remained very interested in "the social question."

Workers, peasants, soldiers, youth and school students! Oppressed and exploited fellow-countrymen! Sisters and brothers! Comrades!

Imperialist contradictions were the cause of the 1914-1918 World War. After this horrible slaughter, the world was divided into two camps: one is the revolutionary camp which includes the oppressed colonial peoples and the exploited working class throughout the world. Its vanguard is the Soviet Union. The other is the counter-revolutionary camp of

7 *Ho Chi Minh: Selected Writings, 1920–1969* (Hanoi: Foreign Languages Publishing House, 1973), 39–41.

international capitalism and imperialism, whose general staff is the League of Nations.

That war resulted in untold loss of life and property for the peoples. French imperialism was the hardest hit. Therefore, in order to restore the forces of capitalism in France, the French imperialists have resorted to every perfidious scheme to intensify capitalist exploitation in Indochina. They have built new factories to exploit the workers by paying them starvation wages. They have plundered the peasants' land to establish plantations and drive them to destitution...

However, the French imperialists' barbarous oppression and ruthless exploitation have awakened our compatriots, who have all realized that revolution is the only road to survival and that without it they will die a slow death. This is why the revolutionary movement has grown stronger with each passing day: the workers refuse to work, the peasants demand land, the students go on strike, the traders stop doing business. Everywhere the masses have risen to oppose the French imperialists...

Workers, peasants, soldiers, youth, school students! Oppressed and exploited fellow-countrymen!

The Vietnamese Communist Party has been founded. It is the Party of the working class. It will help the proletariat lead the revolution waged for the sake of all oppressed and exploited people. From now on we must join the Party, help it and follow it in order to implement the following slogans:

1. To overthrow French imperialism and Vietnamese feudalism and reactionary bourgeoisie;
2. To make Indochina completely independent;
3. To establish a worker-peasant-soldier government;
4. To confiscate the banks and other enterprises belonging to the imperialists and put them under the control of the worker-peasant-soldier government;
5. To confiscate all the plantations and property belonging to the imperialists and the Vietnamese reactionary bourgeoisie and distribute them to the poor peasants;
6. To implement the 8-hour working day;
7. To abolish the forced buying of government bonds, the poll-tax and all unjust taxes hitting the poor;
8. To bring democratic freedoms to the masses;
9. To dispense education to all the people;
10. To realize equality between man and woman.

Ho Chi Minh, The Declaration of Independence of the Democratic Republic of Vietnam (1945)[8]

On Sunday, September 2, 1945, hundreds of thousands of people crowded into Ba Dinh Square in Hanoi. They had gathered to hear the address of Ho Chi Minh, the leader of the pro-independence movement known as the Viet Minh. During the previous three weeks, following the sudden surrender of Imperial Japan and the end of World War II, Viet Minh operatives had seized control of Hanoi and many other cities, towns, and villages across Indochina. They had also proclaimed the formation of an independent Vietnamese government, known as the Democratic Republic of Vietnam (DRV). Ho's address on September 2 marked his first public appearance as the president of the new state. Since he had only recently begun using the alias "Ho Chi Minh," most of the people in Ba Dinh Square that Sunday did not yet know that the DRV president and the famous communist operative Nguyen Ai Quoc were one and the same person. Nevertheless, the atmosphere was electric and the sense that Vietnam had arrived at a historic moment was palpable. After reading the first few sentences of his address, Ho stopped and asked "Compatriots, can you hear me clearly?" "Yes!" the crowd roared in response. As another senior Viet Minh leader later remarked, it was at that moment that "Uncle Ho and the sea of people became one."

Prior to the address, Ho had invited a US Army major named Archimedes Patti to sit on the official platform during the ceremony. Patti was an American intelligence officer with the Office of Strategic Services (OSS), which had cooperated with Ho and the Viet Minh during the last months of World War II. Patti declined Ho's invitation, choosing instead to stand in front of the platform during the address. He did, however, assist Ho by correcting a minor error in his opening quotation from the US Declaration of Independence. Patti later recalled being "uncomfortably aware that I was participating – however slightly – in the formulation of a political entity."

My countrymen,

> "All men are created equal. They are endowed by their Creator with certain inalienable rights, among these are Life, Liberty, and the pursuit of Happiness"

This immortal statement was made in the Declaration of Independence of the United States of America in 1776. In a broader sense, this means: All the nations on the earth are equal from birth, all the nations have the right to live, to be happy and free.

[8] Official English translation of the Declaration of Independence of the Democratic Republic of Vietnam, 2 September 1945. Available at www.chinhphu.vn/portal/page/portal/English/, accessed August 31, 2015.

The Declaration of the French Revolution made in 1791 on the Rights of Man and the Citizen also states: "All men are born free and with equal rights, and must always remain free and having equal rights." Those are undeniable truths.

Nevertheless, for more than eighty years, the French colonialists misused the flag of Liberty, Equality, and Fraternity to invade our Fatherland and oppressed our countrymen. Their action was contrary to humanity and justice.

Politically, they absolutely have deprived our people of every democratic freedom.

They have enforced inhumane laws. They have set up three different regimes in the Central, the Southern and the Northern Parts of Vietnam in order to prevent our nation from being unified and our people from being united.

They have built more prisons than schools. They have mercilessly slain our patriots. They drowned our resistance in rivers of blood. They have fettered public opinion and practiced obscurantism against our people.

They used opium and alcohol to weaken our race.

Economically, they have exploited our people to the bone, so as to impoverish our people and to devastate our country.

They have robbed us of our rice fields, our mines, our forests and our raw materials. They have monopolized the issuing of bank notes and the export trade.

They have levied numerous unjustifiable taxes, which have forced our people, especially our peasantry and tradesmen, into absolute poverty.

They have hampered the prosperity of our national bourgeoisie. They have mercilessly exploited our industrial workers.

In the autumn of 1940, when the Japanese Fascists arrived to occupy Indochina and build new military bases to fight against the Allies, the French colonialists bent their knees and opened our country to the Japanese. Thus, from that date, our people suffered under the double yoke of the French and the Japanese. As a result, from the end of last year to the beginning of this year, from Quang Tri province to the North of Vietnam, more than two million of our fellow-citizens died from starvation.

On March 9, the Japanese disarmed the French Army. The French colonialists either fled or surrendered. As a matter of fact, they were not only incapable of "protecting" us, but had also sold our country twice to the Japanese.[9]

---

[9] Although Imperial Japan had occupied Indochina during 1940–1941, Japanese leaders allowed the French colonial regime to remain in place. This arrangement lasted until March

On several occasions before March 9, the Vietminh League (League of Vietnam Alliance for Independence) urged the French to ally themselves with Vietnam to fight against the Japanese. Instead of responding to this proposal, the French colonialists intensified their terrorist activities against the Vietminh, and before fleeing the country they massacred a great number of our political prisoners detained at Yen Bai and Cao Bang.

Notwithstanding all this, our fellow-citizens have always manifested toward the French a tolerant and humane attitude. Even after the Japanese putsch of March 1945, the Vietminh League helped many Frenchmen cross the frontier, rescued some of them from Japanese jails, and protected French lives and property.

From the autumn of 1940, our country had in fact ceased to be a French colony and had become a Japanese possession.

After the Japanese had surrendered to the Allies, our whole people rose to regain our national sovereignty and to found the Democratic Republic of Vietnam.

The truth is that we have wrested our independence from the Japanese and not from the French.

The French have fled, the Japanese have capitulated, Emperor Bao Dai has abdicated. Our people have broken the chains which for nearly a century have fettered them and have won independence for the Fatherland. Our people at the same time have overthrown the monarchic regime that has reigned supreme for dozens of centuries. In its place has been established the present Democratic Republic.

For these reasons, we, members of the Provisional Government, representing the whole Vietnamese people, declare that from now on we break off all relations of a colonial character with France; we repeal all the international obligations that France has so far subscribed to on behalf of Vietnam and we abolish all the special rights the French have unlawfully acquired in our Fatherland.

The whole Vietnamese people, animated by a common purpose, are determined to fight to the bitter end against any attempt by the French colonialists to reconquer their country.

We are convinced that the Allied nations which at Tehran and San Francisco have acknowledged the principles of self-determination and equality of nations, will not refuse to acknowledge the independence of Vietnam.

9, 1945, when Japanese commanders, fearing that French officials planned to betray them to the Allies, finally removed their French counterparts in a coup.

A people who have courageously opposed French domination for more than eighty years, a people who have fought side by side with the Allies against the Fascists during these last years—such a people must be free and independent.

For these reasons, we, members of the Provisional Government of the Democratic Republic of Vietnam, solemnly declare to the world that Vietnam has the right to be a free and independent country and in fact is so already. The entire Vietnamese people are determined to mobilize all their physical and mental strength, to sacrifice their lives and property in order to safeguard their independence and liberty.

Discussion questions

1. Who was the intended audience for Tam Lang's "I pulled a Rickshaw"? What kind of social change was Tam Lang promoting, and how did he seek to persuade his readers to support it?
2. How did Phan Boi Chau challenge the authority and legitimacy of the colonial state in his 1925 statement? Was his reform vision more radical than Tam Lang's? Why or why not?
3. In his 1930 call for a revolution to overthrow the French colonial regime, was Nguyen Ai Quoc (later Ho Chi Minh) aligning himself with the revolutionary activism of Phan Boi Chau, or was he supporting a different vision?
4. Some historians have argued that Ho Chi Minh was a nationalist who embraced communism because it offered the best means to promote Vietnam's national liberation (the "national question"); others have depicted him as a dedicated communist who used nationalism merely to gain support for the idea of socialist revolution in Vietnam (the "social question"). Based on the documents in this chapter, how do you interpret Ho and his goals?

Chapter 2   The First Indochina War and the Origins of American Involvement

Oral History of Xuan Vu, Viet Minh War Reporter and Propagandist (1987)[1]

Xuan Vu (Xuân Vũ) was the pen name of Bui Quang Triet, one of twentieth-century Vietnam's most prolific and accomplished authors. He was born in the Mekong Delta province of Ben Tre in 1930. Like countless other Vietnamese youths, Xuan Vu embraced the Viet Minh at the time of the August Revolution in 1945. During the subsequent Franco-Viet Minh war, he distinguished himself as a recruiter, war reporter, and propagandist, and even won the DRV's most prestigious literary prize. Although he later became disillusioned with communism and defected to the anticommunist state of

---

[1] Excerpted from David Chanoff and Doan Van Toai, *Vietnam: A Portrait of its People at War* (London: I. B. Tauris, 1987), 5–11.

Original publication details: 2.3 Foreign Relations of the United States, 1946, 1971. 2.4 Excerpted from Văn Kiện Đảng Toàn Tập, 2001, 166-238. Translated by Edward Miller. 2.5 Foreign Relations of the United States, 1950, 1976. 2.6 Blum in Foreign Relations of the United States, 1951, 1976. 2.7 Eisenhower in Foreign Relations of the United States 1952-1954, 1982. 2.8 The Department of State Bulletin, 1954

*South Vietnam in 1968, he never forgot the reasons that had drawn him to
the Viet Minh as a teenager. In this oral history, recorded in the 1980s in the
United States, Xuan Vu recalled the heady idealism of the post-August
Revolution period. He also described the techniques that he and other Viet
Minh supporters used to mobilize the rural population of the Mekong Delta.*

Before the Americans came, there were the French. I was fifteen when war
broke out with them, in tenth grade. The high school I went to was in My
Tho, a city in the Mekong Delta about fifty miles from my home village. By
the time the school year started in 1945, My Tho was blockaded, cut off
from the countryside. Inside the city were the French soldiers, outside were
the Vietminh guerrillas. My village and all the other villages were controlled
by the Vietminh – actually they belonged to the Vietminh, heart and soul.
Everyone was part of the movement, everyone supported it. There was this
great rush of patriotic feeling. To struggle for independence, to be proud of
the nation – that was what everybody wanted. We had been slaves of the
Chinese for a thousand years, slaves of the French for a hundred. Now we
were going to be *free*. The feeling was everywhere – and outpouring – in all
the villages, all the farms. It was unstoppable.

Anyway, I was fifteen, and I was right in the middle of it. I had to join,
it was such an exciting time. Besides, I couldn't get back to school because
of the blockade. So there was no chance of getting on with my studies. Also
I had an uncle who was a university man – where I came from that was a
rare thing (I was the only one from my village who had even gone to high
school) – and this uncle was one of the leaders of the local Vietminh Youth
League. So he took me to help out in the Youth League office. I like to write,
and as I said, I was the only one in the village who had gone past elementary
school. With such magnificent credentials, very soon I was in charge of the
office.

Before long they started sending me and some other guys around to organize. We'd go into a village and just walk around, talking to all of the
teenagers we could find, telling them to come to our meeting tonight, say
at eight o'clock. When eight o'clock came everyone would be there. It was
a little bit of excitement that nobody wanted to miss. The three or four of
us would have a routine prepared. I played the guitar, someone else played
the mandolin, all of us knew how to sing. We'd start off with some patriotic
songs. Everybody would respond to the words and the sentiment (we would
always feel it). Then we'd talk to them, telling stories about the Chinese
domination and the French domination, stories of all the great Vietnamese

heroes who had resisted the invaders or rebelled against them. We'd mix the stories with more songs and with poems.

These were things that everyone knew by heart, words and music they had inside them. The crowd would join in and clap as we played. As part of our preparation we would be given articles to read that we could use in our talks. For example, we would tell them that the French had enslaved the country, that they had built more jails than schools. We told them that the French had spent much more on giving alcohol and drugs to the people than they ever had on medicine. Of course we needed these articles ourselves in order to know what to talk about. Because aside from the popular history that came through the stories and poems, we hardly had any facts at all.

But nobody else did either. And we used that, too. We'd talk about the fact that there were no schools, that the French had built hardly any. And we'd point to people in the audience. "Look, you can't read, you can't write. You are ignorant. Do you know why? You're ignorant because of the French, because of their colonialism. They've kept you like animals – do you like that?" And it was true too. Because maybe only one or two people in the audience had had any significant schooling at all.

Then we'd go around with a sign-up list, for people who wanted to volunteer to join the Youth League. They'd all join. There would be tremendous enthusiasm. Of course no one wanted to be accused of being pro-French either, so there was a lot of unspoken social pressure. But they also wanted to organize. They knew that the chances of their actually becoming real fighters wasn't very good. At that time it was a great honor just to be accepted into the Vietminh army. But at least they could join the Youth League and pay their ten cents dues every month and be part of what was going on.

I traveled all around Ben Tre Province like this for two or three years. I was fifteen, sixteen, seventeen years old. I found out I was an effective speaker, that I could get people to do what I wanted them to. I was proud of it. I felt I was leading them in the right way. We traveled constantly from one village to another. We got no pay for any of this, no food rations, nothing. Our families would do whatever they could to help us. But mainly we relied on the people in the villages. They'd offer us their homes to sleep in, feed us, give us whatever we needed. We didn't even have mosquito nets of our own. Instead we carried woven straw sleeping mats, a little bit like a sleeping bag, except made out of dried grass fiber. We'd carry these mats around rolled up on our backs like a badge of honor. They identified us as revolutionaries. But sleeping in them wasn't quite so rewarding. They were hot as hell – so hot you'd have to stick your head out every once in a while for a breath of fresh air, mosquitoes or not. There was even a famous song called "The Mat

Song of the Resistance" that people sang right through the French war and
the American war, too – right up to 1975.

> Last August on the twenty-third
> We answered our nation's call.
> Everywhere the people cheered
> As we marched to the front
> Our mats and machetes across
> our backs

It was an exhilarating time. I even got to fight in a battle that took place in
my home village in 1947. There was a blockhouse there that sat next to the
road—a big square building that had originally been a rice storehouse and
was barricaded by thick bales of paddy rice. At that time the French had managed to garrison the blockhouse with about thirty soldiers. Since they could
control the traffic on the provincial road, the local Vietminh commander
decided to try and take the blockhouse, even though it was so well fortified.

The road at that point was built up above ground level and the Vietminh
fighters—maybe sixty of them—took up positions behind the embankment.
Then they began firing at the blockhouse. But the only guns they had were
old French musquetons that must have gone back to the nineteenth century.
They were worthless for this kind of attack. While the shooting was going
on, crowds of villagers gathered behind the embankment to watch what was
happening and to help the fighters. They had bamboo stakes, knives, hoes –
anything they could get their hands on. I was part of the crowd.

As we watched, the guerrilla commander – his name was Phan Van Phai –
and two men ran out from behind the embankment toward the blockhouse
to try to set it on fire. Somehow they managed to get to the front without
being shot – to a place where they were safe from the firing coming out of
the windows. Then a grenade came flying out. One of Phai's men grabbed it
and threw it away before it could explode. Two others followed – big potato
masher-type grenades. Phai's men also managed to grab those and get rid
of them. The fourth exploded just as it was being picked up. Phai and both
men were killed.

When this happened the peasants went wild. They practically tore apart
a couple of nearby houses to get flammable material – wood, straw, piles of
coconut palm leaves. They ran our and began throwing this stuff all around
the blockhouse, despite the shooting. I was throwing things too. I hardly
knew where I was. We were all in a frenzy. Some people were shot down,
but others began heaving Molotov cocktails. The palm leaves caught fire
first. Before long the whole building was billowing fire and clouds of smoke.

One French soldier came running out on fire. Phai's men shot him down. The rest of them were trapped inside. We barbecued them all. Once the paddy rice bales started burning, they never went out. They smoldered for months. You could see the bones of the French soldiers in the charred ruins of their blockhouse.

It was no surprise to anyone that the Huong My peasants were daring enough to expose themselves to French fire and burn the blockhouse. Everywhere you turned there was the same kind of passion. Ben Tre Province was one of the centers of revolution. People would listen for hours to the Vietminh speakers, hanging on every word. They'd lean out of windows or perch in trees to get a view of them over the heads of the crowd. The speakers would keep coming back to the revolutionary slogans that by now everyone knew by heart. "Freedom or Death" they would chant. And the crowd would shout back "Freedom or Death, Freedom or Death." "*Muon doc lap phai do mau!*" – "For freedom you have to spend your blood!" And the crowd would yell "*Do mau, Do mau!*" – "Yes! Spend blood! Spend blood!"

For a while I became secretary at a camp my uncle had opened to train propagandists and speakers. It was next to a beautiful beach area in Ben Tre and every district sent people to the training sessions, which lasted about a month. My uncle and the other trainers gave them painstaking instruction. They taught them how to stand up and walk to the front of the crowd or to the stage after they were introduced. "So and so will now talk to us about Tran Hung Dao" [a great hero of the anti-Chinese wars of the thirteenth century]. And the student speaker would learn how to get up from the middle of the crowd where he was squatting, smile, bow, then walk slowly to the front, never turning his back completely on the people. He'd learn how to keep eye contact with the audience, how to modulate his voice and vary the speed of his speech. He'd learn how to gesture, and how to coordinate gestures with intonation. He'd learn when to stop his speech for music or maybe a poem from someone else on his agit-prop team, then how to take it up again smoothly, building on the heightened mood.

The trainees would be given topics for practice speeches that they'd spend all day preparing. Then at night the whole school would gather to listen, and the speaker would go through the entire routine: "We fight for *independence*!" – coming to a crescendo using big, expansive hand gestures; "We fight for the *nation*!" – shouting out "nation." The trainers and other students would respond and clap, playing their own role to create a realistic setting. Afterwards would come the criticism, first from the other students, then from the instructors.

Then there'd be discussion groups. Trainees would be taught how to lead discussions, how to get responses from people, what topics to concentrate on. In all this there was never a mention of communism, Patriotism and independence were the great themes – though of course a certain amount of politics came through too. For example, one topic was "Men and Women Are Equal." That was great, always good for a lively discussion. Up till then nobody had ever heard of the idea.

U.S. Department of State Airgram on French–Vietnamese Relations (1946)[2]

In the wake of the August Revolution, the government of France moved to re-establish its colonial empire in Indochina. The return of French forces to Saigon and other parts of southern Vietnam in the fall of 1945 immediately led to clashes with Viet Minh fighters. Following talks between DRV and French officials in early 1946, Ho Chi Minh agreed to allow French troops to return to Hanoi and northern Vietnam; in exchange, the French recognized the DRV as a "free state within the French Union." However, Paris refused to make any concessions on the crucial issue of Vietnamese independence, and a subsequent round of negotiations between Ho and French officials during the summer of 1946 ended in acrimony. In November of that year, a skirmish between French and Viet Minh naval units near the northern port of Haiphong resulted in the bombardment of the city by French warships. Thousands of Vietnamese civilians were killed. On December 19, 1946, Viet Minh units attacked French positions in Hanoi and then withdrew to the countryside. The First Indochina War had begun.

As Indochina slid toward war in the summer and fall of 1946, the United States government called on French and DRV leaders to pursue a negotiated settlement. Behind the scenes, however, U.S. officials disagreed over what course Washington should take. Some American diplomats advocated quiet support for France's effort to restore its colonial dominion in Indochina, on the grounds that the U.S. needed French cooperation for its policies in postwar Europe. But other State Department officials insisted that the age of European empire in Asia had passed and that the U.S. needed to accommodate Asian aspirations for national liberation. The following secret message, drafted by the U.S. State Department on the eve of the Viet Minh attacks in Hanoi, captured the official American ambivalence, as well as U.S. diplomats' growing exasperation with both sides.

[2] Circular Airgram, 851G.00/12-1746, printed in *Foreign Relations of the United States, 1946.* Vol. 8: *The Far East* (Washington, DC: GPO, 1971), 72-73.

Washington, December 17, 1946 – 1:05 pm
SECRET FOR CHIEF OF MISSION

Basic French-Vietnamese Difficulties

After conversations with French and Vietnamese officials and British, Chinese and US Consuls [in] Hanoi, Mr. Abbot Moffat[3], who is at present in [Southeast Asia], has developed views in which Consul Saigon concurs along the following lines:

The Vietnam Government is in control of a small Communist group, possibly in indirect touch with Moscow and direct touch with Yenan.[4] A nationalist group is utilizing Communist party techniques and discipline with which they are familiar. The people are conservative landowners and attempts to communize the country are secondary and would await successful operation of a nationalist state. Apparently some leaders, like Ho Chi Minh, consider collaboration with the French essential: those like [General Vo Nguyen] Giap would avoid collaboration fearing French domination but might not reject French influence and aid. Nationalist sentiment runs deep among the Vietnamese as does opposition to the French, and they might easily turn against all whites. French influence is important not only as an antidote to Soviet influence but to protect Vietnam and SEA from future Chinese imperialism. Delay in achieving a settlement will progressively diminish the possibility of ultimate French influence.

The honesty of both French and Vietnamese officials is questionable in connection with recent incidents. O'Sullivan believes the Vietnamese were responsible for the November 20 incident, but it seems clear that with a different French commander at Haiphong than Colonel Debes... the trouble might have been confined to the original incidents.

According to the French, the Vietnamese enlarge their claims after each agreement and are so impractical and doctrinaire that all conversations are ineffectual. The Vietnamese feel that the French renege on each agreement and are trying to reestablish control. However, both say they have approximately the same objectives, although Giap says Vietnam opposes a political Indochinese federation but favors a federation dealing with common economic problems. Moffat has mentioned to the French three apparent basic

---

[3] Abbott Low Moffat (1901–1996) was a New York politician and diplomat who served as head of the State Department's Division of South-East Asia Affairs from 1944 to 1947. Moffat met with Ho Chi Minh and other DRV officials during a visit to Hanoi in early December 1946.
[4] Yenan (Yan'an) in north-central China was the headquarters of Mao Zedong's Chinese Communist Party (CCP) from 1936 to 1948.

troubles: (a) complete mutual distrust, (b) failure of the French to resolve their own views on "free state within French Union", (c) almost childish Vietnamese attitude and knowledge of economic questions and vague groping for "independence". Agreement cannot be reached by trying to reach accords on incidental problems. Basic Vietnam powers and relations with France must first be established. Not only new faces are needed but neutral good offices or even mediation may be essential.

BYRNES

Truong Chinh, "We Struggle for Independence and Democracy" (1948)[5]

The text below is excerpted from a speech that Indochinese Communist Party leader Truong Chinh delivered to a secret conference of communist party cadres in northern Vietnam during August of 1948. At the time, Truong Chinh was widely acknowledged to be the second most powerful figure in the ICP after Ho Chi Minh. Many considered him to be the party's leading ideologue. Although the Viet Minh was still diplomatically isolated in 1948 – neither the Soviet Union nor any other foreign government had officially recognized the DRV state – Truong Chinh's remarks showed that he and his colleagues were intensely interested in international affairs. In the excerpts presented here, Truong Chinh discusses the connections he saw between the emerging global wave of anticolonial revolutions and the rising power of the Soviet Union.

I. Development of the Anti-Imperialist Democratic Forces

Since the end of the recent World War, the world situation has been characterized by a general weakening of the imperialist forces, and on the other hand by definite gains for the forces of democracy, Four facts demonstrate the strong development of global democratic forces: (A) the triumph and strengthening of the Soviet Union; (B) the establishment of many new democratic countries; (C) the intensification of the struggle for democracy within the imperialist countries; (D) the boiling over of independence and democracy movements in the colonial and semi-colonial countries.

---

[5] Excerpted from "Chúng Ta Chiến Đấu cho Độc Lập và Dân Chủ: Bào Cảo đọc ở Hội nghị cán bộ lần thứ V (từ 8-8 đến 8-16-48)," in *Văn Kiện Đảng Toàn Tập* (Hanoi: Nhà Xuất Bản Chính Trị, 2001), 166–238. Translated by Edward Miller.

A. The Triumph and Strengthening of the Soviet Union

The Soviet Red Army has wiped out the German fascists and has helped many Eastern European countries to become liberated, thus increasing the prestige and influence of the Soviet Union many times over.

By virtue of its victory in the recent world war, the Soviet Union has recovered the former territories of Russia such as Moldavia, Bukovina, White Russia, the Baltic Countries, Karelia, etc. This has caused the frontiers of the nation of socialism to expand.

The Red Army has been deployed from Central Europe to North Korea. In Eastern Europe, there are many new democratic countries which form the walls and ramparts of the Soviet Union. The Chinese Liberation Army has seized almost all of Manchuria and Northern China.[6] The capitalist siege and encirclement of the Soviet Union has thus been broken.

The fourth five-year plan met its goals in four years and the development of socialism will be the basis on which the Soviet Union advances rapidly towards communism. The Soviet Union is actively using the newest scientific inventions discovered during and since the war to improve the productive capabilities of socialism to quite a high level, and to create the conditions for communist abundance.

B. The establishment of many new democratic countries

Since the war, new democratic regimes have been established in the following countries: Poland, Hungary, Yugoslavia, Bulgaria, Albania, Romania, North Korea and a rather broad portion of China.

The characteristics of the new democratic countries include: a) the vestiges of feudalism—especially landlord regimes—have been wiped out; b) large industrial, transportation and financial enterprises have been nationalized; c) the state is being led by the proletariat class and is no longer the tool of capitalist and landlord oppression, but rather is the means of defending the rights of urban and rural laborers and of the people in general...

What is the political situation in the new democratic countries?

The state apparatus, which was previously a tool of oppression, exploitation and dictatorship in the hands of the propertied classes (capitalists, landlords, etc.), has now become a tool for defending the rights of laborers, peasants and intellectuals.

---

[6] Truong Chinh refers here to recent advances by Mao Zedong's People's Liberation Army (PLA) in its ongoing civil war against Chiang Kai-Shek's Chinese Nationalists. In 1949, Mao would claim victory over the Nationalists and proclaim the formation of the People's Republic of China (PRC).

The state has not taken the form of a dictatorship of the proletariat or the dictatorship of the workers and peasants, but rather the form of the dictatorship of the revolutionary popular classes, or a dictatorship of the laboring and democratic classes.

The new authorities have not finished shattering the old state apparatuses (such as existed previously in Russia) but they have seized control of these old apparatuses and are renovating them so as to repair those parts that are not rational and to purge the evil elements. At the same time, they are attracting and appealing to the progressive elements.

The new democratic regimes are all popular democracies of the following types: parliamentary republics in Poland, Hungary, and Bulgaria; a federal republic in Yugoslavia; democratic republics in Vietnam and China.

Within each country, class struggle continues; however, the new democratic authorities stand completely on the side of the workers and the people by subduing the remaining capitalists and landlords and suppressing those of their lackeys who are still lurking within the state apparatus and scheming with foreign reactionaries to destroy the popular regime...

C. The intensification of the struggle within the imperialist nations

The struggles of the people and the laboring classes in the imperialist and capitalist countries has recently expanded and become fiercer, and has in some places and on some occasions taken on the form of an armed struggle (as in Italy). The struggle movement in France has spread from the working classes to the petty bourgeoisie and small landowners, and involves civil servants while also spreading to peasant farmers. The expanding armed struggled between the the patriotic and democratic forces against anti-nationalist capital has caused the severest kinds of contradictions in several countries.

In Britain and the United States, the struggle movement of the laborers and the people is also growing. The Labor Party holds power in Britain [but] has betrayed the interests of the British people and is losing influence. In the United States, the Progressive Party was recently established in dramatic fashion by Wallace to resist the anti-democratic policies of Truman and Marshall.[7]

The Communist Parties of the imperialist and capitalist countries are growing in strength and numbers, and the masses of people who are

---

[7] The reference here is to the Progressive Party, a short-lived, left-leaning party founded in the United States in 1948 by American liberals and radicals (including some communists) who were dissatisfied with the domestic and foreign policies of President Harry Truman. The Progressive Party's Presidential candidate in 1948 was Henry Wallace, who had served as a cabinet official and Vice President under Truman's predecessor, Franklin D. Roosevelt.

under their leadership have become a multitude. The Communist Party of Italy has 2.5 million members. The French Communist party has 1.5 million.

D. The boiling over of independence and democracy movements in the colonial and semi-colonial countries

These movements have been boiling since the world war. During the war, the resistance of colonized and semi-colonized peoples to fascist invasion became quit pronounced. Since the war, "the colonial nations do not want to go on living as before, and the ruling classes in the metropole also are not able to rule the colonies as they did previously." The movement to fight for independence has gained mass support, and has shaken the imperialist classes of the world.

Hundreds of millions in Asia and Africa have and are rising up to struggle against colonialism. The fiercest of these are the 450 million Chinese, the 20 million Vietnamese, the 70 million Indonesians and the nations that ardently resisted the Japanese fascists and took up arms during the war years to struggle against fascism during the defeat of Japan...

The nationalist and democratic nature of the movement of colonized and semi-colonized perople's is quite apparent. During and after the first World War, the colonial liberation movements contained many bourgeois or feudal leaders (such as Gandhi in India, the Guomindang in China, the Kemalist Party in Turkey, the Wafdist Party in Egypt, etc.) But during and after the last war, as the economies of the colonized and semi-colonial nations strengthened, the liberation movements in those countries became mass movements led by proletarian classes, and the capitalist and feudal classes sold out to the imperialists.

The Soviet Union is victorious and strong. The newly established democratic nations are having a resounding impact on the colonized and semi-colonized areas and are inspiring the masses in their active striving [for liberation].

For all of these reasons, the postwar colonial liberation movement has had not only a *nationalist* character but also a clear *democratic* character. As the colonial liberation movement has chased the imperialist puppet lackeys, it has also swept away the corrupt feudal remnants. Because of this, the revolution in colonial and semi-colonial countries such as China, Vietnam and Indonesia have all had a *bourgeois democratic* character. In a few of these countries (such as China and Vietnam) it has also had a *new democratic* quality, where it has been under the close direction of the worker classes.

U.S. National Security Council, Report on the Position of the United States with Respect to Indochina (1950)[8]

In early 1950, the US government made a major change in its policy for Indochina. After four years of official neutrality in the conflict between France and the DRV, Washington shifted to a stance of firm support for the French war effort. The key decision came in February 1950, when the US extended official diplomatic recognition to a newly established Vietnamese government known as the Associated State of Vietnam (ASV), which had its capital at Saigon. The ASV was a French-backed regime headed by Bao Dai, the former emperor of Vietnam; the new state was unofficially known as the "Bao Dai solution," since French officials hoped to use it to undercut the nationalist appeal of Ho Chi Minh and the DRV. Although many American officials remained skeptical that the "solution" would work, others maintained that the US ought to support France and the ASV on the grounds that they were resisting the advance of communism in Asia.

This report was prepared by the US National Security Council immediately after Washington officially recognized the ASV. It explained the reasons for that decision as well as the strategic rationale for increased military aid for Indochina and for other non-communist governments in the region. This report was an early expression of what would later become known as the "domino theory" – the notion that all the nations of Southeast Asia were lined up like dominoes, and that a communist victory in Indochina would lead inexorably to communist domination of the entire region.

27 February 1950

The Problem

1. To undertake a determination of all practicable United States measures to protect its security in Indochina and to prevent the expansion of communist aggression in that area.

Analysis

2. It is recognized that the threat of communist aggression against Indochina is only one phase of anticipated communist plans to seize all of Southeast Asia. It is understood that Burma is weak internally

---

[8] *Foreign Relations of the United States, 1950.* Vol. 6: *East Asia and the* Pacific (Washington, DC: GPO, 1976), 745–747.

and could be invaded without strong opposition or even that the Government of Burma could be subverted. However, Indochina is the area most immediately threatened. It is also the only area adjacent to communist China which contains a large European army, which along with native troops is now in armed conflict with the forces of communist aggression. A decision to contain communist expansion at the border of Indochina must be considered as a part of a wider study to prevent communist aggression into other parts of Southeast Asia.

3. A large segment of the Indochinese nationalist movement was seized in 1945 by Ho Chi Minh, a Vietnamese who under various aliases has served as a communist agent for thirty years. He has attracted non-communist as well as communist elements to his support. In 1946, he attempted, but failed to secure French agreement to his recognition as the head of a government of Vietnam. Since then he has directed a guerrilla army in raids against French installations and lines of communication. French forces which have been attempting to restore law and order found themselves pitted against a determined adversary who manufactures effective arms locally, who received supplies of arms from outside sources, who maintained no capital or permanent headquarters and who was, and is able, to disrupt and harass almost any area within Vietnam (Tonkin, Annam and Cochinchina) at will.

4. The United States has, since the Japanese surrender, pointed out to the French Government that the legitimate nationalist aspirations of the people of Indochina must be satisfied, and that a return to the prewar colonial rule is not possible. The Department of State has pointed out to the French Government that it was and is necessary to establish and support governments in Indochina, particularly in Vietnam, under leaders who are capable of attracting to their causes the non-communist nationalist followers who had drifted to the Ho Chi Minh communist movement in the absence of any non-communist nationalist movement around which to plan their aspirations.

5. In an effort to establish stability by political means, where military measures had been unsuccessful, i.e., by attracting non-communist nationalists, now followers of Ho Chi Minh, to the support of anti-communist nationalist leaders, the French Government entered into agreements with the governments of the Kingdoms of Laos and Cambodia to elevate their status from protectorates to that of independent states within the French Union. The Associated State of Vietnam was formed, with similar status, out of the former French protectorates of Tonkin, Annam and the former French Colony of Cochinchina. Each state received an increased degree of autonomy and sovereignty. Further steps towards

independence were indicated by the French. The agreements were rat-
ified by the French Government on 2 February 1950.

6. The Governments of Vietnam, Laos and Cambodia were officially rec-
    ognized by the United States and the United Kingdom on February
    7, 1950. Other Western powers have, or are committed to do like-
    wise. The United States has consistently brought to the attention of
    non-communist Asian countries the danger of communist aggres-
    sion which threatens them if communist expansion in Indochina is
    unchecked. As this danger becomes more evident it is expected to over-
    come the reluctance that they have had to recognize and support the
    three new states. We are therefore continuing to press those countries
    to recognize the new states. On January 18, 1950, the Chinese Com-
    munist Government announced its recognition of the Ho Chi Minh
    movement as the legal Government of Vietnam, while on January 30,
    1950, the Soviet Government, while maintaining diplomatic relations
    with France, similarly announced its recognition.

7. The newly formed States of Vietnam, Laos and Cambodia do not as
    yet have sufficient political stability nor military power to prevent the
    infiltration into their areas of Ho Chi Minh's forces. The French Armed
    Forces, while apparently effectively utilized at the present time, can
    do little more than to maintain the status quo. Their strength of some
    140,000 does, however, represent an army in being and the only mili-
    tary bulwark in that area against the further expansion of communist
    aggression from either internal or external forces.

8. The presence of Chinese Communist troops along the border of
    Indochina makes it possible for arms, material and troops to move
    freely from Communist China to the northern Tonkin area now con-
    trolled by Ho Chi Minh. There is already evidence of movement of
    arms.

9. In the present state of affairs, it is doubtful that the combined native
    Indochinese and French troops can successfully contain Ho's forces
    should they be strengthened by either Chinese Communist troops cross-
    ing the border, or Communist-supplied arms and material in quantity
    from outside Indochina strengthening Ho's forces.

Conclusions

10. It is important to United States security interests that all practicable
    measures be taken to prevent further communist expansion in South-
    east Asia. Indochina is a key area of Southeast Asia and is under imme-
    diate threat.

11. The neighboring countries of Thailand and Burma could be expected to fall under Communist domination if Indochina were controlled by a Communist-dominated government. The balance of Southeast Asia would then be in grave hazard.

12. Accordingly, the Departments of State and Defense should prepare as a matter of priority a program of all practicable measures designed to protect United States security interests in Indochina.

Robert Blum, Telegram on US Economic Aid to France in Indochina (1951)[9]

Following Washington's recognition of the Bao Dai government in early 1950, the US government began to provide large amounts of military and economic aid to the French in Indochina. The American presence in Saigon and other Vietnamese cities grew substantially during the early 1950s, as dozens of military advisors, aid experts, and other officials were dispatched to the region. The British writer Graham Greene, who lived in Saigon during this period, found many of the new American arrivals to be fervent idealists who displayed "missionary zeal" in their efforts to prevent a communist victory in Indochina. In 1955, Greene published a novel inspired in part by his encounters with these Americans. The novel, entitled The Quiet American, *told the story of a young American aid official named Alden Pyle who tried to organize an independent anticommunist Vietnamese army in Indochina.*

One of the real-life Americans who may have served as a model for Greene's Pyle was Robert Blum, who arrived in Saigon in 1950. Blum was the head of the Special Technical and Economic Mission (STEM), the US agency charged with oversight of nonmilitary aid programs in Vietnam. Blum annoyed French officials by expressing sympathy for Vietnamese nationalism, and by accusing the French of using US aid to subvert Vietnamese independence. He also locked horns with some of his American colleagues. In this telegram, Blum disagreed with his boss, US ambassador Donald Heath, after the latter suggested that US officials should be more accommodating of French concerns about the American aid program.

Saigon, July 12, 1951

Saigon Legation Telegram No. 2355... raised important fundamental questions concerning American [Indochina] policy in general and STEM

[9] Telegram 841, Blum to ECA, 12 July 1951, printed in *Foreign Relations of the United States, 1951*, Vol. 6, 450–452.

operations in particular. It provides [an] opportunity at close [of] our first year [of] activity... to review STEM policy and work against [the] broader background [of] American policy...

Although I agree fully with the premise of Legtel 2355, that it was and is US policy "to supplement but not to supplant" [the] French and that without French support a free Vietnam [would immediately] collapse, I do not believe the analysis of [the] present [Indochina] situation goes far enough or reaches in all respects valid conclusions, particularly as far as STEM is concerned...

The argument might be made that there [should] be closer and more systematic consultation on our program with the [French]. This point of view has considerable appeal and certainly everything [should] be done to keep the [French] as closely informed of our work as possible. We must realize, however, that there are pitfalls. Basically the [French] are not very sympathetic with our program and [would] much prefer to see our money used for other purposes such as [military] expenditures and to cover budgetary deficits of the three states[10] or the debts inherited by them from [France]. They have said so. We would have to expect that close consultation would be accompanied by constant [French] insistence on this approach and that unless we altered our program constant difficulties and bad feeling would probably result...

If the strengthening of the [French] is an imperative short-term necessity, strengthening local [anti-Communist] aspirations is no less mandatory if the [French] presence is to be continued and for the maintenance of our influence here. During its first year [of] operation the STEM program has been greatly handicapped and its beneficial psychological results largely negated because the US has been pursuing at the same time [a] program of support to the [French]....

We must do everything we can [to] avoid undermining the [French] positions but we must recognized that this undermining is the work of the [Vietnamese] themselves, brought on in part by [French] mistakes, and has been going on for many years. Perhaps the best we can hope for is to conduct here a kind of uneasy holding operation until something else happens in another place. If and when this happens the [French] may have to withdrawn entirely, and unless we are willing [to] abandon this area indefinitely we [should] try [to] maintain [a] position of influence in this part of the world where only [a] break with [the] past offers a firm foundation for the future.

---

[10] Blum here refers to the French-sponsored Associated State of Vietnam and as well as the states of Cambodia and Laos.

I think our position in these matters needs to be explained quite openly and frankly to the [French] who [should] see that it is no narrow selfish interest that inspires us. I do not think the tone [should] be an apologetic one. We are helping [to] defend their interests as well as ours…On the basis of my experience during the past year I am confident that an understanding with the French is possible, provided we hold firmly to the principles that brought us here…

BLUM

Memorandum of a Conversation with President Eisenhower about Dien Bien Phu (1954)[11]

The most important battle of the First Indochina War took place during the spring of 1954, in a remote valley in northern Vietnam. On March 13, Viet Minh forces laid siege to a French garrison in the town of Dien Bien Phu, on the border between Tonkin and Laos. When the assault began, French commanders were stunned and dismayed to discover that the attackers had deployed dozens of artillery and anti-aircraft guns into the mountains overlooking the valley. The revolutionaries had accomplished this feat by disassembling the large weapons and using porters to carry them piece-by-piece over rugged mountain terrain. The big guns made it impossible for the French to send reinforcements to Dien Bien Phu by air. By late March, the Viet Minh appeared to be on the verge of overrunning the garrison – an outcome that would almost certainly destroy whatever remained of the dwindling public support for the war in France. In desperation, French officials turned to Washington and asked for a massive American air assault to force PAVN commanders to raise the siege.

US President Dwight D. Eisenhower gave serious consideration to the French request. In both public and private remarks, Eisenhower endorsed the domino theory and declared that the loss of Indochina would be a disaster that would lead to more communist gains throughout Southeast Asia. Yet the president also knew that the American public and US military commanders would be wary of direct military involvement in Indochina, especially so soon after the end of the bloody and unpopular Korean War of 1950–1953. In this memorandum, Secretary of State John Foster Dulles, Eisenhower's top advisor on foreign affairs, describes a conversation in which the president indicated that he was contemplating using military force at Dien Bien Phu, but only under certain conditions.

---

[11] "Memorandum of a Conversation, by the Secretary of State," 24 March 1954, printed in *Foreign Relations of the United States 1952–1954* (Washington, DC: GPO, 1982), 13(1): 1150.

TOP SECRET

March 24, 1954

MEMORANDUM OF CONVERSATION WITH THE PRESIDENT

...Re: Indochina, I referred to my memorandum of the day before, which the President had read, reporting the talk with Ely, Radford, et. al. The president said that he agreed basically that we should not get involved in fighting in Indochina unless there were the political preconditions necessary for a successful outcome. He did not, however, wholly exclude the possibility of a single strike [at Dien Bien Phu], if it were almost certain this would produce decisive results.

I mentioned that it might be preferable to slow up the Chinese Communists in Southeast Asia by harassing tactics from Formosa [Taiwan] and along the seacoast which would be more readily within our natural facilities than actually fighting in Indochina.[12] The President indicated his concurrence with this general attitude....

Returning to Indochina, I said that I had in mind saying in a paraphrase of the Monroe Doctrine that the freedom of the Southeast Asia area was important from the standpoint of our peace, security, and happiness, and that we could not look upon the loss to Communism of that area with indifference. The President agreed and also authorized us to give Ambassador Heath[13] some discretionary authority to bolster up the morale of the Associated States leaders if there seemed to be evidence of a collapse of the French will. He did not, however, want anything said that would be an explicit promise that we might not be able to live up to.

JFD

Final Declaration of the Geneva Conference (1954)[14]

The Battle of Dien Bien Phu ended with the surrender of the French garrison on May 7, 1954. The timing of the victory could not have been better for the Viet Minh: it came exactly one day before the opening of peace talks in Geneva, Switzerland, between French and DRV government representatives. Those talks took place as part of a conference sponsored by the leading Cold War powers (the United States, Great Britain, the Soviet Union, and China).

---

[12] Dulles here proposed to provide US support to the anticommunist government of the Republic of China (based on Taiwan) for military attacks against communist forces in Indochina.
[13] Donald Heath: the American Ambassador to the French-sponsored governments of Vietnam, Laos, and Cambodia.
[14] *The Department of State Bulletin*, XXXI, No. 788 (August 2, 1954), p. 164.

On July 20, 1954, after months of wrangling, French and DRV officials signed an agreement to end the war. The deal provided for Vietnam to be temporarily divided into two "military regroupment zones" separated at the 17th parallel, in the middle of the country. The DRV would administer the northern zone (which included Hanoi and the Red River Delta), while Bao Dai's Associated State of Vietnam government would take charge of the southern zone (including Saigon and the Mekong Delta). The agreement also specified that nationwide elections to choose a single government for all of Vietnam would be held in July 1956.

After French and DRV officials announced the terms of their deal, other diplomats at the conference drafted the following "final declaration." While the declaration was not signed by any of the participants, it was intended to demonstrate that the peace deal enjoyed broad international support. However, the Eisenhower administration refused to give its unqualified endorsement to the Geneva deal, and promised merely to "refrain from the threat or use of force" to disturb the peace. The Bao Dai government also refused to accept the agreements, accusing the Viet Minh of betraying the cause of national liberation.

---

21 July 1954

1. The Conference takes note of the agreements ending hostilities in Cambodia, Laos, and Viet-Nam and organizing international control and the supervision of the execution of the provisions of these agreements.

2. The Conference expresses satisfaction at the ending of hostilities in Cambodia, Laos, and Viet-Nam. The Conference expresses its conviction that the execution of the provisions set out in the present declaration and in the agreements on the cessation of hostilities will permit Cambodia, Laos, and Viet-Nam henceforth to play their part, in full independence and sovereignty, in the peaceful community of nations.

3. The Conference takes note of the declarations made by the Governments of Cambodia and of Laos of their intention to adopt measures permitting all citizens to take their place in the national community, in particular by participating in the next general elections, which, in conformity with the constitution of each of these countries, shall take place in the course of the year 1955, by secret ballot and in conditions of respect for fundamental freedoms.

4. The Conference takes note of the clauses in the agreement on the cessation of hostilities in Viet-Nam prohibiting the introduction into Viet Nam of foreign troops and military personnel as well as of all kinds of

arms and munitions. The Conference also takes note of the declarations made by the Governments of Cambodia and Laos of their resolution not to request foreign aid, whether in war material, in personnel, or in instructors except for the purpose of effective defense of their territory and, in the case of Laos, to the extent defined by the agreements on the cessation of hostilities in Laos.

5. The Conference takes note of the clauses in the agreement on the cessation of hostilities in Viet-Nam to the effect that no military base at the disposition of a foreign state may be established in the regrouping zones of the two parties, the latter having the obligation to see that the zones allotted to them shall not constitute part of any military alliance and shall not be utilized for the resumption of hostilities or in the service of an aggressive policy. The Conference also takes note of the declarations of the Governments of Cambodia and Laos to the effect that they will not join in any agreement with other states if this agreement includes the obligation to participate in a military alliance not in conformity with the principles of the charter of the United Nations or, in the case of Laos, with the principles of the agreement on the cessation of hostilities in Laos or, so long as their security is not threatened, the obligation to establish bases on Cambodian or Laotian territory for the military forces of foreign powers.

6. The Conference recognizes that the essential purpose of the agreement relating to Viet-Nam is to settle military questions with a view to ending hostilities and that the military demarcation line should not in any way be interpreted as constituting a political or territorial boundary. The Conference expresses its conviction that the execution of the provisions set out in the present declaration and in the agreement on the cessation of hostilities creates the necessary basis for the achievement in the near future of a political settlement in Viet-Nam.

7. The Conference declares that, so far as Viet-Nam is concerned, the settlement of political problems, effected on the basis of respect for the principles of independence, unity, and territorial integrity, shall permit the Vietnamese people to enjoy the fundamental freedoms, guaranteed by democratic institutions established as a result of free general elections by secret ballot.

    In order to insure that sufficient progress in the restoration of peace has been made, and that all the necessary conditions obtain for free expression of the national will, general elections shall be held in July 1956, under the supervision of an international commission composed of representatives of the member states of the International Supervisory Commission referred to in the agreement on the cessation of hostilities.

Consultations will be held on this subject between the competent representative authorities of the two zones from April 20, 1955, onwards.

8. The provisions of the agreements on the cessation of hostilities intended to insure the protection of individuals and of property must be most strictly applied and must, in particular, allow everyone in Viet-Nam to decide freely in which zone he wishes to live.

9. The competent representative authorities of the northern and southern zones of Viet-Nam, as well as the authorities of Laos and Cambodia, must not permit any individual or collective reprisals against persons who have collaborated in any way with one of the parties during the war, or against members of such persons' families.

10. The Conference takes note of the declaration of the French Government to the effect that it is ready to withdraw its troops from the territory of Cambodia, Laos, and Viet-Nam, at the request of the governments concerned and within a period which shall be fixed by agreement between the parties except in the cases where, by agreement between the two parties, a certain number of French troops shall remain at specified points and for a specified time.

11. The Conference takes note of the declaration of the French Government to the effect that for the settlement of all the problems connected with the reestablishment and consolidation of peace in Cambodia, Laos, and Viet-Nam, the French Government will proceed from the principle of respect for the independence and sovereignty, unity, and territorial integrity of Cambodia, Laos, and Viet-Nam.

12. In their relations with Cambodia, Laos, and Viet-Nam, each member of the Geneva Conference undertakes to respect the sovereignty, the independence, the unity, and the territorial integrity of the above-mentioned states, and to refrain from any interference in their internal affairs.

13. The members of the Conference agree to consult one another on any question which may be referred to them by the International Supervisory Commission, in order to study such measures as may prove necessary to insure that the agreements on the cessation of hostilities in Cambodia, Laos, and Viet-Nam are respected.

Discussion questions

1. Why, according to Xuan Vu, did ordinary Vietnamese in the Mekong Delta support the Viet Minh during and after the August Revolution of 1945? Are his claims about the broad popular support for the revolution believable? Why or why not?

2. Some historians argue that the Truman administration's decision not to recognize Ho Chi Minh's DRV government after the August Revolution of 1945 constituted a "lost chance for peace." Do you agree with this assessment?

3. If you had been advising Harry S. Truman on policy for Indochina in 1950, would you have recommended (a) recognition of and aid for the Viet Minh government; (b) recognition of and aid for the Bao Dai government and the French; or (c) continued neutrality in the war between the French and the Viet Minh? Explain your recommendation.

4. Should the United States have endorsed the Geneva Accords of 1954? Why or why not?

Chapter 3   The Two Vietnams

Col. Edward G. Lansdale, Report on the activities of the Saigon Military Mission (1955)[1]

Following the Geneva conference, the task of establishing administrative authority over South Vietnam – as the territory south of the 17th parallel would be called – fell to Ngo Dinh Diem, the newly appointed prime minister of the Saigon government. Diem's task would not be an easy one. When he took office in July 1954, South Vietnam seemed an ungovernable tangle of rival armies, parties, and factions. Warlords and private militias controlled much of the Mekong Delta and even parts of Saigon. The commander of the Associated State of Vietnam's army, General Nguyen Van Hinh, openly threatened to stage a coup to remove Diem from power. Amazingly, however, Diem was able to outmaneuver all of these enemies and to stay in power. In May 1955, after ousting General Hinh and rallying the army to his side, Diem crushed his opponents in a showdown battle fought in the streets of Saigon.

Some historians have attributed Diem's unexpected triumph in 1955 to Colonel Edward G. Lansdale, a CIA operative who headed a small team of Americans known as the Saigon Military Mission (SMM). During this period, Lansdale's men conducted many covert operations in both North and South Vietnam, including some that targeted Diem's opponents. In the secret report

[1] Document No. 15, "Lansdale Team's Report on Covert Saigon Mission in '54 and '55," printed in *The Pentagon Papers As Published by the New York Times* (New York: Bantam Books, 1971), 53–66.

Original publication details: 3.1 Lansdale in The Pentagon Papers as Published by the New York Times, 1971. 3.2 President Ngo Dinh Diem on Democracy: Addresses Relative to the Constitution, 1958. 3.3 Ladejinsky in Walinsky, 1977. Reproduced with permission from The World Bank. 3.4 Excerpted from Journal of Vietnamese Studies, 2010, 243-247. Translation by Tuong Vu from The Complete Collection of Party Documents, 2001.

printed below (written sometime during 1955), Lansdale relates these
exploits in dramatic fashion. This report clearly reflects Lansdale's desire to
take credit for having "saved" South Vietnam from communism. However, it
also affords a glimpse into the political turmoil of the period.

I. Foreword

This is the condensed account of one year in the operations of a "cold war" combat team, written by the team itself in the field, little by little in moments taken as the members could. The team is known as the Saigon Military Mission. The field is Vietnam. There are other teams in the field, American, French, British, Chinese, Vietnamese, Vietminh, and others. Each has its own story to tell. This is ours.

The Saigon Military Mission entered Vietnam on 1 June 1954 when its Chief arrived. However, this is the story of a team, and it wasn't until August 1954 that sufficient members arrived to constitute a team. So, this is mainly an account of the team's first year, from August 1954 to August 1955.

It was often a frustrating and perplexing year, up close. The Geneva Agreements signed on 21 July 1954 imposed restrictive rules upon all official Americans, including the Saigon Military Mission. An active and intelligent enemy made full use of legal rights to screen his activities in establishing his stay-behind organizations south of the 17th Parallel and in obtaining quick security north of that Parallel. The nation's economy and communications system were crippled by eight years of open war. The government, including its Army and other security forces, was in a painful transition from colonial to self rule, making it a year of hot-tempered incidents. Internal problems arose quickly to points where armed conflict was sought as the only solution. The enemy was frequently forgotten in the heavy atmosphere of suspicion, hatred, and jealousy.

The Saigon Military Mission received some blows from allies and the enemy in this atmosphere, as we worked to help stabilize the government and to beat the Geneva time-table of Communist takeover in the north. However, we did beat the time-table. The government did become stabilized. The Free Vietnamese are now becoming unified and learning how to cope with the Communist enemy. We are thankful that we had a chance to help in this work in a critical area of the world, to be positive and constructive in a year of doubt.

II. Mission

The Saigon Military Mission (SMM) was born in a Washington policy meeting early in 1954, when Dien Bien Phu was still holding out against the encircling Vietminh. The SMM was to enter into Vietnam quietly and assist the Vietnamese, rather than the French, in unconventional warfare. The French were to be kept as friendly allies in the process, as far as possible.

The broad mission for the team was to undertake paramilitary operations against the enemy and to wage political-psychological warfare. Later, after Geneva, the mission was modified to prepare the means for undertaking paramilitary operations in Communist areas rather than to wage unconventional warfare....

III. Highlights of the Year

a. Early Days

The Saigon Military Mission (SMM) started on 1 June 1954, when its Chief, Colonel Edward G. Lansdale, USAF, arrived in Saigon with a small box of files and clothes and a borrrowed typewriter, courtesy of an SA-16 flight set up for him by the 13th Air Force at Clark AFB. Lt-General John O'Daniel and Embassy Chargé Rob McClintock had arranged for his appointment as Assistant Air Attache, since it was improper for U.S. officers at MAAG at that time to have advisory conferences with Vietnamese officers.[2] Ambassador Heath had concurred already. There was no desk space for an office, no vehicle, no safe for files. He roomed with General O'Daniel, later moved to a small house rented by MAAG. Secret communications with Washington were provided through the Saigon station of CIA.

There was deepening gloom in Vietnam. Dien Bien Phu had fallen. The French were capitulating to the Vietminh at Geneva. The first night in Saigon, Vietminh saboteurs blew up large ammunition dumps at the airport, rocking Saigon throughout the night. General O'Daniel and Charge McClintock agreed that it was time to start taking positive action. O'Daniel paved the way for a quick first-hand survey of the situation throughout the country. McClintock paved the way for contacts with Vietnamese political leaders. Our Chief's reputation from the Philippines had preceded him. Hundreds of Vietnamese acquaintanceships were made quickly.

---

[2] MAAG: Military Advisory Assistance Group. This team of US military officers (established in 1950) oversaw all American military aid for Indochina.

Working in close cooperation with George Hellyer, USIS Chief, a new psychological warfare campaign was devised for the Vietnamese Army and for the government in Hanoi. Shortly after, a refresher course in combat psywar was constructed and Vietnamese Army personnel were rushed through it. A similar course was initiated for the Ministry of Information. Rumor campaigns were added to the tactics and tried out in Hanoi. It was almost too late.

The first rumor campaign was to be a carefully planted story of a Chinese Communist regiment in Tonkin taking reprisals against a Vietminh village whose girls the Chinese had raped, recalling Chinese Nationalist troop behavior in 1945 and confirming Vietnamese fears of Chinese occupation under Vietminh rule; the story was to be planted by soldiers of the Vietnamese Armed Psywar Company in Hanoi dressed in civilian clothes. The troops received their instructions silently, dressed in civilian clothes, went on the mission, and failed to return. They had deserted to the Vietminh. Weeks later, Tonkinese told an excited story of the misbehavior of the Chinese Divisions in Vietminh territory. Investigated, it turned out to be the old rumor campaign, with Vietnamese embellishments....

Ngo Dinh Diem arrived on 7 July, and within hours was in despair as the French forces withdrew from the Catholic provinces of Phat Diem and Narn Dinh in Tonkin.[3] Catholic militia streamed north to Hanoi and Haiphong, their hearts filled with anger at French abandonment. The two SMM officers stopped a planned grenade attack by militia girls against French troops guarding a warehouse; the girls stated they had not eaten for three days; arrangements were made for Chinese merchants in Haiphong to feed them. Other militia attacks were stopped, including one against a withdrawing French artillery unit; the militia wanted the guns to stand and fight the Vietminh. The Tonkinese had hopes of American friendship and listened to the advice given them. Governor [name illegible] died, reportedly by poison. Tonkin's government changed as despair grew. On 21 July, the Geneva Agreement was signed. Tonkin was given to the Communists. Anti-Communists turned to SMM for help in establishing a resistance movement and several tentative initial arrangements were made.

Diem himself had reached a nadir of frustration, as his country disintegrated after the conference of foreigners. With the approval of Ambassador Heath and General O'Daniel, our Chief drew up a plan of overall governmental action and presented it to Diem, with Hellyer as interpreter. It called

---

[3] Lansdale here confuses the date on which Diem returned to Vietnam from exile (June 26) with the date on which he was officially sworn in as prime minister (July 7).

for fast constructive action and dynamic leadership. Although the plan was not adopted, it laid the foundation for a friendship which has lasted.

b. August 1954

...[SMM team member] Major Conein was given responsibility for developing a paramilitary organization in the north, to be in position when the Vietminh took over. . . . [His] team was moved north immediately as part of the MAAG staff working on the refugee problem. The team had headquarters in Hanoi, with a branch in Haiphong. Among cover duties, this team supervised the refugee flow for the Hanoi airlift organized by the French. One day, as a CAT C-46 finished loading, they saw a small child standing on the ground below the loading door. They shouted for the pilot to wait, picked the child up and shoved him into the aircraft, which then promptly taxied out for its takeoff in the constant air shuttle. A Vietnamese man and woman ran up to the team, asking what they had done with their small boy, whom they'd brought out to say goodbye to relatives. The chagrined team explained, finally talked the parents into going south to Free Vietnam, put them in the next aircraft to catch up with their son in Saigon....

c. September 1954

Highly-placed officials from Washington visited Saigon and, in private conversations, indicated that current estimates led to the conclusion that Vietnam probably would have to be written off as a loss. We admitted that prospects were gloomy, but were positive that there was still a fighting chance.

On 8 September, SMM officers visited Secretary of State for Defense Chan and walked into a tense situation in his office. Chan had just arrested Lt-Col Lan (G-6 of the Vietnamese Army) and Capt Giai (G-5 of the Army). Armed guards filled the room. We were told what had happened and assured that everything was all right by all three principals. Later, we discovered that Chan was alone and that the guards were Lt-Col Lan's commandos. Lan was charged with political terrorism (by his "action" squads) and Giai with anti-Diem propaganda (using G-5 leaflet, rumor, and broadcast facilities).

The arrest of Lan and Giai, who simply refused to consider themselves arrested, and of Lt Minh, officer in charge of the Army radio station which was guarded by Army troops, brought into the open a plot by the Army Chief of Staff, General Hinh, to overthrow the government. Hinh had hinted at such a plot to his American friends, using a silver cigarette box given him by Egypt's Naguib to carry the hint. SMM became thoroughly involved in the tense controversy which followed, due to our Chief's closeness to both President Diem and General Hinh. He had met the latter in the Philippines in 1952, was a friend of both Hinh's wife and favorite mistress. (The mistress was a pupil in a small English class conducted for mistresses of important personages, at their request....)

While various U.S. officials including General O'Daniel and Foreign Service Officer Frank [name illegible] participated in U.S. attempts to heal the split between the President and his Army, Ambassador Heath asked us to make a major effort to end the controversy. This effort strained relations with Diem and never was successful, but did dampen Army enthusiasm for the plot. At one moment, when there was likelihood of an attack by armored vehicles on the Presidential Palace, SMM told Hinh bluntly that U.S. support most probably would stop in such an event...

As a result of the Hinh trouble, Diem started looking around for troops upon whom he could count. Some Tonkinese militia, refugees from the north, were assembled in Saigon close to the Palace. But they were insufficient for what he needed. Diem made an agreement with General Trinh Minh The, leader of some 3,000 Cao Dai dissidents in the vicinity of Tayninh, to give General The some needed financial support; The was to give armed support to the government if necessary and to provide a safe haven for the government if it had to flee. The's guerrillas, known as the Lien Minh, were strongly nationalist and were still fighting the Vietminh and the French. At Ambassador Heath's request, the U.S. secretly furnished Diem with funds for The, through the SMM. Shortly afterwards, an invitation came from The to visit him. Ambassador Heath approved the visit....

The northern SMM team under Conein had organized a paramilitary group, (which we will disguise by the Vietnamese name of Binh) through the Northern Dai Viets, a political party with loyalties to Bao Dai. The group was to be trained and supported by the U.S. as patriotic Vietnamese, to come eventually under government control when the government was ready for such activities. Thirteen Binhs were quietly exfiltrated through the port of Haiphong, under the direction of Lt Andrews, and taken on the first stage of the journey to their training area by a U.S. Navy ship. This was the first of a series of helpful actions by Task Force 98, commanded by Admiral Sabin.

Another paramilitary group for Tonkin operations was being developed in Saigon through General Nguyen Van Vy. In September this group started shaping up fast, and the project was given to Major Allen. (We will give this group the Vietnamese name of Hao)....

Towards the end of the month, it was learned that the largest printing establishment in the north intended to remain in Hanoi and do business with the Vietminh. An attempt was made by SMM to destroy the modern presses, but Vietminh security agents already had moved into the plant and frustrated the attempt. This operation was under a Vietnamese patriot whom we shall call Trieu; his case officer was Capt Arundel. Earlier in the month they had engineered a black psywar strike in Hanoi: leaflets signed by the Vietminh instructing Tonkinese on how to behave for the Vietminh takeover of the Hanoi region in early October, including items about property, money reform, and a three-day holiday of workers upon takeover. The day following the distribution of these leaflets, refugee registration tripled. Two days later Vietminh currency was worth half the value prior to the leaflets. The Vietminh took to the radio to denounce the leaflets; the leaflets were so authentic in appearance that even most of the rank and file Vietminh were sure that the radio denunciations were a French trick....

d. October 1954

Hanoi was evacuated on 9 October. The northern SMM team left with the last French troops, disturbed by what they had seen of the grim efficiency of the Vietminh in their takeover, the contrast between the silent march of the victorious Vietminh troops in their tennis shoes and the clanking armor of the well-equipped French whose western tactics and equipment had failed against the Communist military-political-economic campaign.

The northern team had spent the last days of Hanoi in contaminating the oil supply of the bus company for a gradual wreckage of engines in the buses, in taking the first actions for delayed sabotage of the railroad (which required teamwork with a CIA special technical team in Japan who performed their part brilliantly), and in writing detailed notes of potential targets for future paramilitary operations (U.S. adherence to the Geneva Agreement prevented SMM from carrying out the active sabotage it desired to do against the power plant, water facilities, harbor, and bridge). The team had a bad moment when contaminating the oil. They had to work quickly at night, in an enclosed storage room. Fumes from the contaminant came close to knocking them out. Dizzy and weak-kneed, they masked their faces with handkerchiefs and completed the job.

Meanwhile, Polish and Russian ships had arrived in the south to transport southern Vietminh to Tonkin under the Geneva Agreement. This offered the opportunity for another black psywar strike. A leaflet was developed by Binh with the help of Capt Arundel, attributed to the Vietminh Resistance Committee. Among other items, it reassured the Vietminh they would be kept safe below decks from imperialist air and submarine attacks, and requested that warm clothing be brought; the warm clothing item would be coupled with a verbal rumor campaign that Vietminh were being sent into China as railroad laborers.

...Contention between Diem and Hinh had become murderous.... Finally, we learned that Hinh was close to action; he had selected 26 October as the morning for an attack on the Presidential Palace. Hinh was counting heavily on Lt-Col Lan's special forces and on Captain Giai who was running Hinh's secret headquarters at Hinh's home. We invited these two officers to visit the Philippines, on the pretext that we were making an official trip, could take them along and open the way for them to see some inner workings of the fight against Filipino Communists which they probably would never see otherwise. Hinh reluctantly turned down his own invitation; he had had a memorable time of it on his last visit to Manila in 1952. Lt-Col Lan was a French agent and the temptation to see behind-the-scenes was too much. He and Giai accompanied SMM officers on the MAAG C-47 which General O'Daniel instantly made available for the operation. 26 October was spent in the Philippines. The attack on the palace didn't come off.

e. November 1954

General Lawton Collins arrived as Ambassador on 8 November....

Collins, in his first press conference, made it plain that the U.S. was supporting President Diem. The new Ambassador applied pressure on General Hinh and on 29 November Hinh left for Paris. His other key conspirators followed.

Part of the SMM team became involved in staff work to back up the energetic campaign to save Vietnam which Collins pushed forward. Some SMM members were scattered around the Pacific, accompanying Vietnamese for secret training, obtaining and shipping supplies to be smuggled into north Vietnam and hidden there. In the Philippines, more support was being constructed to help SMM, in expediting the flow of supplies, and in creating Freedom Company, a non-profit Philippines corporation backed by President Magsaysay, which would supply Filipinos experienced in fighting the Communist Huks to help in Vietnam (or elsewhere)....

g. January 1955

The Vietminh long ago had adopted the Chinese Communist thought that the people are the water and the army is the fish. Vietminh relations with the mass of the population during the fighting had been exemplary, with a few exceptions; in contrast, the Vietnamese National Army had been like too many Asian armies, adept at cowing a population into feeding them, providing them with girls. SMM had been working on this problem from the beginning. Since the National Army was the only unit of government with a strong organization throughout the country and with good communications, it was the key to stabilizing the situation quickly on a nation-wide basis. If Army and people could be brought together into a team, the first strong weapon against Communism could be forged.

The Vietminh were aware of this. We later learned that months before the signing of the Geneva Agreement they had been planning for action in the post-Geneva period; the National Army was to be the primary target for subversion efforts, it was given top priority by the Central Committee for operations against its enemy, and about 100 superior cadres were retrained for the operations and placed in the [words illegible] organization for the work, which commenced even before the agreement was signed. We didn't know it at the time, but this was SMM's major opponent, in a secret struggle for the National Army....

The patriot we've named Trieu Dinh had been working on an almanac for popular sale, particularly in the northern cities and towns we could still reach. Noted Vietnamese astrologers were hired to write predictions about coming disasters to certain Vietminh leaders and undertakings, and to predict unity in the south. The work was carried out under the direction of Lt Phillips, based on our concept of the use of astrology for psywar in Southeast Asia. Copies of the almanac were shipped by air to Haiphong and then smuggled into Vietminh territory.

Dinh also had produced a Thomas Paine type series of essays on Vietnamese patriotism against the Communist Vietminh, under the guidance of Capt. Arundel. These essays were circulated among influential groups in Vietnam, earned front-page editorials in the leading daily newspaper in Saigon. Circulation increased with the publication of these essays. The publisher is known to SMM as The Dragon Lady and is a fine Vietnamese girl who has been the mistress of an anti-American French civilian. Despite anti-American remarks by her boy friend, we had helped her keep her paper from being closed by the government....and she found it profitable to heed our advice on the editorial content of her paper.

Ngo Dinh Diem, Message to the RVN National Assembly on the Foundations of the Constitution (1956)[4]

Following his triumph in the Battle of Saigon, Ngo Dinh Diem lost no time in consolidating his authority inside South Vietnam. During the summer of 1955, he announced that his government would not cooperate in holding the all-Vietnam unification elections called for by the Geneva Accords. Instead, he organized a popular referendum in which South Vietnamese voters had to choose between his leadership and that of Bao Dai, the now-discredited ASV chief of state. After winning more than 98 percent of the vote in a blatantly unfair process, Diem announced that the ASV had been replaced by a new state, known as the Republic of Vietnam (RVN). He proclaimed himself its first president. In early 1956, the government held elections for a new National Assembly. Not surprisingly, pro-Diem groups won a large majority of the seats.

In response to complaints that he had become a dictator, Diem insisted that he was in fact a genuine democrat – his definition of "democracy" just differed from the one favored by Americans and Europeans. In the following speech, delivered to the newly elected National Assembly in April 1956, Diem laid out his views on democracy and outlined his state-building goals. Note that Diem criticized not only communist theories of social progress but also classical liberal ideas about individual freedom. For him, the best path for South Vietnam lay in between the twin extremes of Marxist collectivism and liberal individualism – a middle way that would cultivate what he described as the needs of the "human person."

Mr. President, Deputies:

By virtue of the mandate which the nation vested in me by the referendum of October 23, 1955, and by the terms of the Provisional Constitution Act, I have the honor to transmit to the National Assembly my viewpoint on the constitutional problem.

Numerous constitutions have been drawn up and promulgated in the past with the intention of setting up Democracy. During the 18th and 19th centuries, constitutions were drawn up which established political regimes, later known as political democracies, in which individualism and economic liberalism were advocated as proper formulas to emancipate man and lead mankind toward happiness.

While this system in its appreciation brought relative freedom to a minority of its citizens, at the same time it lessened the effectiveness of the state,

[4] *President Ngo Dinh Diem on Democracy: Addresses Relative to the Constitution*, 2nd edn. (Saigon: RVN Presidency, 1958), 13–17.

which became impotent to defend collective interests and to solve social problems.

The events preceding the two world wars revealed these weaknesses more than ever before, and, in certain States led to the birth of fascism, which aims at a concentration of powers and a personal dictatorship.

On the same pretext of organizing power effectively and achieve social justice, another reaction has been manifested in the form of communism and the so-called popular democracies. At the cost of heavy restrictions and the sacrifice of individual liberties, these systems have merely imposed party dictatorships.

Even in the regimes of political democracy which were faithful to the traditional concept of democracy, an important current of ideas has for a number of years led thinkers and jurists to revise the basic notions of modern democracies, as well as their methods and structures.

Most democratic states have endeavored, either by constitutional changes or by legislative enactment, to modify their political institutions in important respects. Although they have been diverse, these transformations of Public Law which aim at reconciling the demands of collective discipline and social justice with those of individual liberty reveal a personalistic tendency. In addition to the negative liberties of a political nature, it is recognized that the human person has positive freedoms of an economic and social nature. At the same time the state, organized on a more democratic basis, is given a wider, more stable and more effective grant of power to bring positive assistance to the citizen against the massive dangers of materialistic civilization, and to guarantee him the right to live and exercise his liberties.

Viet-Nam welcomes gladly the teaching born of the experience of those democratic states, all the more as it is consistent with the political humanism and the historical situation of Viet-Nam.

Placed by its geographical position at the outpost of the Free World, at the confluence of great currents of thought and on one of the great axes of human migration, Viet-Nam is continually exposed to multiple dangers which threaten its political stability. Thus the grave problems which we have to solve now are not transitory or accidental phenomena. The risks of relapsing into anarchy and servitude brought about by the internal feudalism or foreign imperialism that lies in wait for all newly emancipated peoples weigh more heavily on our country than on others, because of our geographic position. This is all the more true since the communism which has been established in the North constitutes a continuing latent menace for South Viet-Nam. Even after reunification, Viet-Nam, located at the nerve center between two great demographic masses, will remain a sensitive zone subject to instability.

These, gentlemen, are the present tendencies of public law among free peoples and the constant geopolitical facts of Viet-Nam.

It is in light of these experiences, of these realities, and of the tradition of Vietnamese humanism that I invite you to examine the problems of the future political regime of our country. In that which concerns us as Vietnamese, we must increase tenfold the dialectical efforts by which our elders in democracy have tried to smooth the conflict between social justice and liberty for the sake of the human person.

Faced with the massive forces of material and political oppression which threaten us constantly, we feel more than other peoples the essential necessity of grounding our political life in a clear cut and solid basis, and to rigorously concentrate the successive stages of our action along the same line towards an increasingly great democratic progress.

Such a basis can only be a spiritualist one; such a line, that which the human person follows in his innermost reality as in his community life, in his transcendent vocation as in his free pursuit of intellectual, moral and spiritual perfection.

Thus we affirm our faith in the absolute value of the human person, whose dignity antedates society and whose destiny is greater than time.

We affirm that the sole legitimate end and object of the State is to protect the fundamental rights of the human person to existence and to the free development of his intellectual, moral and spiritual life.

We affirm that democracy is neither material happiness nor the supremacy of numbers.

Democracy is essentially a permanent effort to find the right political means for assuring to all citizens the right of free development and of maximum initiative, responsibility, and spiritual life.

In the name of these principles, we solemnly declare:

1. Viet-Nam is an independent Republic, one and indivisible,
2. Citizens are born free and equal before the law. The State should assure them equal conditions for the exercise of their rights and the accomplishment of their duties. It owes aid and protection to the family so that harmonious family life can develop. Citizens have a right to a secure and peaceful life, to justify remunerated work, to sufficient individual property to assure a dignified and free life, to democratic freedoms, and to the full development of their personalities.

   They have the duty of developing the national heritage for the Common Good and for universal peace, of safeguarding freedom and democracy, of defending the Nation and the Republic against all those who seek to destroy the foundation of the common life and the Constitution.

3. Sovereignty belongs to the people.

The elected National Assembly is vested with legislative competence.

The President of the Republic, also elected by universal, direct and secret ballot is vested with executive competence. The family vote is admitted, and the voting rights and eligibility of women is recognized. The separation of powers should be clear and the responsibilities of the different organs of the State well defined, and their activities well-coordinated to assure a maximum of stability and efficiency. A High Court of Justice will be established to decide cases of high treason.

4. The judiciary should be independent in order to make an efficacious contribution to the defense of the Republic, of order, of freedom and of Democracy.

5. A Supreme Court should be organized for the control of the constitutionality of laws.

6. Economic forces should associate in the exercise of power in the form of a National Economic Council composed of representatives of union and professional groups and which will present suggestions and opinions on bills of economic interest.

Ladies and Gentlemen, the constitutional principles which have just been outlined are intended to guarantee to the individual the full development of his capacities, and to the state a harmonious and fruitful functioning of its organs by means of the correct working of concerted actions and reciprocal control.

You are to decide upon a question of major interest to the Nation. On the solution that you will have chosen will depend the future and the prosperity of Viet-Nam. I am convinced that you will succeed in this historic mission.

Wolf Ladejinsky, A Visit with President Ngo Dinh Diem (1955)[5]

The U.S. government, though initially uncertain about Diem's prospects and merits as a leader, lent strong support to him and his government as his power grew after 1955. In public, American officials declared their unstinting support for Diem and held him up as a model American Cold War ally; US

[5] Printed in Louis J. Walinsky, ed. *Agrarian Reform as Unfinished Business: The Selected Papers of Wolf Ladejinsky* (New York: Oxford University Press, 1977), 239–243.

journalists dubbed him the "miracle man" of Vietnam. In private, however, US leaders did not view their support for Diem as unconditional. In exchange for the large volume of US aid flowing to South Vietnam, the Americans expected Diem to heed their advice – especially in the critical area of nation building in South Vietnam.

Wolf Ladejinsky was one of the Americans who arrived in South Vietnam in 1955 with hopes of advising Diem on his nation-building policies. Ladejinsky was the US government's top land reform expert and had already worked on land redistribution programs in Taiwan, South Korea, and Japan. He hoped that Ngo Dinh Diem was a leader who appreciated the pressing need for land reform in South Vietnam – especially in the Mekong Delta, where a handful of wealthy families owned huge amounts of farmland, while most of the rest of the population owned little or none. In the report below, Ladejinsky complains that Diem did not seem to share his sense of urgency about the need for land reform.

AT THE INVITATION of President Ngo Dinh Diem, I called on him on June 1 to report on the latest agrarian developments. In the course of the visit, which lasted from 5:00 to 6:30 P.M., a number of other topics were touched upon such as settlement of refugees on land, local administration, the struggle with religious sects, and the U.S. position in regard to France and Vietnam...

...I found the president in a relaxed and self-confident mood. He did not minimize the crucial problems facing free Vietnam; but, while three months ago he was unmistakably a much worried leader about to enter a period of trial of strength with his numerous opponents, now he could speak, as he did, with quiet self-assurance born of recent successful tests. He did not, for example, underestimate the seriousness of the involvement with the Hoa Hao; but he reminded the listener with quiet satisfaction that three months ago he was faced with the "united front" opposition of the Binh Xuyen, Cao Dai, and the Hoa Hao, whereas now he was concerned with the latter only. In one other familiar respect he did not change: he still prefers to talk rather than listen. Nevertheless, this time he seemed to have relaxed this presidential prerogative in favor of a balanced give-and-take.

The nature of my report was threefold: the sad state of the agrarian reform; the poor progress of settling refugees on land; and the problems presented by local administration.

As to the agrarian reform, I told the president that the appointment of a minister for agrarian reform was certainly a step in the right direction but that to date the reform is not off the ground and that there are no indications that the situation will undergo a favorable change in the immediate future. I pointed out why the tenants show no interest in his program, the potent influence of the Communists in this connection, the preference for land ownership to rent reduction, and the political and administrative vacuum in the countryside which prevents the enforcement of most measures sponsored by the national government. I took the liberty of suggesting to the president that, if his government is to make any political capital of the agrarian reform, then the time has come to reexamine the entire problem in the light of the current state of affairs...

The president did not dispute the impasse reached by his program, but he does not intend to give the land reform question a national hearing. He has confidence in his new minister of agrarian reform and is evidently willing to let him try his hand at it for a while longer. The president's reluctance to review the issue with all the care it deserves may be traced also to, what appears to me, a lack on his part of a truly abiding concern with this matter. I am not prepared to say whether the president's attitude stems from the fact that he is not a "land reformer," or that the more pressing day-to-day issues bordering the very survival of his government have primacy in his thinking and his effort to the exclusion of much else, including agrarian reform. Whatever the real reason, this much can be said with certainty: On the occasion of this talk, as during all previous talks, the land reform problems did not appear to loom large in his scheme of things....

As to local administration, I stated that, with few exceptions, it is ineffective and that no application of any national legislation is possible unless the administrators themselves become conscious of the fact that a free and independent Vietnam demands of them a zeal and zest of performance over and beyond the customary. I expressed the view that the real difficulty with the administrators is not their lack of formal public administration training but rather the lassitude, disinterestedness, and seeming failure to sense or comprehend the critical transitional period Vietnam is passing through. I made the point that, just as the national army is in need of political training, the administrators are surely in the same need. The president countered by saying that this problem has been on his mind, that he ordered the delegate for South Vietnam to prepare a secret report on local administration, and that the findings justified his worst fears. However, he did not believe he can deal with the problem outside of the overall issues relating to the country's pacification and stabilization....

The visitor did not argue the presidential preference, nor did he tell him of his most recent experience in one of the most important provinces of South Vietnam, where a new chief of province appointed by the delegate is unmistakably anti-Diem, antireform, and pretty much anti-everything that spells deviating from the current state of inaction.

I did tell the president that the standoffish attitude of the farmers toward the government is not unrelated to the local administration; above all, I suggested that it is closely related to the weak link between the national government and the farmers. I elaborated on an earlier statement under somewhat similar circumstances and suggested that the president himself might devote some time to help create among the farmers a sense of freedom of participation, a sense of belonging with the government in the business of creating a new state, basing this approach on the government's convincing appreciation of the people's fundamental needs. I attempted to impress upon him that he more than any other Vietnamese is in a position to articulate these ideas, which in the long run should prove to be the effective weapon against the Viet Minh and for the stability of Vietnam. But now, as in the past, the president pleaded extreme preoccupation with urgent matters....

...The president spoke warmly of the American attitude toward Vietnam, but he also remarked that the United States is so heavily involved in Europe and is so anxious to maintain friendly relations with France that it cannot see the French position in Vietnam as the Vietnamese see it. He added laughingly that he may be expecting too much.

It is worth noting that sometime back he spoke with asperity of Americans in Saigon who, so he said, didn't understand him and whom he, too, failed to understand. He complained without being specific that Americans gave him contradictory advice and that they were occasionally subjecting him to "shock treatment," offering suggestions at the last moment when he no longer had time for careful consideration of them. I carried away the strong impression that whatever may have given rise to those views, he hardly shares them now. When I thanked the president for his consideration, especially since I had seldom anything cheerful to contribute, he replied that Americans have a way of stating their views straightforwardly, which he appreciates even though he may not agree with them. In general, the United States was the part when the president was at his most mellow and friendly...

Vietnam Worker's Party Politburo, Directive Regarding Land Reform (1953)[6]

Beginning during the early 1950s, Vietnamese communist leaders began to move away from the heavy emphasis on the "national question," which had characterized ICP strategy and policy during the previous decade. Party

---

[6] Excerpted from *Journal of Vietnamese Studies*, Vol. 5, No. 2 (Summer 2010), 243–247. Translation by Tuong Vu. Originally published as "Chi thị của Bộ Chính trị, ngày 4 tháng 5 năm 1953, về mấy vấn đề đặc biệt trong phát động quần chúng" ["Politburo's directive issued on May 4, 1953, on some special issues regarding mass mobilization"], Văn kiện Đảng toàn tập [The Complete Collection of Party Documents] (Hanoi: Chính Tri Quốc Gia, 2001), 14: 201–206.

leaders now placed increased emphasis on the need to promote socialist transformation within Indochina. In 1951, the ICP was reorganized under a new name (the Vietnam Workers' Party, or VWP) and party officials began purging those cadres who were deemed to be insufficiently proletarian in their views and attitudes. This shift was partly a response to pressure from the DRV's foreign allies, the Soviet Union and the newly established People's Republic of China. However, it also reflected the conviction of some VWP leaders that the party needed to return to a focus on the "social question."

The text below is excerpted from a 1953 decree issued by the VWP Politburo, the organ with overall control of party policy. The decree coincided with the launch of the Party's Land Reform campaign in central and northern Indochina. As part of this campaign, VWP cadres were sent into villages to seize land from landlords and other residents who were deemed to own too much of it. The confiscated land was then redistributed to those residents who had little or no property. The campaign continued in North Vietnam until 1956, when it was suspended amid widespread complaints about "errors" and abuses. Many village residents were assaulted, jailed, or even executed during the campaign. The number of those killed remains highly controversial, with estimates ranging from a few thousand deaths to tens or even hundreds of thousands. This document, which was published in an official collection of party materials in 2001, does not settle this debate. However, it does show that top VWP officials were determined from the outset that the program would involve execution and other forms of punishment, and that even those landlords who had been supporters of the Viet Minh could be subjected to this treatment.

Date: May 4, 1953

The previously issued directive of the Central Committee on mass mobilization has explained clearly our mass mobilization policy. [This directive] discusses tactical directions for the campaign that you comrades can rely on while carrying out the policy of the party and the government.

The punishment of reactionary and evil landlords

a. In this campaign, [we] must execute a number of reactionary or evil landlords. In our current situation, the number of executions is fixed in principle at the ratio of one per one thousand people of the total population in the free areas. This ratio will be controlled by the leadership and applied to the rent and interest reduction campaign this year and next year; this does not mean that the ratio will apply only to this year, nor does it mean that every village will execute landlords according to this ratio. (Thus, there may be communes that execute three or four people and others that execute only one or none at all).

Human lives are an important matter. It is not that we do not want to execute those who deserve execution. But the number of executions should not be too many; if so, it would make it difficult [for the people] to agree with us.

b. Executions are intended for the most reactionary who have committed the most crimes, who have killed people, who have caused damages to the revolution, and who are hated most by the people. At the same time, [we must] apply class principles. Landlords who killed peasants or cadres must be executed; [but] peasants who killed landlords who had oppressed them should not be tried if the act occurred long ago, or should be tried in regular court and given a light sentence if the act occurred recently.

c. Landlords who are to be executed but who are still young, educated, and hopefully can be successfully reeducated, or landlords who committed crimes but whose children are soldiers, can be commuted to imprisonment if the masses approve.

d. For very special criminals—leaders or members of the upper elite in ethnic communities, Catholic priests, religious leaders, democratic personalities, famous individuals, and foreign nationals: their executions must be approved [in advance] by a Central Committee.

Execution of criminals who are local cadres from the district level up, and/or who are [officers] from the company level up, must be approved [in advance] by a Central Committee. [The executions of] local cadres at the commune level [and below] may be approved by the Interzone Party Committee. [The executions of] military cadres from the platoon level [and below] may be authorized by the Central Party Committee of the Army.

e. At the central level, we will form a committee to handle these executions. This committee is not public and comprises five members, with one each from the party, the government, the police, the judiciary branch, and the Peasants' Association.

This committee can employ staff to assist it in its work. Its responsibilities include studying, collecting, and preserving documents about criminals; recommending the level of punishment for criminals; submitting its recommendations to the President for approval; and transferring the cases to special People's Courts for sentencing and carrying out the sentences.

Where a mass mobilization campaign has been launched (presently in the Viet Bac Interzone and the Fifth Interzone), a committee to handle [executions] at the zone level is to be established. The character, composition, and

responsibilities of this zone-level committee are similar to those of the committee at the central level. But members of these committees [at zone level]
must be selected carefully. If sufficient numbers of qualified people cannot
be found, three or four [instead of five] are acceptable.

Attention: During the campaign, leaders must prepare in advance the list
of reactionary and evil landlords and the documents or information about
their cases.

Oral History of Han Vi, Musicologist and Communist Party Cadre[7]

*Following the Geneva Conference, around 90,000 Viet Minh cadres and
fighters were "regrouped" from South Vietnam to North Vietnam. Most of
these southerners expected that they would be back within two years,
following the all-Vietnam elections that were supposed take place in
mid-1956. However, because these elections were never held, most of the
regroupees remained in the north longer than they anticipated. Some would
return to the south during the 1960s to participate in the insurgency against
the RVN government and the US military; others remained in the North until
1975 or even longer.*

*One of the regroupees who never returned to the south was Han Vi, a
Vietnamese of Chinese descent from Saigon. He was both a talented musician
and an enthusiastic revolutionary; in 1946, he joined the communist party
and spent the rest of the Indochina War touring the south as a member of a
Viet Minh propaganda unit. He willingly went to the north in 1954, but soon
discovered that the party's postwar plans for building socialism were not to
his liking. Although Han Vi continued to serve the party until the end of the
Vietnam War in 1975, his ethnic Chinese identity became a liability during
Vietnam's postwar confrontation with China in the late 1970s. In 1979 he
was expelled from the party and forced to leave Vietnam. He eventually
settled in the United States, where this oral history was recorded during the
1980s.*

After I left South Vietnam for the North [in 1954], I was transferred from my
propaganda unit into a regular army outfit, as a political cadre. Like all the
other Southerners, I was evaluated for class background and revolutionary
credentials. I ended up with four different classifications: intellectual, South-
erner, wounded veteran, and foreigner (because of my Chinese origin). After

7 Excerpted from David Chanoff and Doan Van Toai, *Vietnam: A Portrait of its People at War*
(London: I. B. Tauris, 1987), 114–121.

a few months of learning how to march, drill, stand at attention, and salute everybody in sight, I was sick of it.

I had spent the entire French war without doing any of these things. Basically I was a free spirit. I loved the propaganda work—living in the countryside, putting on performances, getting to know people, motivating them—that kind of thing. But the regular army life was something else entirely. Eventually I really did get sick, and they sent me to a rest and recuperation area.

I was there when the land reform movement started. Like everyone else, I had to analyze the way my thinking had developed, especially how my class background had influenced it. It turned out that my services over the past eight years weren't enough. First of all, my family was held against me. My father was a traditional doctor who also owned a kind of pharmacy for Chinese medicines. So I was from the merchant class. Before, no one knew who came from what class, but now we had to be organized by background before we could take another step. None of us was happy about it, but what could you do?

While this was going on, the village land reform had also started. All the *bo doi* [Viet Minh soldiers] were sent to live with poor peasants in the village. I was staying with a fifty-year-old widow and her son and daughter. At the same time we were having our meetings, the whole village was being mobilized.

To do this, the Party sent in a team of land reform cadres. They had a system for putting a village through land reform. A series of steps. The first step started with the land reform cadres moving into the cottages of the very poorest peasants. They made friends with these people, and then they set up meetings with other poor people. At the meetings they'd have people tell their stories, talk about how badly they lived. They'd get them worked up and excited about how poor they were, and they'd explain to them about why they were so poor. They molded these people—the bottom proletariat—into the driving force in the land reform. They turned them into the strongest element in the village.

The next step was to classify the entire village—the poor peasants did this for them. There were different definitions they used for the classification. For example, a "landlord" was anyone who didn't work himself but who hired someone else to work for him. Anyone who owned more than the average share of land was also called a landlord. "Rich peasants" were those who worked the land themselves but also hired others to work for them. "Middle peasants" were those who rented land and had their own means to farm it—their own buffalo or ox, and farming implements. They owned their own means of production. The middle peasants consisted of two groups, upper and lower. Upper-middle peasants produced enough for themselves to live on and a surplus in addition. Lower-middle peasants produced just enough to survive, or not enough, so that they were always in debt.

Once the village was classified, the lower-middle peasants were included with the poor peasants—the real proletariat. These people lived a life of utter poverty. Their children were forced to work to help pay off their parents' debts. It wasn't unusual for the poorest peasants to give their children to the landlords or to have to sell them off. The majority of the peasants in the village lived their whole lives in this kind of debt.

So the second step was classifying the village. Once that was done, the land reform cadres formally took over the village administration. They had the authority to fire the Party chief. They kicked him out and they kicked out the whole Party administrative structure. Temporarily, they held all the power. The whole right to govern was in the hands of the land reform team. Then they were ready for the last step—the denunciations.

When they were ready, they gathered all the poor and lower-middle peasants together in a mass outdoor meeting. The rest of the village—the upper-middle and rich—were confined to their homes. The land reform cadres stood behind a cable and told the people about the government's policy of punishment and land redistribution. Then some of the people began coming up to the front—the ones who had the worst stories. As they told them, people were crying and getting really warmed up. Some of them were shouting, "Down with the landlords!"

Then the cadres brought in the richest landlord. He was standing at the front with his head down. People walked up to him, accusing him and screaming at him. They forced him to admit to every crime. Some woman accused him of rape. He said, No, he didn't rape her. The crowd exploded in anger—everyone did. Even his relatives had to parade up to denounce him.

When all of the denouncing was over, the cadres evaluated who were the worst landlords and they sentenced them to death. They had a quota they had to fill. Even some Party members suffered, people who were revolutionaries but who came from the upper classes. The woman I was living with appeared to be quite pleased by it all. All the poor peasants were happy with the land reform—at least at first when land was distributed to them. Later when they were forced into collectives they weren't happy at all.

In our own army meetings it wasn't the same as the villagers' land reform. The main thing was that we had to confess our own errors. My problem here was that in my opinion, my behavior had been beyond reproach. I had always been completely dedicated to the revolution. When we were operating in the highlands among the Montagnard I had even filed down my teeth and learned to live in their way. Of course everybody else in my propaganda unit had done it too. But the point was that I couldn't think of anything about my conduct over eight years of making revolution that I could criticize.

On the other hand, they were taking this self-criticism business so seriously that I knew I would have to say something. I was afraid of being trapped somehow, and I wanted to demonstrate my sincerity and honesty. So I decided to confess my love affairs.

While I was wandering all over the South—from 1946 to 1954—I had met many girls. I had fallen in love with some of them, and some of them had fallen in love with me. I was a young man, a singer and musician, so it was a completely natural thing. I had never thought about any of these affairs in terms of the revolution. But now I realized that they could—from one perspective—be considered antirevolutionary. They certainly demonstrated that I wasn't thinking about the struggle 100 percent of the time. And from a revolutionary point of view, they showed that I had a "decadent" way of living.

Of course none of that was exactly earthshaking, especially when you saw it in the context of everything I had done, so it looked like the perfect thing to confess. It showed off my sincerity and my determination to improve. And it wasn't likely to get me into too much trouble. So I drew up a complete list of all the girls I had slept with. Then when they started badgering me to tell them the whole truth, I added quite a few more, for good effect. The entire list came to one hundred and eight names.

But what I saw as relatively trivial, the interrogators jumped on. Once you mention what you see in yourself as wrong; they use that as the basis for accusation after accusation. Many of my girlfriends had come from landlord families. So they attacked my class way of thinking. My own family was from the "exploiting classes" and here was a new and vicious example of my antirevolutionary, bourgeois habits.

When it was all over, I wasn't feeling well. One afternoon—I remember it very clearly—I was playing volleyball when they called me into the office. The division commander and a political officer were there. They announced that I was being expelled from the Party. They said the decision was based on the views I had expressed in self-criticism and in the land reform sessions. My views on land reform were particularly deficient.

I had to leave all my army clothes behind and all my mementoes from the French war. All I was allowed to take was the pair of shorts I was wearing. A bit later I learned that I wasn't alone; people from all the regiments had been arrested. It was a big purge. A few had committed suicide. Others were in jail.

Instead of putting me in jail they sent me to a little village in Hoang Hoa district to work with the peasants. I was given a small plot of land to cultivate and a cow to take care of. I didn't mind so much. The peasants were friendly to me. I also did a lot of thinking about the Party. I had been sent to the countryside for rehabilitation, so I figured that if I worked well enough, after a while I could begin a campaign to get myself reinstated. I worked like hell for six months. Then I wrote a letter directly to Ho Chi Minh.

In the letter I told Ho about my contribution to the revolution. I gave him my whole resume, explained that I was a Chinese who had come to Vietnam to follow the spirit of the Vietnamese Revolution. I told him how I had sacrificed myself during the French war and how I had been admitted to the Party in 1946. I told him that through all the years when I was fighting nobody had ever asked me anything about my class background. Why was it that after our victory, they began to be so upset about it? In conclusion, I asked Ho to do one of four things with me. The Party could send me back to the South, they could send to China, they could let the ICC decide on my case [the International Control Commission was the three-nation body established to supervise the implementation of the Geneva Agreements], or they could restore my honor—accept me back and compensate me for my sacrifice and humiliation.

After fifteen days I received a short letter over Uncle Ho's signature. It said simply: "I have read your letter. I know of your situation. I hope you will persevere in your tasks." Two weeks after that I was released and sent back to the army. The commander welcomed me back with a profuse apology. They gave me back everything they had confiscated. And they gave me the salary they hadn't paid me for half a year. I was told that my case had been a mistake committed by the Party. They hoped I would understand and continue to be a loyal Party member.

After they took me back they assigned me to be the political officer in the traditional orchestra for Zone 5. Of the hundred people in the orchestra, only ten were Party members, and being the political cadre put me in one of the top positions. My job was mainly to act as an adviser and friend to the orchestra members, to help them through whatever problems they might be having. I was also under pressure to be a model of proper behavior and to always volunteer first if there was some difficult or unpleasant job that had to be done. That was what a Party member had to do.

I liked that job, and I did it well. I also didn't take any chances. During the "Hundred Flowers" campaign, when they asked cultural cadres to freely criticize the government, I kept quiet. At one of the meetings I drew a little cartoon for my friend sitting next to me—a man's face in profile, with a padlock through his lips. I was saying that we'd better shut up. After the campaign was over, a lot of people suffered for the criticisms they had made when things were supposedly open. Even nationally known figures, party members. The atmosphere then was terrible. Many artists went to jail for what they had said. Other people humbled themselves or denounced friends to keep their positions. But I hadn't said a thing. So I just kept working at my job, up until 1960.

Discussion questions

1. Is Edward Lansdale's report on the Saigon Military Mission a reliable account of events in South Vietnam during 1954–1955? Why or why not?
2. Identify the similarities and differences between Ngo Dinh Diem's 1956 speech and Ho Chi Minh's 1945 Declaration of Independence. Is it correct to say that Diem was more committed to democracy than Ho was? Why or why not?
3. Based on the documents in this chapter, what was the main cause of the "errors" in the North Vietnamese land reform campaign in 1953–1956?

Chapter 4   The Rise of the "Viet Cong"

Le Duan, The Path to Revolution in the South (1956)[1]

This document was written by Le Duan, the top VWP leader in South Vietnam, sometime during the spring of 1956. At the time, the communist party's fortunes in the south were clearly ebbing. Shortly after he refused to participate in the reunification elections mandated by the Geneva Agreements, Ngo Dinh Diem launched the "Denounce Communists" (Tố Cộng) campaign. This propaganda and security offensive aimed to arrest or kill all remaining communist operatives in the south. As Diem's crackdown gathered momentum, many communist cadres urged their superiors to resume armed struggle against the Saigon government. However, senior VWP leaders in Hanoi feared that a renewed war in the south might jeopardize their nation-building plans in the north. They therefore ordered their southern comrades to refrain from launching a full-blown insurgency in the south, at least for the time being. Le Duan wrote this essay by way of explaining this policy to his southern comrades. He did so despite the fact that he strongly sympathized with their desire to resume armed struggle – and, indeed, he would lobby vigorously in Hanoi for such a shift in policy during the late 1950s.

[1] Printed in Gareth Porter, *Vietnam: The Definitive Documentation of Human Decisions*, Vol. 2 (Stanfordville, NY: E. M. Coleman, 1979), 24–30.

Original publication details: 4.1 Porter, 1979. 4.2 2320101003, Douglas Pike Collection: Unit 06 Democratic Republic of Vietnam, The Vietnam Center and Archive, Texas Tech University. 4.4 Fall, 1967. Reproduced with permission from D. Fall, Executrix of the Estate of B. B. Fall.

During two years of struggle for peace, unification, independence and democracy, the people of the South have shown clearly their earnest feelings of patriotism and the firm will of Vietnamese.

Meanwhile, the past two years have also made the people of South Vietnam see clearly the poisonous scheme of the aggressive American imperialists, and the traitorous, country-selling crimes of Ngo Dinh Diem.

July 20, 1956, was the anniversary of the day the ceasefire agreement was signed at the Geneva Conference. That agreement required a free national general election to unify Vietnam, but it has not been carried out. The reason is the aggressive American imperialists and dictatorial feudalist Ngo Dinh Diem have sought by every means to sabotage and not carry out the agreement with hope of maintaining long-term division of our country, and turning the South into a colony and military base of the imperialists in order to provoke war and to rob us of our rivers and mountains.

The Vietnamese people, who defeated the French imperialists and American intervention after nine years of heroic resistance, forcing the imperialists at the Geneva Conference to recognize the national independence and territorial integrity of our country, definitely will not allow the imperialists and feudalists to provoke war, or to prolong the division of our country, and the cruel imperialist-feudal regime in the Southern part of our beloved country.

Three Main Tasks of the Whole Nation at Present

In order to cope with that situation created by the U.S.-Diem regime, and in order to complete the work of national liberation, to liberate the Southern people from the imperialist-feudalist yoke, the Party leadership has put forward three main tasks to make a general line for the whole revolution at present for the entire country.

Those tasks are:

1. Firmly consolidate the North.
2. Strongly push the Southern revolutionary movement.
3. Win the sympathy and support of the people who love peace, democracy and national independence throughout the world.

Why must we firmly consolidate the North?

Because the North is one half of the country which has been completely liberated from the yoke of imperialism and feudalism, and which has an independent and democratic government of the people. Independent, democratic North Vietnam is the result of the victory of the revolution due to the fact that the entire people from North to South struggled heroically for 9 years against French imperialism and U.S. intervention. The North at present must be the firm and strong base to serve as rear area for the revolutionary movement to liberate the South. That is why we must firmly consolidate the North.

Why must we push the Southern revolutionary movement?

Because the South at present is still under the yoke of imperialist and feudalist rule, the U.S.-Diem imperialists and feudalists are using a policy of fascist dictatorship by imperialist and class rule in order to occupy the South, sabotaging peace and national unification, oppressing and exploiting our people, scheming to provoke war, and hoping to invade the entire country. In order to resist the U.S.-Diem regime, the Southern people have only one way to save the country and themselves, and that is the Revolutionary path. There is no other path but Revolution.

That is why we must push the revolutionary movement of the South in order to resist the U.S.-Diem regime.

Why must we win the sympathy and support of the people who love peace, democracy, and national independence in the world?

Because our work in maintaining peace, achieving unity and completing our independence and democracy is at present a part of the movement of progressive people throughout the world which is struggling to achieve peace, democracy and independence for all mankind. Because the work of peaceful unification of the country is in keeping with the legal principles recognized by the Geneva Conference, and therefore, all actions opposing peaceful unification of our country are illegal, and are denounced by the world's people. We are strengthened further by that movement, while the enemy will be isolated and weakened, and we will have further favorable conditions to defeat the enemy and finish the complete liberation of our whole nation.

Those are the three tasks of the whole revolutionary line of the entire nation at present. Those three tasks cannot be separated; they are closely linked with each other. Only by fulfilling those tasks, can our people's national liberation revolution succeed.

The entire Party Committee in the South as well as the entire Southern people must clearly realize that general revolutionary line for the whole country.

In order to fulfill its task, the Party Committee of the South must firmly grasp the Revolutionary Path of the South in order to preserve and push the revolutionary movement forward...

Forms of struggle and possibilities of development of the Southern Revolutionary movement

Having realized clearly the goal and needs of the Southern Revolutionary movement and having realized the position and object of the movement, we must have correct struggle line and method, in order to develop the possibilities of the revolution and guide the revolutionary movement to success.

In order to have a correct line and method, we realize even more clearly the concrete situation in the world and in the country and their possible development. We must realize clearly the relationship of forces between the revolution and the counterrevolution at present and its possibilities for development.

What is the situation in the world at present?

The socialist system today has become big and strong, including nearly a billion people from Europe across to Asia, as well as the biggest and most populous countries in the world, such as the Soviet Union and China. The world is no longer under the monopoly of capitalism but is divided into two parallel systems.

The method of production of the socialist economy has surpassed the capitalist method of production. The proof is that the Soviet Union was still an economically backward country before the revolution, but now stands in the first rank among European countries. The goal of development in a socialist economy is to serve the material and spiritual needs of the people, so that the economy has a peaceful, democratic, progressive and mutually-assisting character, so that people can live together advantageously. The peaceful, democratic and progressive character of the socialist economy is in keeping with the needs and the evolution of mankind. So the scope of its relations with other countries, especially those countries whose economies are still undeveloped, is constantly broadening. The result is the creation of a broad zone of peace and democracy encompassing the majority of mankind, for example the relations between the socialist camp and India, Indonesia, Burma, Egypt, etc. . . .

On the other hand, the economy of capitalism has the goal of exploiting working people in their countries, usurping profits in the small and weak countries, and forcing them into poverty in order to subordinate those countries to capitalism and take great profits for the U.S. capitalist, militarist group. With their character of plundering for great profit and contending with one another's interests, the British, French, and U.S. capitalist countries, especially the U.S. imperialists, are seeking by all means to annex the small and weak countries, and to provoke war and disputes among them.

The situation makes the imperialists more and more isolated in the world, and the scope of their influence increasingly narrow.

On the other hand, the political strength of the movement for peace and national independence grows bigger everyday and includes hundreds of millions of people all over the world. The development of atomic and hydrogen weapons which could kill all kinds of people in a horrible fashion is no longer the monopoly of the warmongering imperialists, since the Soviet Union, the representative of the Peace movement in the world, now has atomic and hydrogen inventions more advanced than U.S. imperialism.

The situation forces bellicose states such as the U.S. and Britain to recognize that if they adventurously start a world war, they themselves will be the first to be destroyed, and thus the movement to demand peace in those imperialist countries is also developing strongly.

Recently, in the U.S. Presidential election, the present Republican administration, in order to buy the people's esteem, put forward the slogan "Peace and Prosperity," which showed that even the people of an imperialist warlike country such as the United States want peace.

That general situation shows us that the forces of peace and democracy in the world have tipped the balance toward the camp of peace and democracy. Therefore we can conclude that the world at present can maintain long-term peace.

On the other hand, however, we can also conclude that as long as the capitalist economy survives, it will always scheme to provoke war, and there will still remain the danger of war.

Based on the above world situation, the Twentieth Congress of the Communist Party of the Soviet Union produced two important judgments:

1. All conflicts in the world at present can be resolved by means of peaceful negotiations.
2. The revolutionary movement in many countries at present can develop peacefully. Naturally, in the countries in which the ruling class has a powerful military-police apparatus and is using fascist policies to repress the movement, the revolution in those countries must look clearly at their concrete situation to have the appropriate methods of struggle.

Based on the general situation and that judgment, we conclude that, if all conflicts can be resolved by means of peaceful negotiations, peace can be achieved.

Because the interest and aspiration of peaceful reunification of our country are the common interest and aspiration of all the people of the Northern and Southern zones, the people of the two zones do not have any reason to provoke war, nor to prolong the division of the country. On the contrary the people of the two zones are more and more determined to oppose the U.S.-Diem scheme of division and war provocation in order to create favorable conditions for negotiations between the two zones for peaceful unification of the country.

The present situation of division is created solely by the arbitrary U.S.-Diem regime, so the fundamental problem is how to smash the U.S.-Diem scheme of division and war-provocation.

As observed above, if they want to oppose the U.S.-Diem regime, there is no other path for the people of the South but the path of revolution.

What, then, is the line and struggle method of the revolutionary movement in the South?

If the world situation can maintain peace due to a change in the relationship of forces in the world in favor of the camp of peace and democracy, the world revolutionary movement can develop following a peaceful line, and the revolutionary movement in the South can also develop following a peaceful line. First of all, we must determine: what does it mean for a revolutionary movement to struggle according to a peaceful line?

A revolutionary movement struggling according to a peaceful line means that it takes the political forces of the people as the base rather than using people's armed forces to struggle with the existing government to achieve their revolutionary objective.

The revolutionary movement struggle according to a peaceful line is also different from a reformist movement in that a reformist movement relies fundamentally on the law and the constitution to struggle, while a revolutionary movement relies on the revolutionary political forces of the masses as the base. And another difference is that a revolutionary movement struggles for revolutionary objectives, while a reformist movement struggles for reformist goals.

With an imperialist feudalist dictatorial fascist government like the U.S.-Diem regime, is it possible for a peaceful political struggle line to achieve its objective?

We must recognize that all accomplishments in every country are due to the people. That is a definite law: it cannot be otherwise. Therefore the line of the revolutionary movement must be in accord with the inclinations and aspirations of the people. Only in that way can a revolutionary movement be mobilized and succeed.

The ardent aspiration of the Southern people is to maintain peace and achieve national unification. We must recognize clearly this longing for peace: The revolutionary movement in the South can mobilize and advance to success on the basis of grasping the flag of peace, in harmony with popular feelings. On the contrary, the actions of the U.S.-Diem regime, using fascist violence and provoking war, are contrary to the will of the people and therefore must certainly be defeated.

Can the U.S.-Diem regime, by using a clumsy policy of fascist violence, create a strong force to oppose and destroy the revolutionary movement?

Definitely not. The U.S.-Diem regime has no political strength worth mentioning in the country on which it can rely. On the contrary, nearly all strata of the people oppose them. Therefore the U.S.-Diem government is not a strong government. It is only a vile and brutal government. Its vile and brutal character means that it not only has no mass support in the country but is on the way to being isolated internationally. Its cruelty definitely cannot shake the revolutionary movement, and it cannot survive for long.

The proof is that in the past two years, everywhere in the countryside, the sound of the gunfire of U.S.-Diem repression never ceased; not a day went by when they did not kill patriots. But the revolutionary spirit is still firm, and the revolutionary base of the people still has not been shaken.

Once the entire people have become determined to protect the revolution, there is no cruel force that can shake it.

But why has the revolutionary movement not yet developed strongly?

This is also due to certain objective and subjective factors. Objectively, we see that, after nine years of waging strong armed struggle, the people's movement, generally speaking, now has a temporarily peaceful character which is a factor in the change of the movement from violent forms of struggle to peaceful forms. It has the correct character of rebuilding in order to then advance.

With the cruel repression and exploitation of the U.S. Diem regime, the people's revolutionary movement definitely will rise up. The people of the South have known the blood and fire of nine years of resistance war, but the cruelty of the U.S.-Diem cannot extinguish the struggle spirit of the people.

On the other hand, subjectively, we must admit that a large number of cadres, those who have responsibility for guiding the revolutionary movement, because of the change in the method of struggle and work from public to secret, have not yet firmly grasped the political line of the party, [and] have not yet firmly grasped the method of political struggle, and have not yet followed correctly the mass line, and therefore have greatly reduced the movement's possibilities for development.

At present, therefore, the political struggle movement has not yet developed equally among the people, and a primary reason is that some of the cadres and masses are not yet aware that the strength of political forces of the people can defeat the cruelty, oppression and exploitation of the

U.S.-Diem regime, and therefore they have a half-way attitude and don't believe in the strength of their political forces.

We must admit that any revolutionary movement has times when it falls and times when it rises; any revolutionary movement has times which are favorable for development and times which are unfavorable for development. The basic thing is that the cadres must see clearly the character of the movement's development in order to lead to the correct degree the mass struggle, and find a way for the vast masses who are determined to participate in the movement. If they are determined to struggle from the bottom to the top, no force can resist the determination of the immense masses.

In the past two years, the political struggle movement in the countryside and in the cities, either by one form or another, has shown that the masses have much capacity for political struggle with the U.S.-Diem regime. In those struggles, if we grasp more firmly the struggle line and method, the movement can develop further, to the advantage of the revolution. The cruel policy of U.S.-Diem clearly cannot break the movement, or the people's will to struggle.

There are those who think that the U.S.-Diem regime's use of violence is now aimed fundamentally at killing the leaders of the revolutionary movement in order to destroy the Communist Party and if the Communist Party is worn away to the point that it doesn't have the capacity to lead the revolution, the political struggle movement of the masses cannot develop.

This judgment is incorrect. Those who lead the revolutionary movement are determined to mingle with the masses, to protect and serve the interests of the masses and to pursue correctly the mass line. Between the masses and Communists there is no distinction any more. So how can the U.S.-Diem destroy the leaders of the revolutionary movement, since they cannot destroy the masses? Therefore they cannot annihilate the cadres leading the mass movement.

In fact more than twenty years ago, the French imperialists were determined to destroy the Communists in order to destroy the revolutionary movement for national liberation, but the movement triumphed. It wasn't the Communists who were destroyed but the French imperialists themselves and their feudal lackeys who were destroyed on our soil.

Now twenty years later, U.S.-Diem leaders are determined to destroy the Communists in the South, but the movement is still firm, Communists are still determined to fulfill their duty. And the revolutionary movement will definitely advance and destroy the imperialist, feudalist government. The U.S.-Diem regime will be destroyed just as the French imperialists and their feudal lackeys were destroyed.

We believe that: the peaceful line is not only appropriate to the general situation in the world but also to the situation within the country, both nation-wide and in the South. We believe that the will for peace and peace forces of the people throughout the country has smashed the U.S.-Diem schemes of war provocation and division.

A Communist Party Account of the Situation in the Nam Bo Region of South Vietnam (1961)[2]

As the Diem government's "Denounce Communists" campaign intensified during the late 1950s, conditions became ever more dire for the communist party cadres who remained in South Vietnam. In the years after 1955, tens of thousands of South Vietnamese were detained merely on suspicion of being communists; an unknown number were killed. In rural villages, families who were known to have previously supported the revolution were placed under surveillance and forced to display black signs outside their homes that identified them as potential enemies of the state.

In the long run, the Diem government's harsh anticommunist policies would prove counterproductive. Because government officials had sweeping powers to accuse and detain almost anyone without due process, the crackdown greatly exacerbated the fear and resentment that many rural residents felt toward the Saigon regime. Communist party cadres would eventually turn these feelings to their advantage. However, in the short run, the impact of Diem's crackdown on the party was devastating. The document excerpted here, written in 1961 by an unidentified VWP official in the south, reviewed the recent history of the party in the Nam Bo (Cochinchina) region. As the author frankly admitted, the government had come perilously close to destroying the party's network of cadres in rural areas during the late 1950s.

From 1956, after having eliminated the French and their henchmen and secured control of the army, the administration and the police, the U.S.-Diem [government] started directing their offensive towards the population.

In preparation for the elections in March 1956, the U.S.-Diem launched several campaigns, making propaganda, urging the people "to combat and denounce Communism," slandering the North and defaming the Geneva Accord, organizing rallies and demonstrations with refugees and troops as core elements, and forcing civil servants and students to participate in these campaigns. They set up counter revolutionary organizations such as the Can Lao Nhan Vi Party, the National Revolutionary Movement, the

---

[2] "A Party Account Of The Situation In The Nam Bo Region Of South Vietnam From 1954–1960," 1961, Folder 01, Box 01, Douglas Pike Collection, The Vietnam Center and Archive, Texas Tech University.

People's Council for Denunciation of Communism, the Republican Youth and Republican Women Movements, etc....

They forced government employees to attend courses on the "Denunciation of Communism." In a program allegedly to "depopulate the capital," they expelled people from their dwellings in many workers' neighborhoods, used bulldozers to raze houses and hired hoodlums to burn the people's homes...

Late in 1957, although the U.S.-Diem regime had been able to set up an administrative system at the lowest levels such as the hamlet and the inter-family group, they still could not force the people to carry out their reactionary policies as they wished. Our Party's organization, though split up in some areas, was still basically stable. The people's movement, though not as strong as before, maintained various forms of struggle to oppose the enemy's reactionary policies.

In mid 1958 and especially in early 1959, with a number of wicked agents already trained, with an espionage system already established in hamlets and some reactionary organizations set up in rural areas, the enemy started a larger scale and more vigorous offensive in the hamlets with the aim of erad-icating our movement and our organizations in rural areas.

Through the 10/59 law and the Special Military Courts, they intensi-fied terrorism and denunciation of Communism, and used intimidation as a means of pressuring the masses and their own civil servants and troops to carry out their fascistic policies....

They used reactionary organizations, particularly the People's Self-Defense Corps, to oppress the masses, mobilize the population for guard duty and force them to carry out reactionary policies.

They set up a series of "agrovilles" with the primary purpose of concen-trating the population in remote base areas to keep them under tight control and to attack and destroy our organizations.

Terrorism was prevalent in rural areas, especially in former base areas of the resistance. Many people were beheaded, disemboweled, or had their eyes gouged out; and such acts of terrorism were carried out by the enemy to compel the people to participate in forced labor, enlist in the army, move to "agrovilles," or to cooperate with them in arresting or mistreating our agents and Party cadres. In other words, the enemy forced the people to abandon their homes, gardens and rice fields, to leave the Party and the revolution, to surrender and to carry out the enemy's reactionary policies – failing which they would be outlawed and subjected to punishment under the 10/59 law. For that reason, violent struggle movements took place in Ca Mau, Long My, The Son, Hau My and Thanh Toi, etc. However, although they were highly conscious of the revolution, the people had no arms to defend themselves and soon had to yield to enemy pressure. Within just a few months, the enemy succeeded in dismembering 80-90 percent of our organizations in many base areas, especially in Ca Mau, Long My and Kien Tuong. Tens of thousands of people and Party members became outlaws and fled to the U Minh forest, to Dong Thap and other jungle areas in the East. The enemy then had real control over the townships and hamlets; only a few reactionaries were enough to scare hundreds and even thousands of people and to compel them to obey the enemy's orders. Meanwhile, the enemy placed the people in such a situation that they had to find a way out for their own survival and for the revolution, and which gave rise to the urgent problem of finding an effective way to struggle against the enemy.

In summary, the U.S.-Diem's rural pacification program progressed very slowly on account of opposition on the part of the peasants. Though its organization started in early 1956, the enemy's administrative and police apparatus really began to function and to control the rural areas only in mid-1958. The seesaw struggle took place for nearly three whole years. We must admit that our own mistakes were the main reason why the U.S.-Diem finally succeeded in controlling the rural areas....

The U.S.-Diem regime's policy towards prisoners was extremely severe. With even more savagery than the French colonialists in the past, the regime inflicted horrible physical and mental tortures upon prisoners throughout their detention. Prisoners were forced to attend lectures on denunciation of Communism and to work as informers. Refusal would result in continued torture even for those who had already been indicated. Tens of thousands of the Nam Bo people including comrades of ours have been killed in enemy prisons during the past seven years....

In 1959, the enemy situation in Nam Bo was as follows: Through police, spies, secret agents and tyrants, the enemy controlled the administrative system from the central level down to the townships, hamlets and family groups; and the military apparatus from the main force units down to the militia.

Such an oppressive machinery enabled them to control Nam Bo almost entirely, even the remotest areas. The people's spirit and their struggle movement weakened – just a few spies were enough to control a whole township, and in some townships spies and administrative personnel numbered as many as 500. Some enemy agents were even able to go deep into townships and make arrests overtly...

We say that in 1959, the South Vietnamese administration was relatively stable due to the fact that it controlled the administrative machinery at all levels, controlled the army and was able to implement its major policies, etc. However, to attain this temporary stability, it was forced to oppress the masses with extreme cruelty, with police and military terrorism as the essential means. So, stability was acquired at a very high price – that of complete political failure.

The time the South Vietnamese administration was most stable was precisely the period of optimum development of the very factors that were to cause its weakening and its ruin.

Another weakness of the Diem administration was that it lacked the people's support and depended on its military and administrative apparatus for survival; and even in this apparatus, its supporters were just limited to a body of police and spies and a minority of privileged tyrants, military officers and high ranking officials. And it was through these individuals that the U.S.-Diem ran the army and administration.

So it is no wonder that the South Vietnamese administration's infrastructure was unsteady and collapsed rapidly in the face of the strong revival of the revolutionary movement in Nam Bo during late 1959.

A Poor Farmer's Account of the 1960 "Concerted Uprising" in My Tho Province (1967)[3]

For many communist cadres in South Vietnam, the turning point in their struggle against the Diem government came during 1959. In January of that year, the party's Central Committee in Hanoi secretly authorized cadres in the south to incorporate armed struggle into their resistance activities – exactly the step that Le Duan and some other party leaders had been seeking. However, even before this directive had been transmitted to the south, some low-level cadres there had already taken matters into their own hands. During the summer and fall of 1959, the number of attacks and assassinations of RVN personnel in rural areas of South Vietnam rose sharply. In January 1960, communist operatives in the Mekong Delta province of Ben Tre launched the first of what became known as the "concerted uprisings." Although these local uprisings involved some small-scale military strikes against RVN targets, a lack of weapons and ammunition forced the rebels to rely heavily on nonmilitary tactics, such as mass demonstrations and other forms of popular mobilization.

The interview excerpt below provides an eyewitness description of the "concerted uprising" that began in My Tho province (adjacent to Ben Tre) in February 1960. The interviewee was a poor resident of one of the villages targeted by the insurgents. He was recruited by communist cadres to participate in the uprising and eventually became a party member. Since this

3 Excerpted from Interview No. 203, *Rand Interview Series DT: Activities of Viet Cong within Dinh Tuong Province* (Alexandria, VA: Defense and Documentation Center for Scientific and Technical Information, Cameron Station, 1972).

interview was conducted in 1967, shortly after the one-time insurgent had defected to the South Vietnamese government, his critical comments about the communists and their tactics may have been motivated in part by his desire to distance himself from them. Nevertheless, his description provides a fascinating glimpse of how the revolutionaries used both persuasion and compulsion to enlist ordinary rural residents in their struggle against the government.

The Front started to operate secretly [in my hamlet] beginning in February 1960. At first the secret guerrillas carried out armed propaganda activities in the hamlet at night. They went to the houses of the family group heads and the Hamlet Chief and took them away for one or two hours to propagandize and reform them. When they entered the houses of these officials to arrest them, only those with genuine rifles came in. Those with fake rifles stood outside to lend support. The people who were arrested and their families couldn't distinguish between the real and the fake rifles. They were frightened and told others that the Front was strong and armed with many kinds of weapons. It was the families of the people who were arrested who made unwitting propaganda for the Front and made it appear more powerful than it actually was.

Along with the armed propaganda activities, the cadres collected money throughout the hamlet. They appeared suddenly in people's houses and forced them to turn off all the lamps, then introduced themselves as members of the National Liberation Front of South Vietnam and requested the people contribute money to feed the troops.[4] Before going to see a family, the cadres studied the financial situation of that family and determined how much they would have to contribute, even though when they went to see them they said it was voluntary. No family refused to contribute money to the Front.

Each night the cadres operated in one hamlet. They divided the hamlet into different sectors and each of them took a sector to operate. Before leaving the hamlet, they hung banners, posted slogans, and disseminated leaflets. The cadres collected money from each family two or three times, deliberately making the people commit illegal acts in the eyes of the government [by] contributing money to the Front. By making the people commit illegal acts, the Front built up its real strength…The people who were suspected by the

---

[4] Because the National Liberation Front was not officially proclaimed until December 1960, the interviewee is almost certainly mistaken that the revolutionaries referred to themselves in this way in early 1960. The guerrillas probably referred to themselves as members of the "Liberation Army" at that time.

government of having committed illegal acts naturally were forced to lean toward the Front.

At the start the secret guerrillas were the most important factors in implementing Front policies. They were chosen from the ranks of the poor farmers and the very poor farmers. Only a few were selected because at that time the government was still in control of the village and it was feared if the Front recruited a large group of secret guerrillas, they would be uncovered.

At that time the villagers were frightened out of their wits when they saw how active the Front was and how easy it was for them to operate. The Front members came in and out of the hamlet as though it was deserted. At night, when they saw shadows passing by, people quickly bolted their doors and pretended to be asleep, and didn't dare talk out loud.

When the Front had just emerged and was destroying the government's control, it arrested and killed nine people.[5] They were all from the village... All these people were executed in either August or September 1960. They were killed with machetes. At night the cadres went to the houses of these victims, knocked on their doors, and then killed them with machetes without letting their families witness the execution. After killing these people, the cadres left a condemnation note on their bodies. The cadres absolutely forbade the neighbors to help these families conduct funeral services. The families of the victims were left by themselves and had to bury the dead themselves. No one helped them or went to the funeral.

Usually, the [Communist] Party Chapter chose the executioner. No one volunteered for this job. I witnessed an execution once, and it was so frightening that I almost lost consciousness. The man who was given the task of killing the victim was shaking with fear. He closed his eyes and hit at random. He had to hit the victim up to ten times with his machete before the latter died....

Besides these nine people who were killed, the Front also arrested over 30 people and took them away for warning and thought reform for one day (from the night they were arrested until the evening of the next day). The Front only detained them for one day for indoctrination because it didn't have a secure place to jail them. Those who were released had all been warned. If they committed the same errors again, or if they resumed working for the government, the Front would kill them...

In the face of these horrible executions the people became demoralized and didn't dare to comment on or criticize the killings. They were all shaken

5 Elsewhere in the interview, the farmer indicated that one of the nine was executed for drunkenness and two others for robbery. The remaining six were killed because they were suspected of supplying information to government officials.

up and frightened of everyone. They were constantly worried about their fate, and wondered what would happen to them or whether the Front suspected them or not. Most of the villagers thought that the people who were executed by the Front were innocent, because they had seen that these victims' attitudes or actions hadn't been harmful to the Front...The villagers were extremely frightened and shaken.

Program of the National Liberation Front of South Vietnam (1960)[6]

As the resistance to the Diem government spread across South Vietnam during 1960, communist party leaders decided that the time had come to establish a new organization to direct and guide the emerging insurgency. The National Liberation Front (NLF) of South Vietnam was established during a secret conclave at Tan Lap village in Tay Ninh Province, west of Saigon, on December 20, 1960. Officially, the NLF was a noncommunist organization, open to anyone willing to join the fight against Diem and his American allies; several noncommunists were recruited to serve in prominent posts in its leadership structure. The Front's founding manifesto, which was broadcast to the world on North Vietnamese radio, scrupulously avoided any mention of communism, and Front representatives insisted that the organization was independent and dedicated to neutralism. It was only after the end of the war that communist party leaders acknowledged that they had been in effective control of the Front and its policies from the outset.

I. Overthrow the camouflaged colonial regime of the American imperialists and the dictatorial power of Ngo Dinh Diem, servant of the Americans, and institute a government of national democratic union.

The present South Vietnamese regime is a camouflaged colonial regime dominated by the Yankees, and the South Vietnamese government is a servile government, implementing faithfully all the policies of the American imperialists. Therefore, this regime must be overthrown and a government of national and democratic union put in its place composed of representatives of all social classes, of all nationalities, of various political parties, of all religions; patriotic, eminent citizens must take over for the people the control of economic, political, social, and cultural interests and thus bring about

---

[6] Printed in Bernard Fall, *The Two Viet-Nams: A Political and Military Analysis*, rev. edn (New York: Praeger, 1967), 442–443.

independence, democracy, well- being, peace, neutrality, and efforts toward the peaceful unification of the country.

II. Institute a largely liberal and democratic regime.

1. Abolish the present constitution of the dictatorial powers of Ngo Dinh Diem, servant of the Americans. Elect a new National Assembly through universal suffrage.
2. Implement essential democratic liberties: freedom of opinion, of press, of movement, of trade-unionism; freedom of religion without any discrimination; and the right of all patriotic organizations of whatever political tendency to carry on normal activities.
3. Proclaim a general amnesty for all political prisoners and the dissolution of concentration camps of all sorts; abolish fascist law 10/59 and all the other antidemocratic laws; authorize the return to the country of all persons persecuted by the American-Diem regime who are now refugees abroad.
4. Interdict all illegal arrests and detentions; prohibit torture; and punish all the Diem bullies who have not repented and who have committed crimes against the people.

III. Establish an independent and sovereign economy, and improve the living conditions of the people.

1. Suppress the monopolies imposed by the American imperialists and their servants; establish an independent and sovereign economy and finances in accordance with the national interest; confiscate to the profit of the nation the properties of the American imperialists and their servants.
2. Support the national bourgeoisie in the reconstruction and development of crafts and industry; provide active protection for national products through the suppression of production taxes and the limitation or prohibition of imports that the national economy is capable of producing; reduce custom fees on raw materials and machines.
3. Revitalize agriculture; modernize production, fishing, and cattle raising; help the farmers in putting to the plow unused land and in developing production; protect the crops and guarantee their disposal.
4. Encourage and reinforce economic relations between the city and country, the plain and the mountain regions; develop commercial exchanges with foreign countries, regardless of their political regime, on the basis of equality and mutual interests.

5. Institute a just and rational system of taxation; eliminate harassing penalties.
6. Implement the labor code: prohibition of discharges, of penalties, of ill-treatment of wage earners; improvement of the living conditions of workers and civil servants; imposition of wage scales and protective measures for young apprentices.
7. Organize social welfare: find work for jobless persons; assume the support and protection of orphans, old people, invalids; come to the help of the victims of the Americans and Diemists; organize help for areas hit by bad crops, fires, or natural calamities.
8. Come to the help of displaced persons desiring to return to their native areas and to those who wish to remain permanently in the South; improve their working and living conditions.
9. Prohibit expulsions, spoliation, and compulsory concentration of the population; guarantee job security for the urban and rural working populations.

IV. Reduce land rent; implement agrarian reform with the aim of providing land to the tillers.

1. Reduce land rent; guarantee to the farmers the right to till the soil; guarantee the property right of accession to fallow lands to those who have cultivated them; guarantee property rights to those farmers who have already received land.
2. Dissolve 'prosperity zones' and put an end to recruitment for the camps that are called 'agricultural development centers.' Allow those compatriots who already have been forced into 'prosperity zones' and 'agricultural development centers' to return freely to their own lands.[7]
3. Confiscate the land owned by American imperialists and their servants, and distribute it to poor peasants without any land or with insufficient land; redistribute the communal lands on a just and rational basis.
4. By negotiation and on the basis of fair prices, repurchase for distribution to landless peasant or peasants with insufficient land those surplus lands that the owners of large estates will be made to relinquish if their domain exceeds a certain limit, to be determined in accordance with regional particularities. The farmers who benefit from such land and distribution

---

[7] This is a reference to the Agroville and Land Development Programs, two rural resettlement initiatives instituted by the Diem government in the late 1950s. While participation in these programs was supposed to be voluntary, many rural residents of South Vietnam were forced to build and live in these settlements against their will.

will both be compelled to make any payment or to submit to any other conditions.

V. Develop a national and democratic culture and education.

1. Combat all forms of culture and education enslaved to Yankee fashions; develop a culture and education that is national, progressive, and serves the Fatherland and people.
2. Liquidate illiteracy; increase the number of schools in the fields of general education as well as in those of technical and professional education, in advanced study as well as in other fields; adopt Vietnamese as the vernacular language; reduce the expenses of education and exempt from payment students who are without means; resume the examination system.
3. Promote science and technology and the national letters and arts; encourage and support the intellectuals and artists so as to permit them to develop their talents in the service of national reconstruction.
4. Watch over public health; develop sports and physical education.

VI. Create a national army devoted to the defense of the Fatherland and the people.

1. Establish a national army devoted to the defense of the Fatherland and the people; abolish the system of American military advisers.
2. Abolish the draft system, improve the living conditions of the simple soldiers and guarantee their political rights; put an end to ill- treatment of the military; pay particular attention to the dependents of soldiers without means.
3. Reward officers and soldiers having participated in the struggle against the domination by the Americans and their servants; adopt a policy of clemency toward the former collaborators of the Americans and Diemists [who are] guilty of crimes against the people but who have finally repented and are ready to serve the people.
4. Abolish all foreign military bases established on the territory of Viet-Nam.

VII. Guarantee equality between the various minorities and between the two sexes; protect the legitimate interest of foreign citizens established in Viet-Nam and of Vietnamese citizens residing abroad.

1. Implement the right to autonomy of the national minorities: [establish] autonomous zones in the areas with a minority population, those zones

to be an integral part of the Vietnamese nation. Guarantee equality between the various nationalities: each nationality has the right to use and develop its language and writing system, to maintain or to modify freely its mores and customs; abolish the policy of the Americans and Diemists of racial discrimination and forced assimilation. Create conditions permitting the national minorities to reach the general level of progress of the population: development of their economy and culture; formation of cadres of minority nationalities.

2. Establish equality between the two sexes; women shall have equal rights with men from all viewpoints (political, economic, cultural, social, etc.).
3. Protect the legitimate interest of foreign citizens established in Viet-Nam.
4. Defend and take care of the interest of Vietnamese citizens residing abroad.

VIII. Promote a foreign policy of peace and neutrality.

1. Cancel all unequal treaties that infringe upon the sovereignty of the people and that were concluded with other countries by the servants of the Americans.
2. Establish diplomatic relations with all countries, regardless of their political regime, in accordance with the principles of peaceful coexistence adopted at the Bandung Conference.
3. Develop close solidarity with peace-loving nations and neutral countries; develop free relations with the nations of Southeast Asia, in particular with Cambodia and Laos.
4. Stay out of any military bloc; refuse any military alliance with another country.
5. Accept economic aid from any country willing to help us without attaching any conditions to such help.

IX. Re-establish normal relations between the two zones, and prepare for the peaceful reunification of the country.

The peaceful reunification of the country constitutes the dearest desire of all our compatriots throughout the country. The National Liberation Front of South Viet-Nam advocates the peaceful reunification by stages on the basis of negotiations and through the seeking of ways and means in conformity with the interest of the Vietnamese nation.

While awaiting this reunification, the governments of the two zones will, on the basis of negotiations, promise to banish all separatist and warmongering propaganda and not to use force to settle differences between the zones. Commercial and cultural exchanges between the two zones will be implemented the inhabitants of the two zones will be free to move about throughout the country as their family and business interests indicate. The freedom of postal exchanges will be guaranteed.

X. Struggle against all aggressive war; actively defend universal peace.

1. Struggle against all aggressive war and against all forms of imperialist domination; support the national emancipation movements of the various peoples.
2. Banish all warmongering propaganda; demand general disarmament and the prohibition of nuclear weapons; and advocate the utilization of atomic energy for peaceful purposes.
3. Support all movements of struggle for peace, democracy, and social progress throughout the world; contribute actively to the defense of peace in Southeast Asia and in the world.

Discussion questions

1. Explain what "The Path to Revolution in the South" and "A Party Account of the Situation in Nam Bo" reveal about the position and goals of the communist party in South Vietnam during the mid- and late 1950s. What were the party's main objectives in the south after the Geneva Conference? Why did it mostly fail to realize these objectives?
2. Given the setbacks the party suffered during the post-Geneva period, how was the communist party eventually able to recover and launch a new insurgency against the Saigon government during 1959–1960?
3. In your judgment, who was *most* responsible for starting the conflict that became the Vietnam War? Was it: (i) Ngo Dinh Diem; (ii) US government leaders; (iii) communist cadres in South Vietnam; (iv) Le Duan and other North Vietnamese leaders; (v) some other leader or group?
4. If you lived in a rural village in the Mekong Delta in 1960, would you have supported the NLF? Why or why not?

Chapter 5   The Fall of Diem

The Caravelle Manifesto (1960)[1]

The rise of the communist insurgency during 1959–1960 profoundly altered the political climate inside South Vietnam. By the spring of 1960, the number of attacks on government targets in the countryside had increased sharply since the previous summer. Diem's recently unveiled Agroville program – a scheme to concentrate the population of the Mekong Delta into large town-like settlements – provoked widespread resentment, mainly because local officials had forced thousands of farmers to work on the program under harsh conditions and without pay. Many urban residents were also increasingly dissatisfied with Diem's autocratic style of rule. Even some anticommunists who had previously supported Diem were dismayed by the August 1959 RVN National Assembly elections, which were widely deemed to be less free and fair than the first assembly elections held in 1956.

In April 1960, a group of 18 anticommunist political leaders gathered in Saigon to draft an open letter to Diem. In it, they criticized various government policies and called on the RVN president to institute reforms. The letter was dubbed the "Caravelle Manifesto," after the downtown hotel where the group met. As the Diem government's supporters noted, the 18 signatories spoke only for themselves; none could claim to have a broad popular following inside South Vietnam. Nevertheless, their manifesto attracted considerable attention. While Diem initially seemed content to

---

[1] Source: *The Pentagon Papers*, Gravel ed. (Boston: Beacon Press, 1971), vol. 1, pp. 316-319.

Original publication details: 5.1 The Pentagon Papers, Gravel, 1971. 5.2 Excerpted from Foreign Relations of the United States, 19611963, 1988. 5.4 Foreign Relations of the United States, 1961-1963, 1991. 5.5 Kennedy, 1963.

ignore the manifesto, many of the signatories would later be jailed and
accused of plotting against the government.

The President of the Republic of Viet-Nam, Saigon

April 1960

Mr. President:

We the undersigned, representing a group of eminent citizens and personalities, intellectuals of all tendencies, and men of good will, recognize in the face of the gravity of the present political situation that we can no longer remain indifferent to the realities of life in our country.

Therefore, we officially address to you today an appeal with the aim of exposing to you the whole truth in the hope that the government will accord it all the attention necessary so as to urgently modify its policies, so as to remedy the present situation and lead the people out of danger.

Let us look toward the past, at the time when you were abroad.[2] For eight or nine years, the Vietnamese people suffered many trials due to the war: they passed from French domination to Japanese occupation, from revolution to resistance, from the nationalist imposture behind which hid communism to a pseudo-independence covering up for colonialism; from terror to terror, from sacrifice to sacrifice—in short, from promise to promise, until finally hope ended in bitter disillusion.

Thus, when you were on the point of returning to the country, the people as a whole entertained the hope that it would find again under your guidance the peace that is necessary to give meaning to existence, to reconstruct their destroyed homes, put to the plow again the abandoned lands. The people hoped no longer to be compelled to pay homage to one regime in the morning and to another at night; not to be the prey of the cruelties and oppression of one faction; no longer to be treated as coolies; no longer to be at the mercy of the monopolies; no longer to have to endure the depredations of corrupt and despotic civil servants. In one word, the people hoped to live in security at last, under a regime which would give them a little bit of justice and liberty. The whole people thought that you would be the man of the situation and that you would implement its hopes.

---

[2] Diem was in exile in the United States and Europe between 1950 and 1954.

That is the way it was when you returned. The Geneva Accords of 1954 put an end to combat and to the devastations of war. The French Expeditionary Corps was progressively withdrawn, and total independence of South Viet Nam had become a reality. Furthermore, the country had benefited from moral encouragement and a substantial increase of foreign aid from the free world. With so many favorable political factors, in addition to the blessed geographic conditions of a fertile and rich soil yielding agricultural, forestry, and fishing surpluses, South Vietnam should have been able to begin a definitive victory in the historical competition with the North, so as to carry out the will of the people and to lead the country on the way to hope, liberty, and happiness. Today, six years later, having benefited from so many undeniable advantages, what has the government been able to do? Where has it led South Vietnam? What parts of the popular aspirations have been implemented?

Let us try to draw an objective balance of the situation, without flattery or false accusations, strictly following a constructive line which you yourself have so often indicated, in the hope that the government shall modify its policies so as to extricate itself from a situation that is extremely dangerous to the very existence of the nation.

Policies

In spite of the fact that the bastard regime created and protected by colonialism has been overthrown and that many of the feudal organizations of factions and parties which oppress the population were destroyed, the people do not know a better life or more freedom under the republican regime which you have created. A constitution has been established in form only; a National Assembly exists whose deliberations always fall into line with the government; antidemocratic elections—all these are methods and "comedies" copied from the dictatorial Communist regimes, which obviously cannot serve as terms of comparison with North Vietnam.

Continuous arrests fill the jails and prisons to the rafters, as at this precise moment; public opinion and the press are reduced to silence. The same applies to the popular will as translated in certain open elections, in which it is insulted and trampled (as was the case, for example, during the recent elections for the Second Legislature).[3] All these have provoked the discouragement and resentment of the people.

[3] The 1959 elections for the RVN National Assembly.

Political parties and religious sects have been eliminated. "Groups" or "movements" have replaced them.[4] But this substitution has only brought about new oppressions against the population without protecting it for that matter against Communist enterprises. Here is one example: the fiefs of religious sects, which hitherto were deadly for the Communists, now not only provide no security whatever but have become favored highways for Viet Minh guerrillas, as is, by the way, the case in the rest of the country.

This is proof that the religious sects, though futile, nevertheless constitute effective anti-Communist elements. Their elimination has opened the way to the Viet Cong and unintentionally has prepared the way for the enemy, whereas a more realistic and more flexible policy could have enlisted them all with a view to reinforcing the anti-Communist front.

Today the people want freedom. You should, Mr. President, liberalize the regime, promote democracy, guarantee minimum civil rights, recognize the opposition so as to permit the citizens to express themselves without fear, thus removing grievances and resentments, opposition to which now constitutes for the people their sole reason for existence. When this occurs, the people of South Viet Nam, in comparing their position with that of the North, will appreciate the value of true liberty and of authentic democracy. It is only at that time that the people will make all the necessary efforts and sacrifices to defend that liberty and democracy.

Administration

The size of the territory has shrunk, but the number of civil servants has increased, and still the work doesn't get done. This is because the government, like the Communists, lets the political parties control the population, separate the elite from the lower echelons, and sow distrust between those individuals who are "affiliated with the movement" and those who are "outside the group." Effective power, no longer in the hands of those who are usually responsible, is concentrated in fact in the hands of an irresponsible member of the "family," from whom emanates all orders; this slows down the administrative machinery, paralyzes all initiative, discourages good will. At the same time, not a month goes by without the press being full of stories about graft impossible to hide; this becomes an endless parade of illegal transactions involving millions of piastres.

---

[4] A reference to the National Revolutionary Movement, a pro-Diem political organization that most RVN civil servants were required to join.

The administrative machinery, already slowed down, is about to become completely paralyzed. It is in urgent need of reorganization. Competent people should be put back in the proper jobs; discipline must be re-established from the top to the bottom of the hierarchy; authority must go hand in hand with responsibility; efficiency, initiative, honesty, and the economy should be the criteria for promotion; professional qualifications should be respected. Favoritism based on family or party connections should be banished; the selling of influence, corruption and abuse of power must be punished.

Thus, everything still can be saved, human dignity can be reestablished; faith in an honest and just government can be restored.

Army

The French Expeditionary Corps has left the country, and a republican army has been constituted, thanks to American aid, which has equipped it with modern materiel. Nevertheless, even in a group of the proud elite of the youth such as the Vietnamese Army—where the sense of honor should be cultivated, whose blood and arms should be devoted to the defense of the country, where there should be no place for clannishness and factions— the spirit of the "national revolutionary movement" or of the "personalist body" divides the men of one and the same unit, sows distrust between friends of the same rank, and uses as a criterion for promotion fidelity toward the party in blind submission to its leaders. This creates extremely dangerous situations, such as the recent incident in Tay Ninh.[5]

The purpose of the army, pillar of the defense of the country, is to stop foreign invasions and to eliminate rebel movements. It is at the service of the country only and should not lend itself to the exploitation of any faction or party. Its total reorganization is necessary. Clannishness and party obedience should be eliminated; its moral base strengthened; a noble tradition of national pride created; and fighting spirit, professional conscience, and bravery should become criteria for promotion. The troops should be encouraged to respect their officers, and the officers should be encouraged to love their men. Distrust, jealousy, rancor among colleagues of the same rank should be eliminated.

Then in case of danger, the nation will have at its disposal a valiant army animated by a single spirit and a single aspiration: to defend the most precious possession—our country, Viet Nam.

---

5 A reference to a January 1960 attack northwest of Saigon, in which communist forces overran an ARVN regimental headquarters, inflicted dozens of casualties on government troops, and captured a large number of weapons.

Economic and Social Affairs

A rich and fertile country enjoying food surpluses; a budget which does not have to face military expenditures[6]; important war reparations; substantial profits from Treasury bonds; a colossal foreign-aid program; a developing market capable of receiving foreign capital investments–these are the many favorable conditions which could make Vietnam a productive and prosperous nation. However, at the present time, many people are out of work, have no roof over their heads, and no money. Rice is abundant but does not sell; shop windows are well-stocked but the goods do not move. Sources of revenue are in the hands of speculators who use the [government] party and group to mask monopolies operating for certain private interests. At the same time, thousands of persons are mobilized for exhausting work, compelled to leave their own jobs, homes and families, to participate in the construction of magnificent but useless "agrovilles" which weary them and provoke their disaffection, thus aggravating popular resentment and creating an ideal terrain for enemy propaganda.

The economy is the very foundation of society, and public opinion ensures the survival of the regime. The government must destroy all the obstacles standing in the way of economic development; must abolish all forms of monopoly and speculation; must create a favorable environment for investments coming from foreign friends as well as from our own citizens; must encourage commercial enterprises, develop industry, and create jobs to reduce unemployment. At the same time, it should put an end to all forms of human exploitation in the work camps of the agrovilles.

Then only the economy will flourish again; the citizen will find again a peaceful life and will enjoy his condition; society will be reconstructed in an atmosphere of freedom and democracy.

Mr. President, this is perhaps the first time that you have heard such severe and disagreeable criticism–so contrary to your own desires. Nevertheless, sir, these words are strictly the truth, a truth that is bitter and hard, that you have never been able to know because, whether this is intended or not, a void has been created around you, and by the very fact of your high position, no one permits you to perceive the critical point at which truth shall burst forth in irresistible waves of hatred on the part of a people subjected for a long time to terrible suffering and a people who shall rise to break the bonds which hold it down. They shall sweep away the ignominy and all the injustices which surround and oppress it.

[6] South Vietnam's military expenditures were covered by American aid.

As we do not wish, in all sincerity, that our Fatherland should have to live through these perilous days, we—without taking into consideration the consequences which our attitude may bring upon us—are ringing today the alarm bell, in view of the imminent danger which threatens the government.

Until now, we have kept silent and preferred to let the Executive act as it wished. But now time is of the essence; we feel that it is our duty—and in the case of a nation in turmoil even the most humble people have their share of responsibility—to speak the truth, to awaken public opinion, to alert the people, and to unify the opposition so as to point the way. We beseech the government to urgently modify its policies so as to remedy the situation, to defend the republican regime, and to safeguard the existence of the nation. We hold firm hope that the Vietnamese people shall know a brilliant future in which it will enjoy peace and prosperity in freedom and progress.

Yours respectfully,

1. TRAN VAN VAN, Diploma of Higher Commercial Studies, former Minister of Economy and Planning
2. PHAN KHAC SUU, Agricultural Engineer, former Minister of Agriculture, former Minister of Labor
3. TRAN VAN HUONG, Professor of Secondary Education, former Prefect of Saigon-Cholon
4. NGUYEN, LUU VIEN, M.D., former Professor at the Medical School, former High Commissioner of Refugees
5. HUYNH-KIM HUU, M.D., former Minister of Public Health
6. PHAN HUY QUAT, M.D., former Minister of National Education, former Minister of Defense
7. TRAN VAN LY, former Governor of Central Viet-Nam
8. NGUYEN TIEN HY, M.D.
9. TRAN VAN DO, M.D., former Minister of Foreign Affairs, Chairman of the Vietnamese Delegation to the 1954 Geneva Conference
10. LE NGOC CHAN, Attorney at Law, former Secretary of State for National Defense
11. LE QUANG LUAT, Attorney at Law, former Government Delegate for North Viet-Nam, former Minister of Information and Propaganda
12. LUONG TRONG TUONG, Public Works Engineer, former Secretary of State for National Economy
13. NGUYEN TANG NGUYEN, M.D., former Minister of Labor and Youth
14. PHAM HUU CHUONG, M.D., former Minister of Public Health and Social Action

15. TRAN VAN TUYEN, Attorney at Law, former Secretary of State for Information and Propaganda
16. TA CHUONG PHUNG, former Provincial Governor for Binh-Dinh
17. TRAN LE CHAT, Laureate of the Triennial Mandarin Competition of 1903
18. HO VAN VUI, Reverend, former Parish Priest of Saigon, at present Parish Priest of Tha-La, Province of Tay-Ninh

Report of the Taylor Mission to South Vietnam (1961)[7]

By the fall of 1961, the military and political position of the Diem government appeared more precarious than ever. In September 1961, NLF fighters overran and briefly occupied a South Vietnamese provincial capital less than 50 miles from Saigon. Around the same time, Diem informed Washington that he wanted to negotiate a formal defense treaty between South Vietnam and the United States – a request that appeared to signal the regime's growing sense of desperation.

In response to these developments, US President John F. Kennedy dispatched a high-level fact-finding mission to South Vietnam in October 1961. The mission was headed by General Maxwell Taylor, Kennedy's top advisor on military affairs. In his secret report on his trip, Taylor described "an acute crisis of confidence" in Saigon and advised a large expansion of the scope and scale of the US commitment to South Vietnam. Among other things, Taylor recommended the immediate dispatch of about 8,000 US combat troops to the country. Kennedy strongly resisted this measure, but he endorsed almost all of the report's other suggestions – including a sharp increase in the number of American military advisors in South Vietnam. Kennedy also approved Taylor's advice to try to cajole Diem into reforming his government in ways that would reverse its declining support.

...Perhaps the most striking aspect of this mission's effort is the unanimity of view—individually arrived at by the specialists involved—that what is now required is a shift from U.S. advice to limited partnership and working collaboration with the Vietnamese. The present war cannot be won by direct U.S. action; it must be won by the Vietnamese. But there is a general conviction among us that the Vietnamese performance in every domain can be substantially improved if Americans are prepared to work side by side with

[7] Excerpted from "Letter From the President's Military Representative (Taylor) to the President," 3 November 1961, printed in *Foreign Relations of the United States, 1961–1963*, Vol. 1, *Vietnam: 1961* (Washington DC, GPO, 1988), 491–494.

the Vietnamese on the key problems. Moreover, there is evidence that Diem is, in principle, prepared for this step, and that most—not all—elements in his establishment are eagerly awaiting it.

There is a second conclusion. We have attempted to answer the political and psychological question: would the more substantial involvement of Americans be counter-productive? Our conclusion—based on experience and judgment in Vietnam, Laos, and Thailand—is the following. If Americans come in and go to work side by side with the Vietnamese, preferably outside Saigon, the net effect will almost certainly be positive. The danger lies in excessive headquarters establishments and a failure to do palpably serious jobs. The record of U.S.-Asian relations in field tasks is excellent.

After all, the United States is not operating in Southeast Asia in order to recreate a colonial system doomed by history; it is attempting to permit new nations to find their feet and to make an independent future. Despite Communist propaganda, this is widely understood. When Americans work hard and effectively in this area, they meet friendship.

Such side-by-side partnership requires, of course, men of tact, strongly motivated to come and to get on with the task. They must be led at every level by Americans of first rate technical competence, imagination and human sympathy. It is our conviction that such Americans exist and can be recruited for the specific tasks listed below. On the other hand, the selection of personnel for these operations must be done with extreme care. The operation will fail if the U.S. is not willing to contribute its best men to the effort in adequate numbers and to keep them in the field for substantial periods...

Reforming Diem's Administrative Method

The famous problem of Diem as an administrator and politician could be resolved in a number of ways:

- By his removal in favor of a military dictatorship which would give dominance to the military chain of command.
- By his removal in favor of a figure of more dilute power (e.g., Vice President Nguyen Ngoc Tho) who would delegate authority to act to both military and civil leaders.
- By bringing about a series of de facto administrative changes via persuasion at high levels; collaboration with Diem's aides who want improved administration; and by a U.S. operating presence at many working levels, using the U.S. presence (e.g., control over the helicopter squadrons) to force the Vietnamese to get their house in order in one area after another.

We have opted for the third choice, on the basis of both merit and feasibility.

Our reasons are these: First, it would be dangerous for us to engineer a coup under present tense circumstances, since it is by no means certain that we could control its consequences and potentialities for Communist exploitation. Second, we are convinced that a part of the complaint about Diem's administrative methods conceals a lack of first-rate executives who can get things done. In the endless debate between Diem and his subordinates (Diem complaining of limited executive material; his subordinates, of Diem's bottleneck methods) both have hold of a piece of the truth.

The proposed strategy of limited partnership is designed both to force clear delegation of authority in key areas and to beef up Vietnamese administration until they can surface and develop the men to take over.

This is a difficult course to adopt. We can anticipate some friction and reluctance until it is proved that Americans can be helpful partners and that the techniques will not undermine Diem's political position. Shifts in U.S. attitudes and methods of administration as well as Vietnamese are required. But we are confident that it is the right way to proceed at this stage; and, as noted earlier, there is reason for confidence if the right men are sent to do the right jobs.

The Self-Immolation of Thich Quang Duc (1963)

In the spring of 1963, dissatisfaction with the Ngo Dinh Diem government inside South Vietnam reached new heights. Although the ARVN's battlefield fortunes had improved over the previous year, the regime faced new challenges from noncommunist groups and leaders. On May 8, 1963, government security forces killed eight demonstrators during a demonstration led by Buddhist monks in the city of Hue. The incident set off a wider series of protests by Buddhists, who complained that they had suffered discrimination and even persecution at the hands of Diem government officials, a disproportionate number of whom were Catholic. Although Diem initially seemed inclined to resolve the crisis through negotiations, his brother Ngo Dinh Nhu pressed him to take a hard line. In early June, a compromise agreement between the monks and the government was derailed by Nhu's wife, Madame Nhu, who publicly accused Buddhist leaders of treason.

Madame Nhu's broadside convinced Buddhist leaders to carry out a new and more dramatic kind of protest. Around 9:00 am on June 11, a few hundred Buddhist monks and nuns set out on a procession through the streets of downtown Saigon. When they reached a busy intersection, they abruptly stopped and formed a circle around a car that had been driving slowly at the head of the procession. A septuagenarian monk named Quang Duc emerged from the car and sat down in the middle of the circle in the lotus position, his hands folded together in prayer. One of his fellow monks doused him in gasoline; another then handed him a packet of matches. Quang Duc struck one of the matches and was instantly engulfed by fire. Incredibly, he continued to sit upright and did not cry out, even as he was burning to death. The shocking scene was photographed by an American journalist named Malcolm Browne who worked for the Associated Press. The image below, one of several he captured, was published in newspapers and magazines across the world. It remains one of the most famous photographs ever taken.

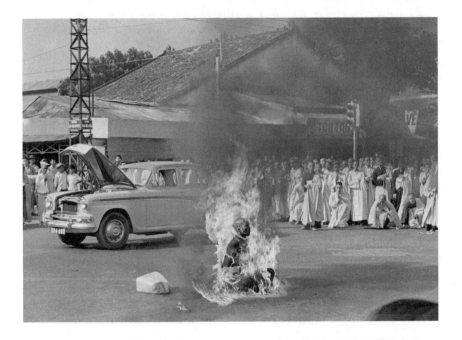

Why did Thich Quang Duc choose to die in such a painful and horrifying way? During and after 1963, observers in Vietnam and elsewhere offered many explanations for his actions. Some Americans interpreted his death as a call for religious freedom. Others portrayed his actions as an antiwar protest, as a gesture of resistance against the US intervention in Vietnam, or as the

expression of ancient Buddhist beliefs. Recent scholarship on Quang Duc has emphasized his nationalist convictions, as well as his prior involvement in a reform movement that aimed to revitalize Vietnamese Buddhist institutions and practices. Today, many Buddhists in Vietnam and elsewhere revere Quang Duc as a bodhisattva – an enlightened being whose extraordinary act of sacrifice revealed him to be a living Buddha.

Transcript of a Phone Conversation between Ngo Dinh Diem and Henry Cabot Lodge, (November 1, 1963)[8]

The 1963 political crisis in South Vietnam culminated in a military coup launched on November 1. The coup, which had been several months in the making, was led by three high-ranking generals in the South Vietnamese army. During the first hours of the uprising, units commanded by the coup plotters surrounded Diem's palace, which was defended by his ultraloyal Presidential guard. After a standoff of several hours, the rebels captured the palace, only to discover that Diem and his brother Nhu had slipped out during the siege. The brothers remained at large until the next morning, when they agreed to surrender in exchange for guarantees of their personal safety. While travelling to the coup leaders' headquarters in an armored personnel carrier, Diem and Nhu were gunned down by some of the soldiers who had been sent to escort them. The officer who fired the deadly shots was apparently acting on the orders of General Duong Van Minh, one of the coup ringleaders.

Diem's last conversation with a US government official took place during the afternoon of November 1, a few hours after the coup began. From the besieged Presidential Palace, Diem telephoned the US Ambassador to South Vietnam, Henry Cabot Lodge. As the transcript of their brief conversation suggests, Diem was in a defiant mood. Although the RVN president was aware that some American officials had been advocating his overthrow, he apparently never learned that Lodge had strongly encouraged the coup plotters to proceed with their plans. The ambassador, for his part, seemed certain that the demise of the Diem government was at hand.

DIEM: Some Units have made a rebellion and I want to know, what is the attitude of the U.S.?

LODGE: I do not feel well enough informed to be able to tell you. I have heard the shootings but am not acquainted with all the facts. Also, it is 4:30 A.M. in Washington and the U. S. Government cannot possibly have a view.

DIEM: But you must have some general ideas. After all, I am Chief of State. I have tried to do my duty. I want to do now what duty and good sense require. I believe in duty above all.

LODGE: You have certainly done your duty. As I told you only this morning, I admire your courage and your great contribution to your country. No one can take away from you the credit for all you have done. Now I am worried about your physical safety. I have a report that those in charge of the current activity offer you and your brother safe conduct out of the country if you resign. Had you heard this?

DIEM: No. [pause] You have my phone number.

LODGE: Yes. If I can do anything for your physical safety, please call me.

DIEM: I am trying to re-establish order.

[call ended]

John F. Kennedy, Comments on the Saigon Coup (November 4, 1963)[9]

In the months leading up to the coup against Diem, President John F. Kennedy was deeply and personally involved in US decisionmaking about Vietnam. However, unlike Ambassador Lodge and some of his other advisors, Kennedy was ambivalent and conflicted about what course to follow. On the one hand, Kennedy worried that Diem's lack of popular support had undermined the Saigon government's ability to win the war against the communists. Yet Kennedy was also anxious about South Vietnam's prospects for survival after Diem was gone. His concerns were heightened by the fact that US military planners were ready to begin a phased withdrawal of US military advisors from South Vietnam – a move that was predicated on the assumption that the war was going well. Historians remain divided over how to interpret the "Kennedy withdrawal" and its implications for understanding Kennedy's thinking at the time. There is no doubt, however, that the president realized that events in South Vietnam had reached a critical point and that his decisions were likely to have far-reaching consequences.

Two days after he learned of the deaths of Diem and Nhu, Kennedy dictated the following comments on the coup. He apparently recorded these

[9] John F. Kennedy, dictated note of November 4, 1963, Cassette M (Dictabelts), John F. Kennedy Presidential Library, Boston, MA.

remarks with the intent of referring to them when writing his presidential memoirs. On the tape, Kennedy spoke frankly about how his top advisors had been sharply split over whether or not support a coup against Diem. He also expressed his deep regret over the assassinations of the Ngo brothers, and his worry over what would happen in South Vietnam in the months ahead.

PRESIDENT KENNEDY: Monday, November 4, 1963. Over the weekend the coup in Saigon took place. It culminated three months of conversation about a coup, conversation which divided the government here and in Saigon...[*Kennedy here explains who among his top advisors had opposed a coup and who had been in favor of it.*]

...I feel that we must bear a good deal of responsibility for [the coup], beginning with our cable of early [*sic*] August in which we suggested the coup. In my judgment that wire was badly drafted, it should never have been sent on a Saturday. I should not have given my consent to it without a roundtable conference at which [*Defense Secretary Robert*] McNamara and [*General Maxwell*] Taylor could have presented their views. While we did redress that [im]balance in later wires, that first wire encouraged [*Ambassador*] Lodge along a course which he was in any case inclined.[10] [*General Paul*] Harkins continued to oppose the coup on the ground that the military effort was doing well. There was sharp split between Saigon and the rest of the country. Politically the situation was deteriorating. Militarily it had not had its effect; there was a feeling, however, that it would. For this reason, Secretary McNamara and General Taylor supported applying additional pressures to Diem and Nhu in order to move them.

[*At this point in the recording, Kennedy was interrupted by his young children, John Jr. and Caroline. After briefly playing and talking with them, he resumed his dictation.*]

[10] Kennedy refers here to the dispatch of a secret State Department cable sent on August 24, 1963, to Ambassador Lodge in Saigon, which authorized Lodge to contact ARVN commanders and encourage them to carry out a coup against the Diem government. That cable, which had been drafted by a small group of State Department officials who favored a coup, was approved and transmitted while Kennedy and most of his senior advisors were out of town for the weekend.

PRESIDENT KENNEDY: I was shocked by the death of Diem and Nhu. I'd met Diem with [Supreme Court] Justice Douglas many years ago. He was an extraordinary character. While he became increasingly difficult in the last months, nevertheless over a ten-year period he'd held his country together, maintained its independence under very adverse conditions. The way he was killed made it particularly abhorrent. The question now is whether the generals can stay together and build a stable government or whether... public opinion in Saigon, the intellectuals, students, etcetera, will turn on this government as repressive and undemocratic in the not-too-distant future.

Discussion questions

1. Summarize the main proposals contained in the Caravelle Manifesto of 1960. If Diem had heeded these suggestions, would he have been able to stay in power beyond 1963? Why or why not?
2. How did the Taylor Report propose to reverse the "crisis of confidence" in South Vietnam in 1961? Did subsequent events confirm the validity of the analysis presented in the report? Explain.
3. Given that most Americans in 1963 knew very little about Buddhism or Vietnam, why did Malcolm Browne's photograph of the self-immolation of Thich Quang Duc garner such attention within the United States?
4. Which of the following leaders was *most* responsible for the demise of the Ngo Dinh Diem government: (i) Henry Cabot Lodge; (ii) John F. Kennedy; (iii) the leaders of the Buddhist movement who led the protests against Diem; (iv) the ARVN generals who led the coup against Diem; (v) communist party leaders; (vi) Ngo Dinh Diem and Ngo Dinh Nhu themselves?

Chapter 6   Escalation

Resolution of the Central Committee of the Vietnam Workers' Party: Strive to Struggle, Rush Forward to Win New Victories in the South (December 1963)[1]

The ouster and assassination of Ngo Dinh Diem in November 1963 altered the course of the Vietnam War. While Ambassador Lodge and some other US officials expected Diem's removal to strengthen the Saigon government, its main effect was to expose the regime's deep weaknesses and dwindling legitimacy. The generals who led the coup remained in power for less than three months before they were themselves overthrown by one of their fellow officers. This began a period of "revolving door" politics in Saigon, during which governments were installed and fell with alarming frequency.

North Vietnamese leaders were keen to take advantage of the post-coup upheaval in South Vietnam. However, they were also anxious not to provoke US President Lyndon Johnson, who had come to power following Kennedy's assassination on November 22, 1963 – just three weeks after Diem's death. During late November and early December, senior VWP officials met in Hanoi to consider their options. After much debate, Le Duan secured

[1] "Resolution of the Ninth Plenum of the Central Committee of the Vietnamese Workers' Party: Strive to Struggle, Rush Forward to Win New Victories in the South, December 1963," in *Van Kien Dang* [Party Documents] (Hanoi: Nha Xuat Ban Chinh Tri Quoc Gia, 2003) Vol. 24 (1963), 811–814, 839–840, 860–861. Translated by Merle Pribbenow.

Original publication details: 6.1 Van Kien Dang, 2003. Translated by Merle Pribbenow. 6.2 Johnson & McNamara, 1964. 6.3 United States Statutes at Large, 1964. 6.4 Morse. Congressional Record, 1964. 6.5 Foreign Relations of the United States, 1964–1968, 1996. 6.6 Foreign Relations of the United States, 1964–1968, 1996.

approval of the controversial secret resolution excerpted here. Known simply as "Resolution Nine," this measure constituted an enormous gamble: Le Duan was betting that by rapidly infiltrating large numbers of North Vietnamese troops into the south the revolutionaries could win a series of large-scale "decisive victories" over the demoralized ARVN, while also triggering a series of party-led popular uprisings in urban areas. These developments, he insisted, would bring about the collapse of the Saigon government before the United States could intervene with its own combat troops. Although the resolution was resisted by Ho Chi Minh and some other VWP leaders who thought it too risky, Le Duan and his supporters carried the day. Resolution Nine thus served to strengthen Le Duan's control over North Vietnamese policy and strategy, even as it also sharply expanded Hanoi's commitment to the war in the south.

The war of aggression currently being waged [in South Vietnam] by the American imperialists is one of the biggest wars in the world today. It is a "special war," one of the types of war included in the new U.S. strategy. The American imperialists are using South Vietnam as a test ground for this kind of "special war," which they intend to use to combat nation liberation movements being conducted by the people of many countries around the world. The American imperialist war of aggression in South Vietnam has created an extremely serious situation. The entire world is now concerned about the problem of South Vietnam.

For the past two years, ever since the U.S. set up a military command headquarters in Saigon and brought in American troops to directly participate in the fighting in South Vietnam, the heroic South Vietnamese people, under the leadership of our Party, overcoming many adversities and hardships, have continued to build on the heroic and unshakable traditions of our people by innovatively coming up with many different forms of struggle and have won glorious victories....

...Our victories and the enemy's defeats have caused a rapid expansion of the internal contradictions within the enemy's ranks. The U.S. and Diem publicly clashed, and the U.S. used a military coup to get rid of Diem and install lackeys who would be easier to control to lead the government. They assembled a number of pro-American, anti-communist elements and laid out a number of deceitful, demagogic policies designed to win over the masses and give the puppet government a firm grip on the army so that they could intensify their war of aggression. However, they still have not been able to overcome the contradictions that continue to grow among the new leaders, who are now vying with one another for power and who have dissolved the rather powerful anti-communist organization structure that had been set up by the Diem-Nhu family. They also have not been able to rebuild the collapsed morale and frightened spirits of the puppet army. Internal disagreements have arisen within U.S. ruling circles regarding the anti-communist policies and stratagems that should be used in South Vietnam. A number of Americans, especially in the intellectual class, have publicly opposed the aggressive policy of the American government in Vietnam... An important point is that after the heavy defeats... and especially after our soldiers and civilians won victory at the battle of Ap Bac, the Americans have begun to lose faith that they will win and have even publicly expressed that loss of confidence. On the other hand, the faith of our people in our final victory is growing each and every day, and the people of the world are increasingly sympathetic to the just struggle of the people of South Vietnam and are increasingly giving us their support...

...While we patiently and steadfastly continue to fight a protracted war, we must direct our effort toward taking advantage of favorable opportunities by massing our forces in a resolute effort to win victories of decisive importance in the next few years.

In order that achieve the goal of this effort, our overall immediate mission is to mobilize our entire Party and our entire population to overcome all difficulties and, on the basis of strongly expanding our people's political awareness, strive to build up our political and armed forces (and especially our armed forces) in order to quickly change the balance of forces between our side and the enemy in our favor and to actively build up and expand our base areas, especially in strategic locations from which our main force army can conduct mobile operations. In this way we will progress toward attacking and destroying and shattering individual portions of the enemy's army, to destroying the majority of the enemy's strategic hamlets, and to gaining control of the mountain jungle regions and of the bulk of the rural villages in the lowlands. This will create conditions that will enable our urban mass movement to conduct powerful uprisings that will drive the U.S.-puppet regime into an even deeper crisis and cause it to deteriorate even more quickly, thereby enabling our movement to gain the strategic initiative and create excellent opportunities for us to win decisive victories.

There are two primary issues involved in our immediate mission as described above, and these are the two primary goals that we must be determined to achieve:

1. Annihilate individual portions of the enemy's army in order to create conditions that will cause the total collapse of the enemy's armed forces, which is the primary tool and source of support of the American imperialists and their lackeys in South Vietnam.

2. Defeat the enemy's resettlement and Strategic Hamlet plan, destroy the majority of the strategic hamlets, gain control of manpower and supplies for the revolution, and gain control of the mountain jungle regions and the bulk of the lowlands.

...In order to accomplish the missions outlined above, not only must our South Vietnamese Party Chapter and the people of South Vietnam make extraordinary efforts, the North Vietnamese Party Chapter and the people of North Vietnam must also make extraordinary efforts. The roles of the two halves of our country in our national revolutionary cause remain unchanged...but the time has come for North Vietnam to increase its assistance to South Vietnam and to more completely fulfill its role as the revolutionary base area for our entire nation.

1. There must be a strong shift in our guidance of the mission of supporting and sending assistance to the revolution in South Vietnam. We must fully understand that under the Party's leadership, our people are building North Vietnam in peace while at the same time carrying out a war against the Americans in South Vietnam. The struggle against the Americans and their lackeys is the duty of our entire nation. Because we must restrict the enemy to "special warfare" and keep the war confined within the area of South Vietnam, the ways in which the two halves of our nation participate in the struggle will be different. However, each half of the nation must make the maximum effort to do everything it can to defeat the enemy's armed forces.

2. We must more fully educate the cadre, Party members, and civilian population of North Vietnam on each individual's duty toward the revolution in South Vietnam in order to raise revolutionary zeal and fighting spirit. We must ensure that each person enthusiastically vies with one another in patriotic zeal, that each person works with enthusiasm, that each person endures all difficulties and hardships, and that, when required, each person is prepared to carry out his or her full responsibility toward the revolution in South Vietnam, no matter what the conditions are and no matter what form the responsibility takes.

3. We must develop a comprehensive plan for sending assistance to South Vietnam, a plan that responds to the needs of the South Vietnamese revolution. Because of the need to provide this assistance to the South, appropriate adjustments must be made to the plan for building up North Vietnam.

4. We must realize that if we want the revolution in South Vietnam to make progress, we must constantly consolidate and strengthen North Vietnam

in all respects. For this reason, we must strive to strengthen North Vietnam's economic and national defense forces. We must constantly maintain a high level of vigilance and be prepared to deal with new enemy plots to increase their sabotage efforts and to provoke North Vietnam...

5. We must strengthen the research agencies that are helping the National leadership direct the revolution in South Vietnam. We must coordinate the efforts of the various branches in North Vietnam that are involved in this effort in order to better support the revolution in South Vietnam...

Recording of a Phone Conversation between Lyndon Johnson and Robert McNamara about Vietnam (April 30, 1964)[2]

During 1964, as DRV leaders intensified their military operations in South Vietnam, the United States also sharply escalated its involvement in the war. Although President Lyndon Johnson knew that the military situation in the south had taken a turn for the worse, he was determined to avoid withdrawal. That spring, he significantly increased the number of US military advisors in South Vietnam; he also approved an expanded program of covert sabotage and commando raids against North Vietnam. However, these measures failed to check the advance of communist forces in the south, which continued to make gains at the expense of the ARVN. In this transcript of a taped telephone conversation with Secretary of Defense Robert McNamara, Johnson expressed frustration with the current situation and made it clear that he expected US military commanders to develop a plan to win the war.

PRESIDENT LYNDON JOHNSON:	Bob.
ROBERT MCNAMARA:	Yes, Mr. President.
LBJ:	I hate to bother you but—
RM:	No trouble at all—
LBJ:	—tell me, I saw a little glimmer of hope on Vietnam in some paper today, where we'd routed some and killed a few and run 'em out or something. Do you have any—are you getting any good cables on them at all?
RM:	Well, I read that article, Mr. President, the, the—

[2] Lyndon Johnson Conversation with Robert McNamara on April 30, 1964, Tape WH6404.16, Lyndon B. Johnson Presidential Library, Austin, TX.

LBJ:	[to someone in the same room, who is not on the phone] Give me another one of those.
RM:	The official battle report wasn't as good as the newspaper report, for once. We got a little—we got a break in the press.
LBJ:	Has Carl Rowan[3] getting any of his propaganda people out there now?
RM:	Yes, I think so and I'm going to check again before I go the end of the week and uh, tell him that I want to talk to Lodge about that while I'm there. I'm just sitting here, as a matter of fact now, writing a cable to Lodge that I'll send Monday, telling him if he agrees, I'd like to stop by on my way home and I will cover that subject with him and be sure before I leave that Rowan's people are actually are on the way.
LBJ:	Have we got anybody that's got a military mind that can give us some military plans for winning that war?
RM:	Well, Bus Wheeler[4] is going out with me.
LBJ:	I know but he went out last time and he just came back with, with planes, that's all he had in mind, wasn't it?
RM:	Well we, uh, yes, well he had more than that but he emphasized the planes. And the planes, Max Taylor agrees, are not the answer to the problem. Whether we should have more planes or not is another question, but it's not going to make any difference in the short run, that's certain.
LBJ:	Let's get some more of something, my friend, because I'm gonna have a heart attack if you don't get me something. I'm just sitting here every day and uh, this war that I'm winning and I'm not doing much about fightin' it, and

3 Carl Rowan: a highly regarded African-American journalist and diplomat. Johnson was referring to Rowan's status as head of the United States Information Agency (USIA), a State Department organization responsible for "public diplomacy" in the United States and around the world.

4 Earle "Bus" Wheeler: the US Army general who at the time of this conversation was serving as Chief of Staff of the US Army (the Army's senior command position). In July 1964, Johnson promoted Wheeler to Chairman of the Joint Chiefs of Staff, a position he would hold until his retirement in 1970.

I'm not doing much about winnin' it, and I just read about it . And uh—let's get somebody that wants to do something besides drop a bomb, but that can go in and take in after these damn fellas and run them back where they belong. It looks like—

RM: Looks like we want to tell Khanh[5]—

[*On the declassified version of this tape, the next thirty seconds of audio has been redacted by the U.S. National Archives for reasons of national security.*]

LBJ: ...and we need... to shoot that guy—we need somebody over there that can give us better plans than we've got, because what we've got is what we've had since '54. We're not getting it done. We're, we're losing, so we need something new. It's uh, if you pitch this ol' southpaw every day and you wind up as the Washington Senators and you lose, well, we'd better go us get us a new pitcher.

RM: I know it—

LBJ: Let's find one. And tell those damn old generals over there to find one for ya', or you gonna go out there yourself.

RM: Well that's one reason I want to go back, and kick them in the tail a little bit, that will help here, at this point, I think.

[*The next 17 seconds of audio has been redacted, on national security grounds.*]

RM: ...a damn good marine coming along behind this one, he wasn't ready for it this time. He's a little tiny guy, but he's out in the Pacific at the moment.

LBJ: Well, what I want is somebody that can lay up some plans to trap these guys and whup hell out of 'em. Kill some of 'em. That's what I want to do. If this Army Chief of Staff is not going to do it, let's get somebody else that'll do it.

---

[5] This is likely a reference to Nguyen Khanh, an ARVN general who had engineered a coup in Saigon in January 1964, and who was the most powerful figure in South Vietnamese politics until he was forced into exile in early 1965.

RM:	I'll try and bring something back that will meet that objective.
LBJ:	OK, Bob.
RM:	Thank you.

[*Conversation ends.*]

The Tonkin Gulf Resolution (August 1964)[6]

When Lyndon Johnson approved an expanded program of covert operations against North Vietnam in the spring of 1964, he also endorsed Pentagon plans for intelligence gathering operations by US Navy warships in the Tonkin Gulf, off the coast of North Vietnam. One of the ships involved in these operations was a destroyer known as the USS Maddox. On August 2, 1964, the Pentagon announced that PAVN torpedo boats had fired on the Maddox in international waters. Two days later, on August 4, US officials reported that both the Maddox and another US ship had been targeted in a second attack. American officials did not disclose that the Maddox had been on an intelligence mission during which it had sailed within a few miles of the North Vietnamese coast. Nor did they reveal what US naval commanders had discovered shortly after the August 4 incident: the report of the second alleged attack had been based on an erroneous sonar reading, and was almost certainly false.

While the Tonkin Gulf incident was far from a straightforward case of "communist aggression," Lyndon Johnson lost no time in using the incident to secure sweeping powers to use military force in Southeast Asia. Within days, both houses of Congress had endorsed the following resolution, the text of which had been drafted by the White House before the incident took place. Johnson immediately used the authority conferred by the resolution to launch retaliatory airstrikes against North Vietnam – the first such US attacks of the war. Although Johnson portrayed these airstrikes as a one-time operation and insisted that the United States sought "no wider war," he would later cite the Tonkin Gulf Resolution as the legal basis for the subsequent massive expansion of the US military involvement in the conflict.

Whereas naval units of the Communist regime in Vietnam, in violation of the principles of the Charter of the United Nations and of international law, have deliberately and repeatedly attacked United Stated naval vessels

---

[6] Public Law 88-408, Joint Resolution to promote the maintenance of international peace and security in southeast Asia, August 10, 1964, *United States Statutes at Large*, 78: 384.

lawfully present in international waters, and have thereby created a serious threat to international peace; and

Whereas these attackers are part of deliberate and systematic campaign of aggression that the Communist regime in North Vietnam has been waging against its neighbors and the nations joined with them in the collective defense of their freedom; and

Whereas the United States is assisting the peoples of southeast Asia to protest their freedom and has no territorial, military or political ambitions in that area, but desires only that these people should be left in peace to work out their destinies in their own way: Now, therefore be it

Resolved by the Senate and House of Representatives of the United States of America in Congress assembled, That the Congress approves and supports the determination of the President, as Commander in Chief, to take all necessary measures to repel any armed attack against the forces of the United States and to prevent further aggression.

Section 2. The United States regards as vital to its national interest and to world peace the maintenance of international peace and security in southeast Asia. Consonant with the Constitution of the United States and the Charter of the United Nations and in accordance with its obligations under the Southeast Asia Collective Defense Treaty, the United States is, therefore, prepared, as the President determines, to take all necessary steps, including the use of armed force, to assist any member or protocol state of the Southeast Asia Collective Defense Treaty requesting assistance in defense of its freedom.

Section 3. This resolution shall expire when the President shall determine that the peace and security of the area is reasonably assured by international conditions created by action of the United Nations or otherwise, except that it may be terminated earlier by concurrent resolution of the Congress.

Approved August 10, 1964.

U.S. Senator Wayne Morse, Speech on the Tonkin Gulf Resolution (August 5, 1964)[7]

Only two members of the US Congress voted against the Tonkin Gulf Resolution in 1964. One of the two was Senator Wayne Morse of Oregon, a former Republican who had become an independent. Morse had previously

---

[7] *Congressional Record,* 18133–18134, August 5, 1964.

criticized both presidents of both parties for seeking broad authorizations to use force in the Middle East and East Asia. In a speech to his Senate colleagues, Morse was skeptical not only of Johnson's justifications for his actions in Vietnam but also of the president's promises to avoid deeper military involvement. In addition, Morse expressed doubts about the validity of the domino theory and the broader geopolitical assumptions that informed US policy.

MR. MORSE: Mr. President, I rise to speak in opposition to the Joint Resolution. I do so with a very sad heart. But I consider the [Tonkin Gulf] resolution, as I considered the resolution of 1955, known as the Formosa resolution, and the subsequent resolution, known as the Middle East resolution, to be naught but a resolution which embodies a predated declaration of war.

Article I, section 8 of our Constitution does not permit the President to make war at his discretion. Therefore I stand on this issue as I have stood before the Senate, perfectly willing to take the judgment of history as to the merits of my cause . . . I am satisfied that history will render a final verdict in opposition to the joint resolution introduced today.

The senior Senator from Oregon has no illusions as to the reactions which will be aroused in some quarters in this Republic. However, I make the speech because it represents the convictions of my conscience and because I consider it essential to make it in keeping the sworn trust that I undertook when I came into this body . . . pledging myself to uphold the constitution.

I have one other remark by way of preface, not contained in the manuscript. I yield to no other Senator or to anyone else in this country in my opposition to communism and all that communism stands for.

In our time a great struggle, which may very well be a deathlock struggle, is going on in the world between freedom on the one hand and the totalitarianism of communism on the other.

However, I am satisfied that the struggle can never be settled by war. I am satisfied that if the hope of anyone is that the struggle between freedom and communism can be settled by war, and that course is followed, both freedom and communism will lose, for there will be no victory in that war.

Because of our own deep interest in the struggle against communism, we in the United States are inclined to overlook some of the other struggles which are occupying others. We try to force every issue into the context of freedom versus communism. That is one of our great mistakes in Asia. There is much communism there, and much totalitarianism in other forms. We say we are opposing communism there, but that does not mean that we are advancing freedom, because we are not.

... I believe the only hope for the establishment of a permanent peace in the world is to practice our oft-repeated American professon [that] we believe in the substitution of the rule of law for the jungle law of military force as a means of settling disputes which threaten the peace of the world ... It makes no difference who says that our objective is peace, even if he be the President of the United States. Our actions speak louder than words; and our actions in Asia today are the actions of warmaking.

As I speak on the floor of the Senate at this moment, the United States is making war in Asia.

George Ball, A Compromise Solution for South Vietnam (1965)[8]

The Tonkin Gulf Resolution gave Lyndon Johnson a free hand to act as he wished in Vietnam. Following his landslide victory in the November 1964 US Presidential election, Johnson moved quickly to turn the Vietnam War into an American War. In February 1965, the US Navy and Air Force launched Operation Rolling Thunder, a strategic bombing campaign against North Vietnam. The following month, Johnson approved a Pentagon request to send a few thousand US ground combat forces to South Vietnam for the first time. During the summer of 1965, he authorized the deployment of over 100,000 additional troops, and indicated that he was prepared to send more if US commanders requested them.

While most of Johnson's top advisors supported these escalatory moves, a few expressed reservations. Some of the most incisive criticisms came from George Ball, a veteran diplomat and the second-ranking official in the State Department. In this memo, written during the late spring or early summer of 1965, Ball argued that escalation would not lead to victory, and that Johnson should instead seek a negotiated settlement to the conflict.

---

[8] *Foreign Relations of the United States, 1964–1968*, Vol. 3, *Vietnam, January–June 1965* (Washington, DC: GPO, 1996), 106–109.

A Compromise Solution for South Viet-nam

1. *A Losing War:* The South Vietnamese are losing the war to the Viet Cong. No one can assure you that we can beat the Viet Cong or even force them to the conference table on our terms no matter how many hundred thousand white foreign (US) troops we deploy.

    No one has demonstrated that a white ground force of whatever size can win a guerrilla war—which is at the same time a civil war between Asians—in jungle terrain in the midst of a population that refuses cooperation to the white forces (and the [South Vietnamese army]) and thus provides a great intelligence advantage to the other side. Three recent incidents vividly illustrate this point:

    (a) The sneak attack on the Danang Air Base which involved penetration of a defense perimeter guarded by 9,000 Marines. This raid was possible only because of the cooperation of the local inhabitants.
    (b) The B-52 raid that failed to hit the Viet Cong who had obviously been tipped off.
    (c) The search-and-destroy mission of the 173rd Airborne Brigade which spent three days looking for the Viet Cong, suffered 23 casualties, and never made contact with the enemy who had obviously gotten advance word of their assignment.

2. *The Question to Decide:* Should we limit our liabilities in South Viet-Nam and try to find a way out with minimal long-term costs?

    The alternative—no matter what we may wish it to be—is almost certainly a protracted war involving an open-ended commitment of US forces, mounting US casualties, no assurance of a satisfactory solution, and a serious danger of escalation at the end of the road.

3. *Need for a Decision Now:* So long as our forces are restricted to advising and assisting the South Vietnamese, the struggle will remain a civil war between Asian peoples. Once we deploy substantial numbers of troops in combat it will become a war between the United States and a large part of the population of South Viet-Nam, organized and directed from North Viet-Nam and backed by the resources of both Moscow and Peiping.

    The decision you face now, therefore, is crucial. Once large numbers of US troops are committed to direct combat they will begin to take heavy casualties in a war they are ill-equipped to fight in a non-cooperative if not downright hostile countryside.

    Once we suffer large casualties we will have started a well-nigh irreversible process. Our involvement will be so great that we cannot—without national humiliation—stop short of achieving our complete objectives. Of the two possibilities I think humiliation would be more likely than the achievement of our objectives—even after we had paid terrible costs.

4. *A Compromise Solution:* Should we commit US manpower and prestige to a terrain so unfavorable as to give a very large advantage to the enemy—or should we seek a compromise settlement which achieves less than our stated objectives and thus cut our losses while we still have the freedom of maneuver to do so?

5. *Costs of Compromise Solution:* The answer involves a judgment as to the costs to the United States of such a compromise settlement in terms of our relations with the countries in the area of South Viet-Nam, the credibility of our commitments and our prestige around the world. In my judgment, if we act before we commit substantial US forces to combat in South Viet-Nam we can, by accepting some short-term costs, avoid what may well be a long-term catastrophe. I believe we have tended greatly to exaggerate the costs involved in a compromise settlement. An appreciation of probable costs is contained in the attached memorandum. (Tab A)

6. With these considerations in mind, I strongly urge the following program:

A. *Military Program*

   1. Complete all deployments already announced (15 battalions) but decide not to go beyond the total of 72,000 men represented by this figure.
   2. Restrict the combat role of American forces to the June 9 announcement, making it clear to General Westmoreland that this announcement is to be strictly construed.
   3. Continue bombing in the North but avoid the Hanoi-Haiphong area and any targets nearer to the Chinese border than those already struck.

B. *Political Program*

   1. In any political approaches so far, we have been the prisoners of whatever South Vietnamese Government was momentarily in power. If we are ever to move toward a settlement it will probably be because the South Vietnamese Government pulls the rug out from under us and makes its own deal or because we go forward quietly without advance pre-arrangement with Saigon.
   2. So far we have not given the other side a reason to believe that there is any flexibility in our negotiating approach. And the other side has

been unwilling to accept what in their terms is complete capitulation.

3. Now is the time to start some serious diplomatic feelers, looking towards a solution based on some application of the self-determination principle.

4. I would recommend approaching Hanoi rather than any of the other probable parties (the National Liberation Front, Moscow or Peiping). Hanoi is the only one that has given any signs of interest in discussion. Peiping has been rigidly opposed. Moscow has recommended that we negotiate with Hanoi. The National Liberation Front has been silent.

5. There are several channels to the North Vietnamese but I think the best one is through their representative in Paris, Mai Van Bo. Initial feelers with Bo should be directed toward a discussion both of the four points we have put forward and the four points put forward by Hanoi as a basis for negotiation. We can accept all but one of Hanoi's four points and hopefully we should be able to agree on some ground rules for serious negotiation—including no preconditions.

6. If the initial feelers lead to further secret exploratory talks we can inject the concept of self-determination that would permit the Viet Cong some hope of achieving some of their political objectives through local elections or some other device.

7. The contact on our side should be handled through a non-governmental cutout (possibly a reliable newspaperman who can be repudiated.)

8. If progress can be made at this level the basis can be laid for a multi-national conference. At some point obviously the government of South Viet-Nam will have to be brought on board but I would postpone this step until after a substantial feeling-out of Hanoi.

9. Before moving to any formal conference we should be prepared to agree that once the conference is started (a) the United States will stand down its bombing of the North, (b) the South Vietnamese will initiate no offensive operations in the South, and (c) the DRV will stop terrorism and other aggressive acts in the South.

10. Negotiations at the conference should aim at incorporating our understanding with Hanoi in the form of a multi-national agreement guaranteed by the United States, the Soviet Union and possibly other

parties, and providing for an international mechanism to supervise its execution.

George W. Ball

Notes of a Meeting at the White House (July 21, 1965)[9]

George Ball delivered his warning about the danger of escalation just as Johnson and his advisors were debating a US military proposal to deploy an additional 44 combat battalions to South Vietnam. At the White House meeting described in this document, Johnson's team compared Ball's memo with another one written by Defense Secretary Robert McNamara, who argued in favor of sending the troops. The document shows that Johnson listened carefully to Ball's advice. But it also suggests that he had already made up his mind about which course of action he would follow.

Washington, July 21, 1965, 10:40 a.m.

SUBJECT: Viet Nam

PRESENT: McNamara, Rusk, Vance, Mac Bundy, Gen. Wheeler, Geo. Ball, Bill Bundy, Len Unger, Helms, Raborn, Lodge, Rowan, McNaughton, Moyers, Valenti

...

(The President entered the meeting at 11:30 am.)

McNamara: To support an additional 200,000 troops in [South Vietnam] by first of the year the reserves in the US should be reconstituted by like amount. I recommend calling up 235,000 a year from now, replace the reserves with regulars.

    In mid-1966 we would have approximately 600,000 additional men.

President: What has happened in recent past that requires this decision on my part? What are the alternatives? Also, I want more discussions on what we expect to flow from this decision. Discuss in detail.

---

[9] *Foreign Relations of the United States, 1964–1968*, Vol. 3, *Vietnam, January–June 1965* (Washington, DC: GPO, 1996), 189–197.

Have we wrung every single soldier out of every country we can? Who else can help? Are we the sole defenders of freedom in the world? Have we done all we can in this direction? The reasons for the call up? The results we can expect? What are the alternatives? We must make no snap judgments. We must consider carefully all our options.

We know we can tell SVN [South Vietnam] "we're coming home." Is that the option we should take? What flows from that?

The negotiations, the [bombing] pause, all the other approaches—have all been explored. It makes us look weak—with cup in hand. We have tried.

Let's look at all our options so that every man at this table understands fully the total picture.

MCNAMARA: This is our position a year ago (shows President a map of the country with legends). Estimated by country team that VC [Viet Cong] controls 25%—SVN 50%—rest in white area, VC in red areas. VC tactics are terror, and sniping.

PRESIDENT: Looks dangerous to put US forces in those red areas.

MCNAMARA: You're right. We're placing our people with their backs to the sea—for protection. Our mission would be to seek out the VC in large scale units.

WHEELER: Big problem in Vietnam is good combat intelligence. The VC is a creature of habit. By continuing to probe we think we can make headway.

BALL: Isn't it possible that the VC will do what they did against the French—stay away from confrontation and not accommodate us?

WHEELER: Yes, but by constantly harassing them, they will have to fight somewhere.

MCNAMARA: If VC doesn't fight in large units, it will give ARVN a chance to re-secure hostile areas. We don't know what VC tactics will be when VC is confronted by 175,000 Americans.

RABORN: We agree—by 1965, we expect NVN [North Vietnam] will increase their forces. They will attempt to gain a substantial victory before our build-up is complete.

PRESIDENT: Is anyone of the opinion we should not do what [McNamara's] memo says—If so, I'd like to hear from them.

BALL: I can foresee a perilous voyage—very dangerous—great apprehensions that we can win under these conditions. But, let me be clear, if the decision is to go ahead, I'm committed.

PRESIDENT: But is there another course in the national interest that is better than the McNamara course? We know it's dangerous and perilous. But can it be avoided?

BALL: There is no course that will allow us to cut our losses. If we get bogged down, our cost might be substantially greater. The pressures to create a larger war would be irresistible. Qualifications I have are not due to the fact that I think we are in a bad moral position.

PRESIDENT: What other road can I go?

BALL: Take what precautions we can—take losses—let their government fall apart—negotiate—probable take over by Communists. This is disagreeable, I know.

PRESIDENT: Can we make a case for this—discuss it fully?

BALL: We have discussed it. I have had my day in court.

PRESIDENT: I don't think we have made a full commitment. You have pointed out the danger, but you haven't proposed an alternative course. We haven't always been right. We have no mortgage on victory.

I feel we have very little alternative to what we are doing.

I want another meeting before we take this action. We should look at all other courses carefully. Right now I feel it would be more dangerous for us to lose this now, than endanger a greater number of troops.

RUSK: What we have done since 1954-61 has not been good enough. We should have probably committed ourselves heavier in 1961.

ROWAN: What bothers me most is the weakness of the Ky government. Unless we put the screws on the Ky government, 175,000 men will do us no good.

LODGE: There is no tradition of a national government in Saigon. There are no roots in the country. Not until there is tranquility can you have any stability. I don't think we ought to take this government seriously. There is no one who can do anything. We have to do what we think we ought to do regardless of what the Saigon government does.

As we move ahead on a new phase—it gives us the right and duty to do certain things with or without the government's approval.

PRESIDENT: George, do you think we have another course?

BALL: I would not recommend that you follow McNamara's course.

PRESIDENT: Are you able to outline your doubts—and offer another course of action? I think it is desirable to hear you out—and determine if your suggestions are sound and ready to be followed.

BALL: Yes. I think I can present to you the least bad of two courses. What I would present is a course that is costly, but can be limited to short term costs.

PRESIDENT: Then, let's meet at 2:30 this afternoon to discuss Ball's proposals. Now let Bob tell us why we need to risk those 600,000 lives.

                   ....

[1:00 pm—Meeting adjourned until 2:30 pm.]
[Resume same meeting at 2:45 pm]

BALL: We can't win. [The war will be] long [and] protracted. The most we can hope for is messy conclusion. There remains a great danger of intrusion by [Chinese Communists].

Problem of long war in US:

1. Korean experience was galling one. Correlation between Korean casualties and public opinion (Ball showed Pres. a chart) showed support stabilized at 50%. As casualties increase, pressure to strike at jugular of NVN will become very great.
2. World opinion. If we could win in a year's time—win decisively—world opinion would be alright. However, if long and protracted we will suffer because a great power cannot beat guerrillas.
3. National politics. Every great captain in history is not afraid to make a tactical withdrawal if conditions are unfavorable to him. The enemy cannot even be seen; he is indigenous to the country.

[I] Have serious doubts if an army of westerners can fight orientals in Asian jungle and succeed.

PRESIDENT: This is important—can westerners, in absence of intelligence, successfully fight orientals in jungle rice-paddies? I want McNamara and Wheeler to seriously ponder this question.

BALL: I think we have all underestimated the seriousness of this situation. Like giving cobalt treatment to a terminal cancer case. I think a long protracted war will disclose our weakness, not our strength.
                   The least harmful way to cut losses in SVN is to let the government decide it doesn't want us to stay there. Therefore, put such proposals to SVN government that they can't accept, then it would move into a neutralist position—and I have no illusions

that after we were asked to leave, SVN would be under Hanoi control.

What about Thailand? It would be our main problem. Thailand has proven a good ally so far—though history shows it has never been a staunch ally. If we wanted to make a stand in Thailand, we might be able to make it.

Another problem would be South Korea. We have two divisions there now. There would be a problem with Taiwan, but as long as Generalissimo is there, they have no place to go. Indonesia is a problem—insofar as Malaysia. There we might have to help the British in military way. Japan thinks we are propping up a lifeless government and are on a sticky wicket. Between a long war and cutting our losses, the Japanese would go for the latter...

PRESIDENT: Wouldn't all those countries say Uncle Sam is a paper tiger—wouldn't we lose credibility breaking the word of three presidents—if we set it up as you proposed? It would seem to be an irreparable blow. But, I gather you don't think so.

BALL: The worse blow would be that the mightiest power in the world is unable to defeat guerrillas.

Discussion questions

1. Was it a mistake for Le Duan and other North Vietnamese leaders to adopt the strategy of escalation outlined in Resolution Nine of December 1963? Why or why not?

2. What, if anything, does Lyndon Johnson's April 30, 1964 conversation with Robert McNamara reveal about the motives behind Johnson's decisions to expand the US military involvement in Vietnam? What does it reveal about his relationship with McNamara?

3. Compare Wayne Morse's 1964 criticism of the Tonkin Gulf Resolution with George Ball's 1965 memo advising Johnson against troop increases in Vietnam. Was Ball's argument against escalation substantially the same as Morse's?

4. Based on the documents in this chapter, why did Lyndon Johnson decide not to heed Ball's advice in 1965?

Chapter 7   On the Battlefield

A South Vietnamese Account of the Battle of Ap Bac (1995)[1]

*On January 2, 1963, a force of approximately 1500 ARVN soldiers and Civil
Guardsmen converged on the small hamlet of Ap Bac near the city of My
Tho in the Mekong Delta. US and South Vietnamese intelligence reports
suggested that the hamlet would be defended by a force of about 120
insurgents, all of whom could be expected to withdraw as soon as the attack
began. In reality, there were two full-strength NLF companies in and around
the hamlet – around 350 fighters. The commander of these companies saw
the attack on Ap Bac as a chance to test the insurgents' new "stand and fight"
tactics. By delivering disciplined and concentrated fire from heavily fortified
positions, the defenders hoped to inflict heavy losses on the enemy before
conducting an orderly retreat. These tactics proved spectacularly successful.
During the day-long battle, the revolutionaries killed or wounded more than
180 of the attacking troops while suffering fewer than 60 casualties on their
own side. They also shot down five US-piloted helicopters and damaged nine
others, while destroying several of the American-made armored personnel
carriers (APCs) that the ARVN had committed to the battle.*

*In the aftermath of the battle, some of the US military advisors on the
scene blamed ARVN commanders for the carnage. According to these*

---

[1] Lý Tông Bá, *Hồi ký 25 năm khói lửa: của một tướng cầm quân tại Mặt Trận* [*A Memoir of
25 Years of Fire: By a General Who Served at the Front*] (San Marcos, CA: s.p., 1995), 55–84.
Translation by Merle Pribbenow.

Original publication details: 7.3 OH0333, John Thomas Esslinger Collection, The Vietnam
Center and Archive, Texas Tech University. 7.4 1540148004, My Lai Collection, The Vietnam
Center and Archive, Texas Tech University. 7.5 OH0291, Ted Acheson Collection, The Vietnam
Center and Archive, Texas Tech University.

American officers, their South Vietnamese counterparts were cowards who had hung back and refused to follow US advice at critical moments during the battle, thus turning victory into defeat. This interpretation, though widely accepted by American journalists and later by historians, has been vigorously disputed by some South Vietnamese participants. In the translated memoir excerpt printed here, former ARVN officer Ly Tong Ba describes his experience as commander of an APC company that was mauled during the battle. While Ba admits that ARVN tactics at Ap Bac were severely flawed, he rejects the accusations of cowardice and insists that the battle was a rare defeat amid a string of victories won by his men.

In the early 1960's, faced with increasing Viet Cong attacks in the Mekong Delta, most notably in the Plain of Reeds, the U.S. Government supplied a new weapon to the Army of the Republic of Vietnam (ARVN) – the M-113 Armored Personnel Carrier (APC). In South Vietnam the M-113 served as a light armored vehicle. In addition to its amphibious capabilities, it had a composite metal outer shell strong enough to withstand enemy bullets of all types, from rifles to heavy machine guns. A 50-caliber machine gun was mounted on top of the vehicle.

Before the vehicles were given to larger units, like regiments and task forces, two M-113 companies were formed to serve as test units. I was one of the two company commanders selected by the Armored Command to command one of these two companies: the 7th Mechanized Company (M-113)....

...When discussing feats of arms and military victories, everyone recognizes that a price must be paid for such achievements – they do not just happen on their own. In the 7th Mechanized Company, my fellow soldiers and I endured pouring rain and blazing sun, rolling from place to place, night and day, in response to the needs of the battlefield. Sometimes we plowed through soggy rice fields, and sometimes we were transported by ship. No matter what the situation, no matter what the environment, 7th Company not only carried out every operational plan with precision, it also decisively pursued and destroyed the enemy, to say nothing of the fact that we also had to study the terrain beforehand when the situation permitted and when we had the opportunity.

...During this period, whenever they fought the 7th Mechanized Company (M-113), the Viet Cong always suffered heavy losses. The 7th M-113 Company, performing as if it was hunting for wild birds or driving rats from their holes, swept away a line of enemy positions from Tan Chau and Hong Ngu districts in Chau Doc province up to Duc Hoa and Duc Hue in Tay Ninh province. These were important operations that must never be forgotten.

During the two-year period between 1962 and 1964, I can safely say that no Viet Cong unit ever dared to try to hold their position and stand up against any of the units under my command that were equipped with M-113s, from the 7th Mechanized Company (M-113) up to the Regiments and task forces at My Tho. Only once, during the Battle of Ap Bac, did the Viet Cong temporarily manage to hold off the 7th Company for a short time before finally being overrun and dispersed...

I don't think I need to devote a lot of space to the battle of Ap Bac. It was a very difficult day – the company had to cross rice paddies covered with deep mud and three successive canals to reach and fight the enemy on a piece of ground he had chosen. The losses on both sides were even – eight Viet Cong lay dead on the ground, and eight ARVN troops sprawled dead in our vehicles. That was especially painful to me – all eight armored troopers were killed by the enemy's initial volley. Our vehicle commanders and 50-caliber gunners did not have bullet shields. The enemy was lying in wait for us in camouflaged dug-in positions looking out from the edge of the hamlet, and our gunners were just sitting ducks for them. I believe that no matter how bad the enemy's marksmanship was, it wouldn't have made any difference.

I had recognized the danger several months earlier, when my company destroyed an entire enemy battalion in Kien Phong. At that time I suggested to my superiors that, whether we liked it or not, we had to install gunshields on our M-113s as soon as possible. Even then, I had already guessed that at some future date the enemy would concentrate his forces to take revenge on us and to regain his lost morale...

It was my opinion that the Viet Cong would never again accept a stand-up fight against the 7th Mechanized Company in flooded, uninhabited rice paddies, as they had before. Instead they would secretly concentrate their forces and build a network of solid fortifications on the edge of a hamlet where the terrain was completely unfavorable for the M-113. The enemy would inflict casualties on us and then go to ground, stealing away and disappearing. It is unfortunate that both the American and Vietnamese side, with their standard lethargy, did not do what I recommended. For this reason, the battle of Ap Bac did not go as we planned – just as I had predicted! This was a significant blunder on our part. I believe that the higher-ups wanted to use our battles (in which the mistakes were made by the senior levels) to turn our ARVN troops into "Texas cowboys," and to do that in just one day was simply not possible!

In addition, it is my opinion that, "We were always one step behind the Viet Cong in everything from equipment to organization, and even in tactics!" Only after they had AKs did ARVN get M-16s, only after they got AT-3 missiles did we get TOWs,[2] and only after they began conducting operations at the platoon and company level did we finally agree to begin increasing our own troop strength! And every time, it was only after we suffered casualties and lost a number of our best fighters that our side finally would agree to make changes and that the U.S. would finally agree to provide us with the needed aid, etc. As a classic example of this, it was only after we suffered these losses that the U.S. finally agreed to install the solidly protected turrets for the 50-caliber machineguns on our M-113s that my readers will recall seeing later on.

It was truly a case of, "wanting to catch a tiger but only trying to chase after it from behind and grab at its tail!" We wanted to defeat the Viet Cong, who fought a guerrilla war using "dirty" tricks and a protracted-war strategy, but not once did we pour onto the battlefield the kind of overwhelming force in manpower and weapons that was needed to crush our opponent right from the very beginning, to destroy their capacity so that they could not prolong the war as they wanted. If we had been decisive in this way the VC would never have had time to conduct their whispering propaganda campaign, to exploit our weaknesses, or to conduct their psychological warfare campaign to erode the core fighting ability of the Republic of Vietnam. And in the battle of Ap Bac, my company would not have lost, in one fell swoop, so many experienced battlefield soldiers, men like Platoon Commander 2nd Lt. Nguyen Van Nho, Company Sergeant Major Nguyen Van Nao, and a number of vehicle commanders and gunners. They were eliminated from the battlefield only because our vehicles did not have shields to protect against enemy fire, even though we were capable of providing such shields and even though I had recommended them. We were not afraid to die, but what did we have to do to avoid unhappy surprises while simultaneously responding to developments in order to turn things around to save lives. Meanwhile the enemy always had the ability to select the terrain and tactics he desired, with surprise being his most effective weapon!

During the initial moments of the battle, after losing the personnel I mentioned above, I was forced to spend almost an hour re-assessing the situation because the morale of my company had collapsed. I personally had to fire my weapons with one hand while holding my radio transmitter in the other to maneuver and command my unit. Sometimes I fired the 50-caliber, sometimes I fired my carbine, and sometimes I threw hand grenades, because the enemy was sitting there in foxholes and bunkers not more than 20 meters away. During that period VC bullets were constantly zipping over our heads, sometimes sending up a string of sparks as they hit the shells of our vehicles,

---

[2] TOW: a kind of anti-tank missile.

looking like a string of firecrackers going off during a New Year's Dragon Dance.

While I hesitated as I went over the formula, "the enemy and the terrain," in my head, I reluctantly ordered my company to hold its position, giving priority to using the maximum possible firepower to pin the enemy in place until we could get a handle on the situation. Then the first flight of B-26s arrived. After the planes made their bombing attack, I ordered one final assault to seize our battlefield objective. The time was about 16:30 hours. At that time a bugler riding in my command vehicle was felled by enemy bullets. He was carrying out my orders by blowing the "Charge" call on his bugle to buck up the morale of the company.

He was only a hands-breadth to my right, standing in the square hatch where I stood, issuing orders to command my troops. He fell to the floor, and the only thing left of his hand was his little finger, dangling by a shred of skin. It was a truly appalling sight...

...We also realized that in the first battle of Ap Bac the Viet Cong had for the first time taken a small step forward in finding new tactics for use in engaging units equipped with M-113s....On this occasion the enemy truly took full advantage of the terrain and did not neglect any of our weaknesses, at least the weaknesses of which they were aware. They studied the lessons they had learned before, when we wiped out an entire VC battalion. They studied how to change their combat formations and their other combat methods. Exploiting our weakness, the fact that our M-113s did not have gun-shields to protect our gunners, when we closed in on our objective and failed to detect their forces, their first volley knocked out our gunners. At that time our firepower was immediately strangled. The soul of the M-113, its firepower, was temporarily cut off. When that happened, naturally each individual vehicle crew, and the entire unit by extension, became confused and disorganized for hours until we had time to regroup and replace our personnel losses. If the terrain in the lowlands of the Mekong Delta and the Plain of Reeds had been hard and flat as a desert, which would allow the M-113 to exploit its mobility, the battle would certainly have had a different outcome...

...In fact, over the course of those two years, from early 1962 until the end of 1964, and not counting the first battle of Ap Bac...the Viet Cong in the Plain of Reeds were just a bunch of fried rats – no more, no less! Every time we engaged the enemy a pleasant aroma wafted across the rice paddies, increasing the combat ardor of the ARVN troops in general, and of our invincible Black Berets in particular.[3] That golden era was a concrete

3 Black berets were part of the dress uniform worn by ARVN armored branch personnel.

manifestation of the perfect tactics being employed by our armored troops, who wielded these tactics like an enchanted sword against their opponents.

Interrogation of a Captured NLF Fighter (1967)[4]

As the war in South Vietnam escalated during the mid-1960s, many Vietnamese rural residents felt compelled to choose sides. In this interview, an unnamed woman from a village in Dinh Tuong province in the Mekong Delta explains why she decided to join the National Liberation Front in 1965, when she was just 17 years old. Abandoned by her widowed father and raised by her maternal grandparents, this enterprising girl had briefly set up her own tailor shop in her home village. However, she abandoned the business venture after being robbed several times by South Vietnamese soldiers. Against her grandparents' wishes, she left home to join the Front. After months of training, she became the deputy leader of a demolition cell.

At the time this interview was recorded in 1967, the woman was a prisoner, following her arrest by South Vietnamese Civil Guardsmen a few months earlier. By her own account, she had been savagely beaten and tortured by her captors; at one point, she became so despondent that she attempted suicide. However, as she made clear to her interrogator, she did not regret her decision to join the revolution.

PRISONER: When I set up my tailor shop, [my grandmother's] village was still a contested area. The Front's pressure was then much more felt than that of the GVN.[5] Nevertheless, the Front propaganda over there was not widespread and it didn't touch me since I was well guarded by my grandparents. They didn't allow me to frequent other people or to go around the village very often.

I was then a grown-up, and I began to think a lot about the situation. The sight of misfortunes which happened every day in my village shocked me a great deal. They made me feel that the cause of the Front is right, while the GVN, despite its repeated statements of helping the

---

[4] Excerpted from Interview No. 213, *Rand Interview Series DT: Activities of Viet Cong within Dinh Tuong Province* (Alexandria, VA: Defense and Documentation Center for Scientific and Technical Information, Cameron Station, 1972).

[5] GVN ("Government of Vietnam") was an acronym used by Americans and others to refer to the South Vietnamese government.

people enjoy a good life, is simply doing harm to the people by setting [their] houses on fire and extorting money by means of arbitrary arrest.

The Front's cadres... worked without pay, without any advantages whatsoever. Many of their families didn't even have enough rice to eat, but still they agreed to continue to work for the villagers in the hamlet. They are willing to accept any sacrifices required of themselves and of their relatives for the country. They helped the people in their work in the fields; they dug ditches to improve the villagers' crops. Since I witnessed the cadres' sacrifices, I paid much respect to the Front although I didn't know much of this organization or what it represented. I viewed the cadres as living embodiments of heroes of our legends. They are those who stand up to fight the evil in order to protect the people. That's why I respected the Front a great deal...

INTERVIEWER: Did you really witness killings, dismemberments of people and setting houses afire by GVN soldiers, or did you only learn of them from hearsay?

PRISONER: I did witness GVN soldiers setting houses afire, [and] dismembering people... I cried a lot because of these misdeeds. That's why when a woman cadre invited me to attend the burial of the four dismembered men, I agreed to follow her right away despite my grandparents' objection. They feared that attending this burial would be very dangerous because it could be the target of a sweep. This was the first time I disobeyed my grandparents. This was also the first time I [made] a resolution... After I listened to the cadres' speech dealing with misdeeds perpetrated by GVN people, I felt most angry. That night, I couldn't sleep.

A month later, that is, in early 1965, a woman... [who] was working for the Village [Worker's Association] Chapter called on me and advised me to join the Front. She said that the Front is always willing to help all those who are generous and enthusiastic in fighting for the Revolution . . . "I am ready to give my own life to the Front," I told her, "but I had to make necessary preparations before I leave my grandparents behind. When I join the Front, I will ask for assignments in distant places. I don't want to work in the village because I am afraid that my possible arrest would cause my grandparents a lot of trouble with the GVN."

Seven or eight months passed. I continued to work for a living but I couldn't help becoming more and more angry at the GVN. Every time GVN soldiers came into my village, they seized poultry and people's belongings. They didn't spare me either. Four or five times they robbed all the clothes I had made from the stuff that customers brought me. I had to indemnify these losses from my own money.

It was not until September 1965 that another female cadre came to see me quite unexpectedly. She introduced herself as the head of the Village Liberation Women's Committee... She asked to stay overnight in my house. When the night was far advanced, she asked me: "Are you ready to leave your family behind to join the Front now? Do you love your grandparents?"

I replied that I had not arranged anything yet since I had lost all my savings in indemnifying the customers. "As for my grandparents, I love them very much. But why did you put this question to me? It sounds quite absurd."

"If you love them, you ought to think about how to secure them a good life," she went on.

"What do you mean about securing them a good life?" [I asked.]

"I mean that if you do love them very much you ought to see to it that they could enjoy a good life in the years to come. A good life for them could be secured only if the Revolution becomes a success. It will be then that they could live with freedom and welfare. No one might oppress and exploit them, as the enemy is doing to the people at present. But the enemy is loafing now and they are in trouble. The Revolution is moving closer to the final victory and you should join it right away in order to be able to pay back your grandparents all the past worries and care they had granted you."

Her words, in fact, sounded right. So I agreed to [leave] my grandparents but I didn't know how to tell my grandparents about my decision. I urged [the cadre] to take care of it.

My grandparents were shaken when they listened to [the female cadre] advocating to let me join the Front....

They asked the female cadre to let me stay home and said: "Our granddaughter is still very young. She has never lived far from us. Her comprehension is very limited and she wouldn't be able to work efficiently for the Front. If you have any compassion for us, please, let her stay home for a few more years. When she grows wiser, we will be most willing to let her follow the Revolution. But at present, she is still a child, and she couldn't stand hardships."

"Never mind about it," [the cadre] answered. "The Front is responsible for educating [your granddaughter] to become a good citizen. We will enjoy freedom and happiness later on if we agree to withstand present hardships. Moreover, if [your granddaughter] didn't come right now to seek protection from the Front, she would be arrested by the GVN police very soon. The enemy won't fail to torture and assault her since they know that [she] has entertained close relations with the Front and attended the funerals of the four [murdered] men."

Her answer made my grandmother burst out crying. She cried: "Oh! My granddaughter! How can you be so ungrateful to me! Your mother died when she gave birth to you and I have raised you ever since! And now how can you be so awful towards me by leaving me alone!"

After that, my grandparents left us behind and went outdoors. [The female cadre] and I stayed home until 4:00 PM before we set out. I didn't meet my grandparents anew because they didn't come back home. Either out of discouragement or out of anger at me, they stayed with the neighbors seemingly to avoid us.

I felt very sorry for them. They were very old, and yet they had to live under risks of being killed by bombs and bullets every day. But the deeper I felt sorry for them, the quicker I thought I had to join the Front...

Later on, I learned that my grandmother wept endlessly for days. This was reported by the cadres who gave me two black suits that my grandmother had sent me through them.

That day, [the female cadre] and I left at 4:00 PM. We marched all night and early in the morning we arrived at the Chau Thanh District liaison station... As a matter of fact, I felt a little homesick while we were marching away.

It was the first time I left my relatives behind to start a new life of my own. [The cadre] seemed to be aware of my feelings and we talked abundantly, trying, I suppose, to alleviate my pain and to build up my morale. She said: "You are a true daughter of the Revolution"...

INTERVIEWER: In case the GVN wins over and succeeds in pacifying all of Dinh Tuong province and you are freed, will you agree to live peacefully under the protection of the laws?

PRISONER: How [is it] that the GVN can succeed... when its soldiers rob the people, burn houses, assault women wherever they go? What I just told you were happenings I had witnessed in my hamlet. They weren't lies. In case the GVN freed me from jail and torture, I would be very grateful of it but it wouldn't certainly be for this reason that I would agree to stop fighting. As far as soldiers, exploitation, oppression would plague the countryside, I would continue to fight the GVN. If I am freed now, I will return to my grandparents to take care of them until their death. After that, I'll join the Revolution again. They are now very old and I think that it won't be long before they die.

Oral History of Tom Esslinger, US Marine Lieutenant and Veteran of the Battle of Khe Sanh (2003)[6]

John Thomas "Tom" Esslinger was born in rural Pennsylvania in 1943. He attended Yale on a full scholarship and graduated in 1965 with plans to become a doctor. The following year, after opting not to pursue a career in medicine, he decided to enlist in the US Marines. Upon graduating from Officer Candidate School, he was commissioned as a lieutenant and received three months of Vietnamese language training. He arrived in Vietnam in August 1967 and was assigned to the Third Battalion of the 26th Marine Regiment, which was operating north of Hue, near the demilitarized zone (DMZ) that separated North and South Vietnam.

In December 1967, the company in which Esslinger was serving as executive officer was sent to Khe Sanh, a Marine firebase which overlooked the DMZ. His unit was subsequently ordered to occupy Hill 881, just to the west of the firebase. The area was fairly quiet until January 21, 1968, when

[6] Excerpted from Interview with Tom Esslinger, 21 August 2003, John Thomas Esslinger Collection, Vietnam Center and Archive, Texas Tech University. http://www.vietnam.ttu.edu/virtualarchive/items.php?item=OH0333 [accessed 23 September 2015].

North Vietnamese (PAVN) forces began raining rocket, mortar, and artillery fire onto the Marine positions. The PAVN attacks continued without letup for 77 days. Although the battle unfolded against the backdrop of communists' Tet Offensive (which began on January 31, 1968, and which involved attacks all across South Vietnam), US commanders made the defense of Khe Sanh a top military priority. Thanks to the use of massive amounts of American airpower and elaborate resupply operations, PAVN commanders eventually decided to raise the siege, prompting American leaders to claim the battle as a victory. However, because US forces subsequently withdrew from Khe Sanh in June 1968, North Vietnamese leaders maintained that they were the real victors. A total of 274 American soldiers and marines were killed and more than 2,500 wounded during the battle; estimates of North Vietnamese dead and wounded ran as high as 15,000.

INTERVIEWER: Tell me how you got to Khe Sanh. Was it more of an emergency call that they needed more bodies there?

ESSLINGER: We were told we were moving out of Camp Evans. We took a truck convoy north. The word was that we were going out. They were in the process then of building the McNamara Wall. They were putting a new series of firebases sort of slightly in front of and in between the existing ones. So this one was going to be called A-3. It was going to be just to the west and slightly north of Con Thien. In the fall of 1967 Con Thien was the hot point in the northern Marine Corps area of Vietnam, just below the DMZ. It was a small hill in terms of elevation, but it looked over the DMZ. There was always a battalion up there. They were always taking incoming and there were a lot of probing attacks. It was just the hot spot. We all felt like, "Wow, we're going right up there to the DMZ. We're going from a rice paddy war to the real war." So we were pretty nervous. So we packed up got in the trucks and went to Dong Ha. We got there; early evening sort of left the airfield to places where we were going to bivouac for the night. Just about the time we got where we were supposed to pitch camp for the night the word came, "Get back on the trucks, we're going back to the landing zone and we're going to Khe Sanh." I had told you about the reaction I had to the tactical position at Khe Sanh when we were coming through Okinawa. My thought was, "Oh my God they're attacking Khe Sanh and we're going to fly right into the middle of it." So we got on helicopters and they flew us out there. They landed us on the airstrip; we had our flak jackets buttoned, our helmets buckled and our weapons at high port. We came off there ready to go to war. I remember I was running off next to Matt Caulfield who had been my company commander and was now the major, the S-3. You know we took a look around and we saw these mountains to the north and west hovering over the airfield. Even as we were running I turned to Caulfield and says, "It looks like Dien Bien Phu to me."...

...We get off the airstrip and life is normal. Guys are strolling down the road on their way to the enlisted man's club to have a beer. Nothing's going on. They sort of wondered what they hell we were doing there...They didn't even have any room for us. So they sent us outside the wire to the west area a little bit. Said, "Here, you guys can camp here." So that's what we did. We built sort of an add-on, an annex to the base. We extended the wire and dug our little holes and that's where we lived....

INTERVIEWER: How long did you stay in that position before you moved out to the hill?

ESSLINGER: I stayed there until we moved out to [Hill 881]. What we did was what we were doing before, we would run operations. I remember my company ran a couple of operations out into the jungle. The terrain there was very different than what we had been used to. The mountains were a lot higher. The vegetation was a lot heavier. It was very difficult terrain to move in. We ran a patrol along the ridgeline, a high ridgeline that overlooked Route 9. We were on the south side of Route 9. Route 9 ran east and west and was the only surface line that Khe Sanh had with the rest of Vietnam. It had actually already been compromised because it was so easy to ambush Route 9 virtually anywhere along it. I think at that point in late December it had already been in effect closed by the NVA. We ran a couple of other operations.

INTERVIEWER: What were the operations?

ESSLINGER: It was basically taking the company and patrolling, looking for signs of the NVA... You talk about intelligence. Now looking back on it and having read books I know that at a much higher level they had learned that the normal infiltration pattern by which units coming down the Ho Chi Minh Trail and Laos would turn east and infiltrate toward Quang Tri City and Hue. The Marines had been at Khe Sanh from April and May of '67 all through that summer. Basically after those hill fights there was very little contact. What basically happened, we figured out later, was the Marines from Khe Sanh would patrol out about four thousand meters in any direction. So the enemy just started passing them to the south about five thousand meters away. There just was no contact.

But intelligence had discovered that those patterns were changing. They were infiltrating both south and north of us at a much greater volume than they had been. So Westmoreland was concerned about a build up around Khe Sanh. Nobody's ever quite convinced anybody else as to why Khe Sanh was there. Westmoreland says that it was there, we were basically bait because he was hoping the enemy would mass and try and do a Dien Bien Phu and then he could blow them away…

INTERVIEWER: What was the mood on the base in December 1967?
ESSLINGER: Pretty relaxed. I remember Christmas Day sitting there in this little—we just dug a little hole and went down about two feet and had a little poncho tent over it. I was sitting there with a gunny. They served us a turkey dinner, which wasn't bad. There were some helicopters flying around playing Christmas carols and trailing red and green smoke, troops playing softball. We played softball until the softball went into the wire where the trip wires were, so then they switched to football. Everybody was sitting there writing letters home, it was pretty relaxed. That changed pretty quickly. Again we didn't know about this build up. We didn't even know why we were there…

…At that point intelligence knew that there were three divisions of NVA surrounding the Khe Sanh combat base and that we were effectively cut off on Hill 881 South. They flew a few helicopters in and got the battalion staff out but they decided to leave Mike Company up there. So the hill sort of was two knobs connected by a saddle. So India Company took the bigger knob and they sent Mike Company down to the smaller knob and that's where we stayed for the rest of the siege.

INTERVIEWER: Tell me about how you lived there on that hill.

ESSLINGER: Well, when we first got there, they had a trench line and there was a wire, of course. The trench line was maybe eighteen inches deep. Most of the troops lived in sort of square sandbag bunkers that were fairly sizeable. Inside they might have been ten [feet] by ten [feet]. There would be six or eight guys in there and that's where they'd sleep. They'd man the trenches during the day. The reason given for the fact that the trenches weren't deeper was this was just really hard clay, almost like rock. Digging was really difficult. You'd bend your E tool trying to dig this stuff up. Well, [Hill] 881 started taking incoming almost immediately before anybody realized there was a Tet Offensive. We were getting these mortars and rockets that were landing up there. It was just terrifying. I remember I was just scared to death.

    ...We quickly figured out that anytime [we went out] that we were obviously under observation. Anytime anybody moved on the hill [the enemy] would shoot at them. They had snipers shooting at them and mortars. I told you earlier about the RPG that blew off Sobel's leg. We had a number of other casualties. It became obvious immediately that these sandbag bunkers were death traps. So the word went out we were moving into the trenches. Well, under impetus of enemy incoming [fire], the dirt got a lot softer. It wasn't long before we had these trenches. In fact they ended up digging them too deep some places. Some of these places the trench lines were down eight feet. So I had to have them dig firing steps so they could step up and see out over the trench line so they could use them as defensive firing positions. In relatively short order, I'd say within a week, we were living in the trenches. Troops would live in there and the interior wall of the trench they would scoop out a hole. That's where they would sleep. That's what we did.

INTERVIEWER: So you were protected unless a round fell in the trench itself?

ESSLINGER: That's right. We quickly learned that moving around during daytime was an invitation to death or worse, death or injury. So during daytime we just stayed in the trenches and kept a look out. At nighttime we'd have a more aggressive lookout. We would put out listening posts, and at least initially a few ambushes, but not very far out…

… As the Tet Offensive began and the siege went on, we got word directly from Westmoreland's headquarters that nobody was to go outside the wire under any circumstances. I must admit that I was not willing to sit inside that wire blind all night every night.

INTERVIEWER: Essentially that order came from Saigon?

ESSLINGER: Because when it came I disputed it in my Marine Corps chain of command. They told me that they didn't decide it, that it was decided in Saigon. It wasn't up to me. So I just ignored them and I sent my listening posts out every night anyway.

INTERVIEWER: Did you really?

ESSLINGER: Yeah. How was Westmoreland going to know? He certainly never visited. Nobody did. Anyway that's how we lived…

… When this first started I remember just being so scared. It was almost like paralysis. I just was convinced that Khe Sanh was the focus of the free world. President Johnson and everybody between him and me was doing everything they could to get us out of there or to do something. It turns out I wasn't that far from correct. I discovered later Johnson did have a mock-up of Khe Sanh in the basement [of the White House] and would prowl around there at night, offering suggestions. But if you had told me on the first couple of days that we were going to be up there for seventy-seven days I don't know what I would have done. I might very well have shot myself. I don't think I could have taken that. It was hard enough to take it hour-by-hour or day-by-day. But then within a couple of weeks you adjust. I mean it was just amazing how resilient human beings are.

INTERVIEWER: How do you adjust to that fear?

ESSLINGER: Well, for one thing you sort of overcome the fear. It's hard to believe that sitting there getting mortared and rocketed you can adjust to that, you can accept it, but you do…

…January thirty-first [1968] is when I became company commander because Captain Gilece decided to move from one side of the hill to other instead of going around a trench line during the middle of the day. Jumped up and ran across the top of the hill. And a sniper shot him in the leg. So I got him medevaced...We got him out of there. It was a flesh wound. It went straight through the thigh but didn't hit any bone or anything, or an artery. I figured he'll be back in three weeks. That was January thirty-first [1968]. That was the beginning of the Tet Offensive. As it turned out, anybody who was stabilized they put them back [in the field] to keep beds available for the more seriously wounded. The next time I heard from him he was in the Philadelphia Naval Hospital and he never came back...

...So going back to this adjustment, this resilience. We quickly settled into a pattern of staying underground and out of sight during the day and doing whatever we needed to do at night. But you sort of got tired of that. You sort of started feeling like a rat, particularly since it was sort of monsoonal up there and it was foggy and rainy and cold a lot of the time. So one day in mid-February it was a nice sunny day. One of the first we've had. I'm sitting outside the bunker. The bunker entrance to it the door was down about two feet because of a dip in the terrain protruded about two feet above the surface. In order to prevent any shrapnel from blowing through that door we had to put a sandbag wall about two feet away from it. So I'm sitting on top of this sandbag wall, sort of drying out and looking around and soaking up the sun. By this time most of what the enemy shot at us was 120 mm Russian mortars, which were pretty devastating.

INTERVIEWER: Could you hear them coming?

ESSLINGER: You could hear them come out of the tube. You could hear the thump. We had figured out you had twenty-six seconds from the time you heard the thump until the round landed, a high trajectory. So I'm sitting up there and I hear this thump and I'm saying to myself, "You know these guy are watching me. I'm not going to scurry into my hole like a rat. I'm just going to sit here."

INTERVIEWER: Were you counting in your head?

ESSLINGER: Yeah. So about fifteen seconds go by and I say, "You know this could be pretty dumb if you heard it come out of the tube and because of false pride it landed on you." So slowly—showing my disdain—slowly I got off the hill and sort ambled in through the door of the hooch. Just as I get through the door the round lands, and it lands right on the sandbag wall and blew me through the trench, up against the far wall, and filled the back of my legs and my butt with shrapnel, just small pieces. It landed above me and mainly it would blow dirt and pebbles and rocks down there. There really wasn't very much shrapnel. The shrapnel all went out and up. But the blast blew me across the place and into the far wall and so forth. So I really wasn't very badly hurt. I was shook up a little bit but I wasn't badly hurt at all. But I often reflect on the potential devastating effect of false pride...

INTERVIEWER: What happened with your wounds? Were you able to stay? Were you medevaced?

ESSLINGER: By that time we had already recognized that the most dangerous thing that happened there was the landing of a helicopter. So we only medevaced emergencies. So the doc patched me up a little bit. Picked a few pebbles and stuff out of the wounds and patched them up and that was that.

We only had three places [for a helicopter to land] on the hill...By this time, we'd already had three helicopters shot down. They were still there, and like I said earlier, we took the speakers and stuff out of them and the .50 caliber machine guns. They sort of decorated our landing area. So it became obvious that the enemy had at least one mortar zeroed in on each of those three areas. As soon as they saw a helicopter approach when they figured that was the zone it was going to land in they started pumping those rounds. So we would have helicopters feint into one landing zone and then land in another. But still they only had thirty or forty seconds. We'd have the medevac; we had a trench line out to the landing zone. We'd have the medevac in the trench with a couple of guys. As soon as the helicopter—it didn't even land. As soon as it got close to the ground they'd run out, throw the guy into the helicopter, jump back into the trench, and the helicopter would get out of there. This all had to be done within thirty-five seconds. So there weren't any coming and going from the hill. There wasn't any medevacs except for emergencies.

Varnado Simpson, Testimony about the My Lai Massacre (1969)[7]

Of the many documented cases in which Americans committed battlefield atrocities during the Vietnam War, the My Lai massacre is by far the most infamous. On the morning of March 16, 1968, a US Army infantry unit known as Charlie Company (First Battalion, 20th Infantry Division) assaulted a hamlet located in the central Vietnamese province of Quang Ngai. The hamlet was part of Son My village, but it appeared on American maps as My Lai 4 (pronounced "Mee Lye"). The more than 100 men of Charlie Company had been told to expect fierce resistance from a North Vietnamese battalion that was believed to be operating in the area. But there were no enemy soldiers in My Lai 4 that morning – only several hundred Vietnamese women, children, and old men. Over a four-hour period, the men of Charlie Company destroyed the hamlet and committed rape and murder on a horrific scale. Some inhabitants were shot in their homes; others were rounded up and then gunned down en masse. The rape victims included both women and girls, some as young as ten years old. A total of between four and five hundred people were slaughtered.

A subsequent US Army investigation of the massacre showed that many – though not all – of the members of Charlie Company had participated in the killings. At least some had done so on the direct orders of superior officers. One such soldier was Varnado Simpson, an infantryman from Mississippi who had arrived in Vietnam in November 1967. In this statement given to Army investigators in late 1969, Simpson described his role in the carnage. He also testified that Captain Ernest Medina, Company C's commanding officer, had told his men the night before the massacre to kill everyone in the hamlet – a claim confirmed by some of Varnado's fellow soldiers, but vigorously disputed by others and by Medina himself.

Statement of Varnado SIMPSON, taken at Jackson, Miss., 9 November 1969

I, Varnado SIMPSON, want to make the following statement under oath: I volunteered for the draft 9 January 1967 and had my basic training at Ft Campbell, Kentucky. Then I was assigned to Company C, 1/20th Infantry, then in Hawaii. I went to Vietnam during November 1967. I took part in the operation around MyLai (4), which I remember took place in March 1968.

Before we went to MyLai (4) Captain MEDINA, our company commander, gave us a briefing. During this briefing he said that when we went to

7   Statement of Accused or Suspected Person (Varnado Simpson), 9 November 1969, Item Number: 1540148004, Folder 48, Box 01, My Lai Collection, The Vietnam Center and Archive, Texas Tech University.

MyLai (4) we were to leave nothing standing and that we were to kill everything in the village: men, women, children, cats, and dogs.

The next day we went to MyLai (4). I was in the second or third lift [helicopter flight]. Another Platoon, the First Platoon of Company C, went in ahead of us. I was with my unit, the Third Squad, 2d Platoon. My Platoon Leader was Lt BROOKS. My Squad Leader was Sgt LaCROIX. My Platoon Leader or rather Platoon Sergeant was Sgt BUCHANON. Members of my squad were LAMARTINA, RUCKER (deceased), DELGADO, HUTTON, HUTSON, WRIGHT, and MOWER. (HUTTO, HUTSON, and WRIGHT were the machine gun team.)

After we landed we advanced by fire into the village. We started on the left, but during the advance through the village the troops were all mixed up. Some of the 1st Platoon got with the 2d Platoon and so forth.

Just after we got into the village, I came upon WOOD and STANLEY with four or five Vietnamese detainees. STANLEY said they were going to take them to the Platoon Collection area. They were asking these people some questions in Vietnamese. Then ROSCHEVITZ, who had come up with me, said to kill all the people and told me to kill them. I hadn't killed anyone yet, so I said that I would not. Then ROSCHEVITZ grabbed my M16 away from me and put it on automatic fire and killed all of the Vietnamese who had been standing there. These people were not armed and were not trying to escape.

Q: What happened then?
A: I continued on into the village and found a place where a boy had been shot by a well near a hut. A woman, carrying a baby, came out of the hut crying and carrying on. ROSCHEVITZ, LAMARTINA, and LACROIX were there. WRIGHT, HUTTO, and HUDSON were there also. I think BROOKS may have been around. BROOKS told me to kill the woman, and, acting on his orders, I shot her and her baby. I have been shown a group of photographs and I identify the photograph of the woman and the baby as being the ones I shot as related here. I remember shooting the baby in the face.
Q: Would you initial and date this photograph for future identification?
A: Yes.
Q: What happened then?
A: There were four or five people — mostly children — still in the hut. HUTTO, WRIGHT, and HUDSON went into the hut and HUDSON fired the machine gun into the children. I had gone into the hut at that time and saw that the bodies were all torn up and I have no doubt they were

all killed. There was a little old hole in the hut where the people took shelter from attack, and WRIGHT dropped a grenade into the hole, in case someone was hiding there.

Q: What happened then?

A: As we moved into the village we heard a lot of firing and then came on an area where the platoon ahead of us had rounded up 25 or 30 people and executed them. We did not see the shooting, but it had just happened. MEDINA was there when we got there, but I don't know if he had witnessed the killing while it was going on. I heard about another execution that day, not far from this scene, (but didn't see it either during the killing of the people or afterwards), and also found a ditch full of people at MyLai (4).

Q: What happened next?

A: We were on the left, moving ahead and burning huts and killing people. I killed 8 people that day. I shot a couple of old men who were running away. I also shot some women and children. I would shoot them as they ran out of huts or tried to hide.

Q: Did you see anyone else killed?

A: Yes. I saw WRIGHT, HUTTO, HUDSON, RUCKER (deceased), and MOWER go into a hut and rape a 17 or 18 year old girl. I watched from the door. When they all got done, they all took their weapons, M-60, M16's, and caliber .45 pistols and fired into the girl until she was dead. Her face was just blown away and her brains just everywhere. I didn't take part in the rape or the shooting.

Q: Did each of these men — HUTTO, WRIGHT, HUDSON, RUCKER, and MOWER — have sexual intercourse with that girl?

A: Yes, they did.

Q: Did you see anyone else killed?

A: I witnessed a lot people being killed, but there was a lot of confusion going on and I can't relate details of every killing I saw. I estimate there were 400 people killed in MyLai (4). I would like to stress that everyone was ordered by MEDINA to kill these people; that the killing was done on his orders.

Q: You said you saw a ditch full of people. Please tell me about that?

A: The First Platoon had been there and gone when we arrived. We saw an irrigation ditch with 30-40 dead Vietnamese in it. They had all been just killed. Some had been killed in the ditch, but they were all dead. I don't know who did this by name, but it was the First Platoon.

Q: Did you see a helicopter that day at MyLai (4)?

A.   I saw a Huey land that day at MyLai (4). We were chasing some people through a field or they were moving ahead of us because they knew they were going to be killed and the helicopter landed between us and the people and took them out. I didn't see anyone talk to the people in the helicopter.

Q: Did anything unusual happen that night after you were in your night defensive position?

A: Yes, the [South Vietnamese] National Police killed two or three Vietnamese and showed their bodies to some other suspects. I didn't see any Americans take part in this, but heard the next day from MEDINA's radio man that MEDINA had killed one of them by shooting around him to scare him and then shooting off a finger and then finally by killing him with a shot between the eyes.

Oral History of Wilson Key, US Navy Pilot and Prisoner of War (2004)[8]

Prisoners of War (POWs) have played a prominent role in American collective memories of the Vietnam War. In 1973, North Vietnam released a total of 591 American prisoners, some of whom had been held in prisons and detention camps for as long as seven years. While a few of these prisoners were US soldiers and civilians who had been captured in South Vietnam, most were Air Force and Navy aviators shot down during air combat missions over North Vietnam and Laos. Because DRV leaders considered the US war in Vietnam to be illegal, they declared their captives to be "pirates," to whom international conventions about the treatment of POWs did not apply. Until 1969, most of the Americans who were held in North Vietnam were tortured or spent long periods in solitary confinement, often as punishment for refusing to denounce US policies. When these men returned home in 1973, they were hailed as heroes by President Nixon and by many other Americans, who viewed their stories of endurance as a means to expunge the nation's feelings of failure and guilt over Vietnam.

One of the POWs who returned in 1973 was Wilson Key, a US Navy pilot from North Carolina. A graduate of the US Naval Academy, Key flew dozens of bombing and attack missions against North Vietnam before his A4 Skyhawk was downed by a surface-to-air missile (SAM) in November 1967. In the oral history excerpted below, Key recalls his shootdown and capture, as well as the years he spent in prisons in and around Hanoi. Like many of his fellow POWs, Key largely succeeded in resisting his captors' efforts to force him to participate in anti-US propaganda campaigns. Nevertheless, he expresses mixed feelings about the US military's strict "Code of Conduct," which forbade POWs providing any information to the enemy other than one's name, rank, date of birth, and serial code.

---

[8] Excerpted from Interview with Wilson Key, 5 Nov 2004, Item No. OH0412, Oral History Collection, The Vietnam Center and Archive, Texas Tech University.

INTERVIEWER: When you were shot down, were you on an alpha strike[9] that day?

WK: Yes I was. We were attacking a barge construction yard in the outskirts of Hanoi... I guess because [there were] so many aircraft in the air, the Vietnamese decided just to fire a lot of SAMs, and they did...

...We had our own intelligence, or our own photo-reconnaissance aircraft and usually at most, the intelligence was what we had gotten the previous afternoon, if we're going on a morning alpha strike and sometimes we'd go on an afternoon alpha strike and have... a reconnaissance aircraft that morning bring back pictures. So we had very current intelligence on the operational SAM sites. They moved them around a lot, so it had to be very current. And we were assigned I think three SAM sites, so we had a primary, a secondary, and a tertiary SAM site... Our four aircraft and we were supposed to check out the first one. If it wasn't firing, to go the second one, if it wasn't firing, go to the third one. And we made, I think, we made it, the first two were not firing and we were I think on our way to the third one when I got hit...

INTERVIEWER: ...Did you see the SAM that actually hit you?

WK: No, I never did see [it]... We had seen several SAMs go by, but this one I didn't see. I just all of a sudden, I felt an explosion behind me, I mean, I could tell it was behind me and out of the corner of my eye, I saw my RPM gauge go to zero. It looked like, you know, in retrospect after thinking about it, it looked like it made the engine cease because it didn't wind down, it just went to zero within about three seconds. Well, maybe five seconds. Of course, I lost power immediately... when I got my power back on, [my wingman] was screaming at me [on the radio] to get out, get out... I think I ejected in the neighborhood of six, seven hundred feet... I was going, you know, a hundred and forty knots probably at that time...I was straight and level pretty much except I was heading down pretty fast. And so I ejected... The A4 has a rocket seat in it and it was very, no problem at all. I didn't stay in the air long. I probably stayed in the air probably ten seconds after

---

[9] Alpha strike: the US Navy's term for a large air attack carried out by an aircraft carrier air wing, often involving dozens of aircraft.

the chute opened and then I hit the ground. The aircraft landed about a hundred yards from me and it blew up...

...The only person I saw [when I landed] was a kid, looked like maybe ten to twelve years old, maybe thirty, forty feet from me yelling at me with his hands over his head, I guess like to say to give up, or put your hands up, or something like that...I made one big mistake here. I tried to get away instead of just sitting down and calling my [fellow pilot] and tell him I was okay...[instead] I ran into a little patch of woods in the area and hid in a little hole there for awhile. And it took them about fifteen minutes to flush me out.

INTERVIEWER: Now, were you hurt at all in the ejection or from your jet blowing up a hundred yards from you?

WK: No. I hit the ground pretty hard, normally, but I wasn't hurt in any way at that point.

...it wasn't long until I heard people yelling and screaming and coming in the woods where I'd run. And these woods were not part of the jungle, they were just woods associated with the hamlet. All the hamlets have woods, you know, to give them shade and I just happened to be in one corner of the hamlet... Anyway, they found me after a few minutes. And they were upset, you know, of course, and they wouldn't let me take time to take my flight gear off. They cut it off and they were, of course, agitated I guess, which I guess is understandable. But I was kind of surprised and then I think I was in a little bit of shock at this time too because of all that just happened. But once they got my flight gear off and they took my boots off, yeah, and then they started marching me into the hamlet. And then they took me into, and I guess the thing that was kind of surprising, while they were marching me along, the kids and the old women were very upset with me. They were throwing stones and trying to get at me with sticks. The young women who were basically in charge, they were the ones that had the guns, they were the militia because I guess all the young men were away. They were very professional. They kept the kids away and admonished them to quit throwing rocks. But I passed old men and they were actually respectful. They actually, you know, gave a traditional Vietnamese greeting which is a bow. They would actually bow, which is, I just found that to be kind of amazing, you know, these different mindsets among all these different groups...

...after they searched my flight gear, they offered me some water, which I accepted [but] couldn't drink, it was so horrible. It was horrible tasting. So then I put my flight suit back on without my shoes. They kept my flight boots and then we walked to a bigger village, which was maybe a quarter mile or half mile away. And there, they put me in a little bigger house... The house had basically no furnishings. It had rattan bed. You know, rattan is a bark off of a tree and the bed was made out of rattan. They had one or two benches, dirt floor. They had a picture of who I later learned to be Ho Chi Minh on the wall and they had one of these big water pipes. But anyway, this was at eleven o'clock in the morning basically and I stayed there until dusk...And while I was there, they blindfolded me and I just sat there blindfolded inside the house and all the villagers came by and some shouted at me and cursed at me, I guess. I didn't know what they were saying....

INTERVIEWER: When they took you to Hanoi, did they take you to the "Hanoi Hilton"?

WK: The Vietnamese name was Hoa Lo [which was] a French-built prison... The Vietnamese called it Hoa Lo. We called it the Hanoi Hilton. It was the big, great, huge prison in the middle of Hanoi. And I got there and there was an air strike underway. This was at night, in the middle of the night...SAMs were taking off; you could hear SAMs being fired...After the air strike, they took me into the Hilton and put me into what I learned later was called the Knobby Walled Room...It was called that because on the walls...they had made the wall very rough, [covered with] little sound cones...because they had a lot of screaming going on in there, so they were trying to cut down on the noise outside, I guess....

...[The interrogation] started off with them just asking questions. What's your name, what is your rank, what is your serial number, date of birth, which I gave. Then they wanted, they just keep going. 'Okay, what is your squadron?' And I said, 'I'm sorry, I can't tell you any-more than my name, rank, serial number, and date of birth by the Geneva Convention.' And he quickly informed me that because we had not declared war, that the [Geneva]

Conventions did not apply. Because when they signed the Geneva Conventions, which they had, they made a provision that they would only serve it for declared wars...And so then they asked me, started asking me again what was my squadron. And I, you know, I stuck to name, rank, serial, and date of birth and they just didn't...you know, that was it. Then they turned me over to what some of us called the Heavy, who was a big Vietnamese guy, strong, and he just came up and took his fist... he just knocked me with his fist in the jaw across the room. I mean, he just hit me as hard as he could...I guess maybe they asked me again and I refused, then they put me in what's called a rope. You know, we called [it] a rope trick or a pretzel, where you're just tied up in a little ball...They first tied a ball of string in your mouth. Anyway, and then they proceeded to put me in this rope... It was kind of like an inch and a half wide piece of a strip, nylon strip, probably fifteen feet long or twenty feet long...So, that's what he had to do this little torture session. And they just put me in it and left the room... Thirty minutes later, they came back and took me out of it and started asking me these questions again. And once again, I refused and so they didn't do anything. They just put me right back into it. This time, I guess they stayed away two hours or something like that. Well, I can't, you know, it was just something where you finally say, 'Well, maybe there's a better way.' And what I decided to do, which is basically I think what everyone decided to do is to answer their questions, but just tell them lies. And so that's what I did...

My aircraft had landed a hundred feet from me and my squadron [designation] was right on the tail, and I said, well, they probably know that, so the things I knew they knew I would answer truthfully and the things they didn't...I would lie about. And that got me through until they got to my squadron members and of course, I started lying about them. [The] problem was that [they] already had two guys who had gotten shot down before me who had been the through the same thing and they probably told them different lies. So, they obviously knew I was lying too. So, back into the rope trick again. And whenever they catch you in a lie, you'd just go back in it. So you had to be really careful...

...For the first two days I was in solitary confinement and then they came and got me and put me into a room with three other guys, all of whom were injured to some degree or the other. One guy, another Navy guy had gotten shot down two days before I had....unfortunately he'd gotten shot down near Haiphong... I think they were concerned about maybe rescue attempts, because he was pretty close to the beach. They took off his boots and then they ran him he estimated for ten miles. And so by the time he got to Hanoi, all of his skin had been torn off the bottom of his feet, so he could not walk. And then another one of my other roommates had a broken arm and the other one had a broken ankle. So, they were all cripples basically except me... So, anywhere we went, I carried the guy with the bad feet for you know, the first month I guess. And he eventually got better, fortunately. And that was in November of, early part, well, December, we were all together. And then in January, mid-January, then I got put in solitary confinement for about six months. Both the guy with the bad feet and I did for making the Vietnamese mad.

INTERVIEWER: During this period, did the torture and interrogations continue?

WK: Well, not the torture. We didn't get tortured anymore after that initial period for some time. We had what's called attitude checks... where the Vietnamese played propaganda programs all day long from maybe 8:00 am till 8:00 pm... it was a constant barrage of mostly POWs reading this stuff that they were being forced to read by the Vietnamese over the camp radio. So we had to, you know, we just listened and listened and listened. We basically tuned them out...after we'd listen to the stuff for ten or fifteen days, then they would bring us in for an attitude check and see if it was getting through, I guess. At least that was what we assumed they were doing. And I think what they were looking for any weaknesses on our part. If we started agreeing with them, then I guess they figured they were doing something right and then they had somebody they could exploit... We were very careful, you know, to never let them think that we were ever being swayed by that stuff....[T]hat just went on twelve hours a day for the whole time we were there...Well, at least for the first two or three years...

...We had these camp regulations, posted on all the doors. We had all these rules that you were not supposed to do. And communicating [with prisoners in other cells] was the biggest taboo of all. So, a lot of people had gone through the ringer because they'd been caught communicating...

WK: Well, it depended on the season. Probably the single most common meal was a bowl of pumpkin soup and a plate of pumpkin that was taken from the pumpkin soup and a piece of French bread... Once in a while, we would have a bowl of green soup and a bowl of greens or a plate of greens.... The French bread was I guess our staple; we always had that. Later on when we got out to Son Tay, I guess they were out in the farm country and there, once in a while, we would have black-eyed peas, which was probably the best meal we ever got there. We would have once in a while cabbage in the wintertime. And once in a while, we would have bean curd or whatever that's called, tofu. We called it tofu. We called it bean curd there, but I guess the official name of it was tofu. But that was a good meal, too. And then oddly enough, about once every three weeks, we'd have a bowl of sugar. I think they had, someone told them that Americans need sugar or something. So, that was our meal, just a bowl of sugar. So, we'd try to save that, you know, to spread it out because we could eat with our bread....

INTERVIEWER: How about the Code of Conduct, did it provide enough guidance for you?

WK: No, I don't think it did. You know, it was very depressing when you learned you couldn't [give] them more than name, rank, serial number, and date of birth. And I think we all came to believe that the Code of Conduct should be a little more flexible than that...None of us, to my knowledge, were able to stick to that. So, we felt that maybe the Code of Conduct should...that the Code of Conduct was a little too not flexible enough. We made up an appendix to the Code of Conduct you might say... It recognized that we could not stick to strictly name, rank, serial number, and date of birth. It's a good theoretical guideline and if you know, if people who capture you will go by the Geneva Conventions or recognize them, then yeah, they'd probably be great, great guidance. In our situation, it was not flexible enough... We felt, for example, that to resist giving them anything but date, rank, or name, rank, date of birth, and serial number until you were, had lost your mental faculties, which happened in a few cases, was probably more detrimental to the United States than saying, 'Okay, I've gone to my limit' and then when you get there...you give them enough to get you out of that situation and you just lie, basically.

You just make up something. And that's kind of the way we did it later on once we got organized. We would never give them anything free, but if they tortured us...later on, when they had more time, they weren't interested in immediate military information like they were when we were first shot down. They had more time and they didn't use the rope there, they would just...either you were kneeling or more commonly [sitting on] a stool. They would just put you on a stool and sit you there; you would sit there until you decided to do what they wanted, which was typically write something. You know, write off a letter to Senator Fulbright[10] for example...And they didn't care if it took two days or two months, you know, you just sat there until you wrote something. And so our rules at least from our SRO [Senior Rank Officer] at Son Tay was to resist until you couldn't resist anymore, but don't resist to the point that you lose your mental faculties and then end up giving them more than you would otherwise.

A North Vietnamese soldier remembers the Bombing of North Vietnam (1970)[11]

In February 1965, the US Navy and US Air Force launched Operation Rolling Thunder, a strategic bombing campaign against North Vietnam. According to US military and civilian leaders, the main goal of the campaign was to compel North Vietnamese leaders to cease their support for the NLF insurgency in South Vietnam. In addition, the US hoped that the campaign would impede the flow of enemy soldiers and supplies from north to south,

[10] Senator William Fulbright, D-Arkansas, was chairman of the Senate Foreign Relations Committee and an early critic of the US intervention in the Vietnam War.
[11] Nguyen Van Mo, "Hanoi Under Attack," in David Chanoff and Doan Van Toai, *Vietnam: A Portrait of its People at War* (London: I. B. Tauris, 1987), 126.

*and boost the morale of the South Vietnamese government and army. A
central feature of Rolling Thunder was the gradual escalation of the number
and tempo of air attacks; American military planners believed that this
escalation would quickly push North Vietnam to its "breaking point," where
it would be compelled to negotiate on US terms. Although Rolling Thunder
continued for more than three-and-a-half years and comprised more than
300,000 attack sorties by US combat aircraft, this "breaking point" was
never reached.*

*While the US bombing did not shatter North Vietnam's will to fight, it did
have profound and devastating effects on the people of North Vietnam. In
this account, Nguyen Van Mo, a native of the northern province of Ha Dong,
recalls how the bombing impacted life in Hanoi during the mid-1960s, when
he worked in the city as a barber. In 1968, Mo was drafted into the People's
Army of Vietnam and sent to fight as a sapper in South Vietnam. He
abandoned his unit and surrendered to an ARVN unit in Quang Ngai
province in January 1970. He made these remarks while being interrogated
by US and South Vietnamese interviewers, who wanted to know how the
bombing had affected the morale and outlook of the northern
population.*

The people in North Vietnam hated the bombing. They were enraged about
the air raids. In the beginning, the Americans carried out their attacks very
carefully—the attacks on the Long Bien Bridge, for example, and the Gia
Lam Airfield, and on Van Dien. We used to watch them, to see how accurate
the bombers were, and to judge how good the pilots were at avoiding anti-
aircraft fire and rockets. We had to admit that during the early attacks they
hit proper military targets and that their flying techniques were pretty good.
If they hadn't been, our ground fire would have shot down a great number
of them.

But later—and I didn't understand why—the Americans dropped bombs
all over the place. The people in Hanoi had already gained a lot of confidence
in the accuracy of the bombing, and large groups of them would gather to
watch the attacks. At one point the pilots dropped a couple of beehive bombs
on the Bach Mai and Hung Ky Street area, in the vicinity of the "Eighth of
March" factory, and on Hue street. These beehive bombs contained hundreds
of little steel balls. A large number of civilians were unexpectedly killed. After
that people began to hate the Americans. If the local authorities hadn't intervened, they would have beaten shot-down American pilots to death.

In my opinion, in the early days, the Americans didn't have any intention of bombing populated areas. Later, because the anticaircraft fire had gotten so heavy, the pilots had to escape themselves, and they dropped their bombs carelessly, without paying any attention to the lives of the people. They were afraid of dying, and they didn't think about the adverse political effects.

Kim Phuc and the Napalm Attack on Trang Bang Village (1972)

On June 8, 1972, two South Vietnamese Skyraider warplanes attacked the village of Trang Bang, which lies on a highway a few miles northwest of Saigon. Over the previous two days, Trang Bang had been wracked by fighting between South Vietnamese and "Viet Cong" soldiers. One of the Skyraiders dropped canisters of napalm, a jellied form of gasoline that creates huge fireballs and burns at temperatures of up to 1200 degrees Celsius (2200 degrees Fahrenheit). The napalm struck a group of Vietnamese civilian residents of the village as they were attempting to flee. At least two children were burned to death. The scene was captured on film by several Vietnamese and foreign journalists who had been observing the battle from a military post on the town's outskirts, and who watched in horror as the terrified survivors of the attack ran towards them.

The picture below was taken by Huynh Cong Ut, an Associated Press photographer. The naked girl in the center of the picture was nine-year-old Tran Thi Kim Phuc. Although the photograph does not reveal it, Kim Phuc had suffered severe burns on her arms and back. During the attack, she had pulled her burning clothes off of her body. In the days following the strike, Ut's photograph and the accompanying caption (which did not identify Kim Phuc by name but did indicate that she had been badly burned) appeared in newspapers around the world. The picture eventually won a host of photographic prizes, including the Pulitzer Prize for spot news.

Kim Phuc survived the attack, but her life was forever altered by her injuries and by Ut's photograph. Ut himself transported Kim Phuc to a hospital before returning to Saigon to develop his film. Two days later, two other journalists who were pursuing a follow-up story on the "girl in the picture" arranged for Kim Phuc to be transferred to one of the only clinics in South Vietnam capable of performing the skin grafts that she desperately needed. However, not all of the attention that the picture brought was welcome. After the war had ended, government officials in Vietnam compelled Kim Phuc to

suspend her university studies so they could use her and the famous picture for propaganda purposes. In 1992, she defected to Canada. Although she is still known as "the girl in the picture," she has found ways to use her fame to advance her efforts to provide support and healing to child victims of war.

Discussion questions

1. What explanation does Ly Tong Ba give for the defeat of US and ARVN forces at the Battle of Ap Bac? Is his explanation persuasive? Why or why not?

2. What does the testimony of the captured female NLF cadre reveal about the motives of South Vietnamese who joined the insurgency during the 1960s? Does her account contradict that of the Dinh Tuong farmer presented in Chapter 4? Why or why not?

3. Compare Tom Esslinger's account of the Battle of Khe Sanh in 1968 with the other descriptions of battlefield experiences included in this volume. How was the war in the area near the 17th parallel different from the war in other parts of Vietnam?

4. What explanation(s) for the My Lai massacre does Varnado Simpson present in his testimony about the event? How does he represent his own participation in the slaughter?
5. What do the accounts of Wilson Key and Nguyen Van Mo reveal about the military effectiveness of Operation Rolling Thunder?
6. Of the thousands of published photographs depicting the suffering of soldiers and civilians during the Vietnam War, why did Huynh Cong Ut's image of Kim Phuc become so famous?

Chapter 8   The Tet Offensive

Resolution of the 14th Plenum of the VWP Central Committee (January 1968)[1]

This resolution, adopted by the VWP Central Committee in mid-January 1968, authorized the military campaign that would become known as the Tet Offensive. Remarkably, the resolution was approved just two weeks prior to the launch of the offensive on January 31, 1968 – even though the committee had been discussing the plans and strategy for the offensive for several months. As the resolution indicates, VWP leaders did consider the possibility that the offensive might not achieve all of the party's major goals in South Vietnam. However, the resolution also shows that they were optimistic that a decisive victory over US and South Vietnamese forces was within reach.

[1] *Van Kiên Đảng Toàn Tập* (Hanoi: Nhà Xuất Bản Chính Trị Quốc Gia, 2004), 29:41–68. Translated by Merle Pribbenow.

Original publication details: 8.1 Van Kiên Đảng Toàn Tập, 2004. Translated by Merle Pribbenow. 8.2 Foreign Relations of the United States, 1964–1968, 2002. 8.4 Major General Huynh Công Thân, 1994. 8.6 Lyndon B. Johnson, 1968. Peters & Woolley, The American Presidency Project. http://www.presidency.ucsb.edu/ws/?pid=28772

I. Situation and Prospects for the Resistance War Against the Americans to Save the Nation

...The Revolution in the South is growing under the following conditions and special characteristics:

The South Vietnamese revolution is holding high the flag of resistance against the new colonialism of the American imperialists following the defeat inflicted by the population of our entire nation on the aggression of the French imperialists, beginning the collapse of colonialism throughout the world. It continues the glorious traditions of our August Revolution in 1945 and of our resistance war against the French, during which our people, with our glorious victory at Dien Bien Phu, completely liberated one half of our nation...

...The revolution in South Vietnam represents a new stage in the Vietnamese people's national democratic revolutionary movement, led by the laboring class. It is an integral part of the high tide of world revolution that is currently in an offensive posture, systematically pushing back and crushing individual imperialist forces in order to gradually and completely eliminate all imperialist positions throughout the world...

... Even though the American imperialists, the impetuous leaders of imperialism who possess massive material and technological power, planned and aspired to achieve hegemony over the entire world, they have encountered ferocious resistance from a nation of more than 30 million people who use the peasants and workers as the regular, main-force soldiers of the revolution, who are led by a resolute and experienced Marxist-Leninist Party, a people who have continuously conducted three glorious revolutions against imperialism for more than twenty years (the August 1945 Revolution, the resistance war against the French, and our present war of resistance against the Americans to save the nation). The South Vietnamese revolution also has a large, direct rear area of support, the socialist North, which is in turn linked to an even larger rear area, meaning the socialist camp.

Under these conditions and special characteristics, the people of Vietnam are capable on their own of creating sufficient political and military power to defeat any imperialist aggressor. For that reason, the American failure in South Vietnam is clear and their total defeat is unavoidable....

We are confronted with great strategic prospects and opportunities.

The American imperialists are now at a strategic dead end. When compared with their limited political and military goals in South Vietnam, the American War effort (and their heavy losses) in Vietnam has reached its peak.

The basic scheme of the American imperialists in South Vietnam at present is still to seek every possible way to maintain their neo-colonialist position.

For the short term, they are striving to stabilize the puppet army and puppet regime and to reinforce American and satellite troops to a limited extent in an effort to preserve their posture in South Vietnam against any unexpected disruptions. They are continuing their "pacification" and "search and destroy" policies at a certain level in order to maintain a firm hold on their important positions and headquarters and to weaken our forces and push us into a desperate struggle against them. At the same time they are increasing their attacks against the North and are carrying out a devious diplomatic policy aimed at isolating us and eventually causing us to become discouraged and to enter into negotiations under conditions imposed by them.

Although these are the enemy's basic and short-term schemes, because of their string of recent defeats the puppet army today is not sufficiently strong to carry out its "pacification" mission and American and satellite troops are no longer capable of effectively carrying out their "search and destroy" mission. The enemy's forces are now being stretched thin on the battlefield and are now being encircled and strangled...Their strategic posture has been disrupted and the morale of their soldiers is increasingly collapsing and weakening. The internal contractions of the Americans and the puppets are increasing by the day, and they are being faced with increasingly serious political, military, and economic problems. The strategic position of the Americans is steadily weakening not only in South Vietnam and domestically, within the U.S., but even on the world stage, and they have never been as isolated as they are at present....

As for our side, we have defeated the enemy both strategically and tactically, and our posture and strength is growing more powerful than ever before. Our military and political forces have become stronger than they have ever been in the history of our revolutionary war. We now have the initiative throughout the entire battlefield, we have implemented measures which have expanded our control over individual areas in order to destroy the enemy and to annihilate large numbers of the enemy to further expand our control over large areas of the rural lowlands and the mountain jungles...

The masses of the population in the cities and in areas of South Vietnam temporarily under enemy control have many times risen up in many different forms of insurrection. Millions of the masses are seething with revolutionary spirit and are ready to rise up, prepared to sacrifice everything for the causes of independence, freedom, peace, prosperity, and land....

At present we still have a number of weaknesses in such areas as local recruitment of our armed forces, fighting battles of annihilation against large American units, and building real political strength and guiding the urban movement. We still have certain difficulties in logistics, supply, and transportation, and in our enemy proselyting and puppet proselyting operations.

We need to strive to overcome these weaknesses and difficulties during the course of the development of the revolution. However, the basic feature of the current situation is still that we have a victorious and favorable posture, we have the initiative, while the enemy is in a posture of defeat, of passivity and difficulty.

This situation allows us to move the revolutionary war of the people in South Vietnam into a new era, the era of offensives and uprisings to secure decisive victory.

II. Our Directions and Missions During this New Era

...The strategic goals which our party has set forward in this new era are as follows:

a. to annihilate and disperse the vast bulk of the puppet army, overthrow the puppet governmental administration at all levels...
b. To annihilate an important segment of U.S. troop strength and their implements of war, to prevent American troops from being able to accomplish their political and military missions in Vietnam.
c. On these foundations, crush the American will to commit aggression, force the U.S. to concede defeat in Vietnam and to end all acts of war against the North, while enabling us to defend the socialist North and achieve the short-term objectives of the revolution in South Vietnam. [These objectives are] freedom, democracy, peace, and neutrality, which will lead to national reunification.

How will we Carry Out the General Offensive and Uprising?

First of all, we must clearly recognize that the upcoming general offensive and uprising is a phase, a process of very powerful and complex strategic offensives. It combines military attacks with political attacks... in coordination with diplomatic attacks. It is a phase that will be made up of many large campaigns by revolutionary armed forces in important strategic areas in coordination with uprisings and insurrections taking many different forms by the revolutionary popular masses in the cities and rural areas temporarily under enemy control. It will consist of attacks combined with uprisings in the enemy's "capital city" and in other large cities...

The attacks launched by our armed forces on the primary battlefields and the uprisings of the people in the large cities are the two primary offensive spearheads which will work closely together, support each other, and encourage an all-out general offensive and general insurrection in all three areas: cities, rural lowlands, and mountain jungles. In particular the attack by our armed forces and the uprising of the popular masses in the large cities will be a sharp dagger through the throat of the enemy that will be of decisive importance to the over-all battlefield and the over-all course of the war....

...From the military standpoint, the enemy still has more than one million troops and a vast capacity for war, but the enemy's army has suffered a series of continuous strategic and tactical defeats, and although his numbers are large the morale of his troops is weak and has begun to collapse. Politically, the enemy has sunk into a serious and complete crisis, demonstrating that he cannot any longer govern the people of South Vietnam and that the people of South Vietnam refuse to live any longer under his yoke of oppression. Meanwhile, we are in a victorious position and have the initiative throughout all battlefields. Our armed forces have become large and powerful in all respects, our mass political forces are very powerful, and the bulk of the popular masses in the areas temporarily under enemy control have been honed and tested through years of arduous struggle and have demonstrated a high revolutionary resolve.

Under these conditions...our poicy is not to simply launch a general offensive but to simultaneously launch a general insurrection. [This means] we will use our powerful armed forces to attack the enemy's large regular units and strike powerful blows against the "capital city" and other cities to create conditions which will enable millions of people living in cities and in rural areas still temporarily under enemy occupation to rise up in insurrection, coordinating with our armed forces to annihilate and disintegrate the enemy army, overthrow the leadership agencies of the puppet governmental authority, disrupt the American and puppet war apparatus and paralyze it to its very roots, turn the enemy's rear area and his strategic stockpiles into OUR rear area and OUR strategic stockpiles, rapidly change the balance of forces in our favor and against the enemy, and secure a decisive victory for our side.

Assessing Possible Developments in the Situation.

There are three possibilities:
POSSIBILITY ONE is that we will gain major victories on the important battlefields, that our attacks and uprisings will finally succeed in the large cities, and that we will gradually be able to crush enemy counter-attacks, causing the enemy to fail to a point from which he is no longer capable of recovering, and crushing the enemy's will to commit aggression. The enemy

will be forced to concede defeat and enter into negotiations to end the war in a manner that meets our goals and requirements.

POSSIBILITY TWO is that, although we secure important victories in many locations, the enemy will strive to concentrate his forces and send in reinforcements from the outside, regaining and maintaining a firm hold on important locations, securing control of the large cities, especially his "capital city," utilizing his large bases to continue the battle against us.

POSSIBILITY THREE is that the enemy will mobilize and send large numbers of reinforcements to expand his "limited war" into North Vietnam, Laos, and Cambodia with the objective of reversing the direction of the war and reversing his current posture of defeat.

We must make extraordinary efforts, devoting all our spiritual and material resources to a resolve to fight to secure, at any cost, the maximum possible victory in accordance with POSSIBILITY ONE, because, more than ever before, we now have a favorable opportunity to gain a decisive victory in our great patriotic war and secure the strategic goals we have set for ourselves.

If, however, the situation develops along the lines of POSSIBILITY TWO, because of the important victories we will secure our forces will not be weakened but will instead double in strength, both militarily and politically. Our liberated zones in the rural lowlands and in the mountain jungles will be expanded and strengthened, enemy troops will be surrounded in their bases as we build on our successes by continuing both military and political attacks until the enemy is completely defeated.

In the immediate future there is little chance that POSSIBILITY THREE will occur, but we must maintain constant vigilance and make preparations to be ready to seize the initiative in any situation that might develop...

U.S. Central Intelligence Agency Report on the Communist Tet Offensive (January 31, 1968)[2]

The Tet Offensive began in the early morning hours of January 30, 1968, with a wave of NLF and PAVN attacks on US and South Vietnamese government targets in central Vietnam. The next day, communist forces struck Saigon and most of the cities and towns in the Mekong Delta. Some of the most dramatic battles took place in Saigon, where a team of NLF commandos briefly took over part of the US Embassy, and in the city of Hue, much of which was overrun by PAVN troops. Despite these initial communist successes, the offensive did not trigger the popular "general uprising" that

[2]   CIA Intelligence Memorandum SC No. 01909/68, 31 Jan 1968, printed in *Foreign Relations of the United States, 1964–1968* (Washington: GPO, 2002), 6: 92.

North Vietnamese leaders had anticipated, and the revolutionaries eventually suffered heavy losses due to US and RVN counterattacks. However, in the chaotic first hours and days of the offensive, its outcome and implications were far from clear.

In this memorandum, written during the first 48 hours of the offensive, analysts from the Central Intelligence Agency offered their assessment of the communists' main objectives. While the memo acknowledged that the offensive was intended in part to produce new battlefield victories, it stressed that the ultimate goals of the offensive were probably psychological rather than military. The authors apparently did not realize that communist leaders hoped and expected the offensive would result in the destruction of the ARVN, the collapse of the Saigon government, and a rapid US withdrawal from Vietnam.

The Communist Tet Offensive

1. The current coordinated series of enemy attacks in South Vietnam, so far targeted primarily against population centers and US installations from I Corps to the delta, appears primarily designed for maximum psychological impact. The Communists appear to be trying to demonstrate to the South Vietnamese, to US and world opinion and probably to their own forces that, almost three years after the intervention of US forces, they can still enter major towns and bases, threaten the US Embassy itself, and seriously disrupt the country, if only temporarily.

2. Extensive harassment of US airfields, logistical centers, and command and communications centers appears–in addition to its shock effect– partly designed to inhibit immediate allied reaction and retaliation. It may be preparatory to or intended to support further impending enemy actions in the Khe Sanh/DMZ/northern Quang Tri area. So far this area has been relatively quiet during the latest round of attacks, but the enemy concentration in this area remains the most ominous in the country.

3. Evidence has been building up for the past several weeks that the Communists intended a major nationwide offensive in connection with the Tet season. Enemy propaganda, however, had stressed an intention to honor a seven-day cease-fire regardless of the period of the allied stand-down. This line may have been intended to enhance the surprise factor of attacks on the day of Tet itself. It may also be that the Communist timetable–in past years calling for stepped up action just prior to and immediately following the Tet truce–was sufficiently flexible to call for action during the Tet if the allies could be put in the position of apparently bearing the onus. In any event, Communist propagandists were

clearly ready with the line that the enemy attacks were "punishment" for allied violations.

4. It is clear that the Communists made careful and, most recently, urgent preparations for the current offensive. These preparations seem to point, in coming days or weeks, to a major assault around Khe Sanh, possibly in conjunction with a campaign throughout the northern I Corps area. The Communists probably hope, in addition to psychological gains, to score some dramatic battlefield successes, ideally (from their standpoint) the overrunning of Khe Sanh or a US withdrawal from this or some other key garrison. In launching a series of bold actions, they incur the risk of serious defeats or retaliation, with possible repercussions on their own forces. Nonetheless, they probably hope to gain the strategic initiative and to pin down substantial numbers of allied troops over wide areas in which the Communists hold some military advantages. A major objective of the entire Communist "winter-spring" campaign since autumn appears to be to draw off US forces while the VC attempt to erode the pacification effort through guerrilla-type actions. Furthermore, the Communists certainly hope to make political mileage out of heightened US casualty rates and a demonstration of continued VC strength.

5. There seems to be little question that the present Communist offensive activity bears a relation to Hanoi's recent offer to open talks.[3] Foremost, the Communists probably hope to improve their political and military image in the event that any negotiations are initiated in coming months. Prior to the initiation of the "winter-spring" campaign, Communist forces throughout the country were intensively indoctrinated on the importance of the campaign. At least in some areas, the campaign itself was linked, directly or by implication, to the possibility of a political settlement. Some of this indoctrination may have been propaganda intended to instill a victory psychology among troops possibly discouraged by hardships and talk of "protracted war." Although the current surge of Communist activity involves both a military and political gamble, it is highly questionable that the Communists are making a final desperate effort for a show of strength prior to suing for peace. Despite evident problems of manpower and supply, enemy forces continued to display improved fire-power, flexibility of tactics, and a considerable

[3] This is apparently a reference to the DRV's recent reiteration of its offer to begin peace talks on the basis of a four-point proposal that Hanoi had issued in 1965. The US rejected that proposal on the grounds that its terms would hand control of South Vietnam over to the NLF.

degree of resiliency. Their current offensive is probably intended to convey the impression that despite VC problems and despite half a million US troops, the Communists are still powerful and capable of waging war.

The Execution of Nguyen Van Lem

February 1, 1968, was the second day of the Tet Offensive in Saigon. That morning, an Associated Press photographer named Eddie Adams headed to the district of Cho Lon to check out reports of a firefight between South Vietnamese army troops and NLF guerrillas. Shortly after arriving on the scene, Adams saw several ARVN soldiers escorting a handcuffed Vietnamese prisoner down the street. Adams began taking pictures. As he did so, a South Vietnamese officer approached the prisoner and pulled out a handgun. Adams, who did not know who the officer was, expected him merely to threaten the prisoner – a practice Adams had witnessed many times before in Vietnam. Instead, the officer put the pistol to the man's head and fired once, instantly killing him. By chance, Adams clicked his shutter just as the shooter pulled the trigger. The resulting photograph captured both the gunman's apparent nonchalance and the prisoner's terrified grimace at the very moment of his death.

*As the prisoner's lifeless body fell to the ground, the gunman spoke in English
to Adams. "He killed many of my men and many of your people," the officer
said. Then he calmly walked away.*

*The man who pulled the trigger was Nguyen Ngoc Loan, the chief of the
South Vietnamese National Police. The man he killed was Nguyen Van Lem,
a Saigon native and an NLF operative. After Adams' stunning photograph
appeared in newspapers around the world, Loan and his supporters tried to
defend the impromptu execution, claiming that Lem was a Viet Cong assassin
who had killed several police officers and their families. Communist party
sources later confirmed that Lem was a member of a team that was supposed
to target South Vietnamese officials during the offensive. However, neither
General Loan nor anyone else ever presented evidence showing that Lem had
actually killed anyone. Even if Lem was guilty of murder, Loan's summary
execution of him was obviously a war crime, as that concept is defined under
international law.*

*For millions of people who saw it, Adams' photograph was indisputable
proof of both the brutality of the Vietnam War and of the vicious and
corrupt nature of the South Vietnamese regime. In this regard, the
photograph contributed to the growing opposition to the war in the United
States and elsewhere. However, many of those who supported the war
insisted that the photograph distorted the public's perception of the conflict,
insofar as it seemed to assign blame only to one side. Among those who came
to this conclusion was Eddie Adams. In 1993, Adams visited Loan in
Virginia, where he had settled after the war, and apologized for taking the
photograph. "Two people's lives were destroyed that day." Adams later told
an interviewer. "The general's life was destroyed, as well as the life of the
Vietcong. I don't want to destroy anybody's life. That's not my job."*

General Huyng Cong Than, The General Offensive and Uprising in the Southern Sector of Saigon (1994)[4]

*Huynh Cong Than was a native of Long An, a province in the western
Mekong Delta. After serving with the Viet Minh in the war against the
French, he chose to remain in the south after the 1954 Geneva agreements
and joined the communist-led insurgency against the Diem government that
began in the late 1950s. At the time of the Tet Offensive in 1968, he was an
NLF sub-regional commander. In this capacity, he took part of the fighting in
Saigon during the initial wave of attacks in January and February, and also*

4   Excerpted from Huỳnh Công Thân, Ở Chiến Trường Long An: Hồi Ức [On the Long An Battlefield: A Memoir] (Hanoi: Nhà Xuất Bản Quân Đội Nhân Dân, 1994), 126–131. Translated
by Merle Pribbenow.

participated in a follow-up series of attacks on the city a few months later. In his 1994 memoir, Than explained how and why the offensive did not go as the revolutionaries expected.

...Near the end of the 1967 rainy season, Long An received orders to prepare for a new mission and instructions for a major re-organization of the battlefield. Long An was removed from Region 8 and was split into two sub-regions directly subordinate to COSVN[5] Military Headquarters. At the same time we were ordered to prepare our forces to join the other sub-regions in launching an attack against Saigon whenever the order was issued.

At that time this was all we knew about the mission. We viewed this as a strategic policy decision by the Party that had to be kept absolutely secret, so we didn't worry about it. We concerned ourselves only with properly carrying out our orders. ...

. ...Our preparations were carried out on a very urgent basis because our superiors told us time was short and because there was much difficult, unfamiliar work to be done. We did not know the situation in the city outskirts and in the inner city, so we had to send cadres to contact our people who were operating in those areas. ...

...With respect to the organization and preparation of our military forces, a number of the reinforcement units promised to the Sub-Region by higher authorities had still not arrived, and other units were under-strength in terms of both troops and weapons. Almost all of our district local-force troops and village guerrillas were called up and assigned to our [main-force] battalions on an urgent basis to strengthen them. In addition, we also had to mobilize hundreds of civilian youths into our armed forces. This left the rural areas virtually devoid of military forces...

There were mountains of work to be done, but the atmosphere was very enthusiastic. ... Our enthusiasm was based on our understanding that, this time, total victory was certain. Even though problems of every sort confronted us, even though we had not found solutions for all our problems, everyone believed that these were just local difficulties encountered only by our own individual units or individual areas. Our national-level leadership, our superiors, had made careful calculations for this offensive. Certainly they would only have made this decision if it were certain we could win, because this was a major decision—it was not just one single battle to be fought in just one locality.

---

5 COSVN: Central Office for South Vietnam, the headquarters of the Vietnamese Communist Party in South Vietnam.

When the mission and the combat coordination requirements were disseminated to us, we all became even more enthusiastic. So, it was to be a "General Offensive-General Insurrection" in which the general insurrection would be the key to victory! The Sub-Region's spear-head battalions were assigned the mission of attacking strategic targets in the city in support of our urban commandos and of thousands of civilians, youth, and students who were to rise up to take over control of the governmental apparatus. Our mission was to send in troops to provide support while the primary task, seizing control of the governmental apparatus, would be performed by our personnel inside the city, who would organize the people to conduct an uprising. In this case, we were sure that victory would be ours.

While our preparations were carried out on an urgent basis, no one yet knew the exact date of the offensive. Time flew by, the 1967-68 dry season arrived, and the Tet lunar new year was fast approaching. Both Liberation Radio and Radio Saigon announced a cease-fire that would last several days to allow the population to celebrate the new year in the traditional manner. Everyone thought this meant any attack would have to be launched after Tet. ...

Because of this understanding of the timing of the mission, we issued normal guidance to our units for the conduct of Tet celebrations. As had been the case during previous Tet celebrations, units were to remain combat-ready, but a set number of cadre and soldiers would be allowed to return home to visit their families or to invite their families to come visit them for the Tet holiday. ...On the 30th day of the lunar calendar, the eve of the Tet lunar new year, I intended to try to get a little rest so that the next morning I and Muoi Xuong could make another inspection trip up Route 4. Just before midnight on Tet eve, however, we were startled to hear [South Vietnamese President] Nguyen Van Thieu make a proclamation over the radio canceling the cease-fire because the Viet Cong had attacked the cities in Central Vietnam, including Hue. At that moment no one could understand how this could have happened. Was it possible that all our preparations had only been an elaborate deception operation to conceal our real attacks, which would be made in the north? If this was not the case, then why hadn't we received our attack orders? We had not even received any cables reiterating our mission assignments or reminding us of the work that had to be done. Was it possible that Saigon and the South would be ordered to launch their attacks AFTER the attacks in Hue and Central Vietnam? Could there be any possible military advantage to mounting the offensive in this manner? I could not understand what doing things in this way would accomplish from the stand-point of the entire battlefield throughout South Vietnam, but I knew that from the purely parochial standpoint of Saigon, conducting the attack in this manner would cost us at least part of the element of surprise when we did launch our own attacks.

Everyone excitedly discussed this subject amongst each other, but no one could figure out any rational explanation. We greeted the New Year in an atmosphere of worry and confusion. We waited through the night for an explanatory cable from higher authority, but there was only silence from above.

At around 4:00 in the morning all of us leapt out of bed when we heard that the cadre of the Forward Headquarters for the Southern Sector of Saigon had arrived. When we saw them we knew that something extremely important was in the wind. Almost before we finished our greetings to them they blurted out, "The situation is extremely critical. We have orders that Saigon must be attacked tonight! Sub-Region 3's battle plan must be put aside. The battalions must find a way to get into Saigon tonight!"

After hearing these orders, all I could do was stand there moaning, "Oh my God! Oh my God!"

Chin Can was calmer. He told me, "No matter how much you appeal to the gods, no one else is going to do our work for us. We all will have to work together to try to get the job done. That's all we can do!"

He was right! No feat of magic could resolve our problems. We had only 20 hours, and half that time was daylight, when our forces would not be able to move across the open fields, so how could we have enough time to organize our battle forces? We had to assign missions to and deploy almost 10 battalions, which were currently scattered and dispersed all across the countryside and had a number of their cadre and soldiers away on Tet leave. We also would have to issue them additional food and ammunition. We would also have to replace some of 1st Battalion's equipment to enable it to fight, because 1st Battalion had been very lightly equipped as disguised commandos pretending to be enemy troops. And what about approach routes and river-crossing equipment? Our guides still had not arrived, so how could we choose what routes to take to get into the city and reach our targets? All of these were very important questions that had no answers, but they were issues whose resolution could not be postponed. ...

...On the afternoon of the first day of Tet we were forced to order our troops to begin their approach march at 1600 hours, even though we knew how dangerous this was. Enemy outposts might spot our troops and call in artillery on them. We had no other alternative, however, because if our troops started any later they might not reach the city until after daylight. As soon as we reached each unit we issued them their mission orders and ordered them to move out immediately...

... Events during the first day of fighting in Saigon were completely differ-ent from what we had expected. The spearhead battalions were not able to advance rapidly because they carried only small, light weapons and had little ammunition, while enemy forces were numerous and used the thick building walls and the tangle of streets and alleys in the cities to put up a ferocious resistance. The civilian population had a very good attitude towards our troops when they encountered our men, but we never saw any large demon-strations erupt in the city. Only a small number of youths and students made contact with our troops, and this group did not launch the kind of struggle demonstrations we had seen them conduct in the past.

This meant we had to conduct a purely military struggle. We were not playing a supporting role for an uprising of the masses as we had thought. These battles were conducted under very difficult conditions: our forces had to launch assaults in order to move forward, but we didn't have assault weapons with us. On the second day of the offensive there were no major changes, either militarily or politically, in the over-all situation. The rate of advance of our spearhead battalions began to slow. The enemy launched powerful counter-attacks in a number of locations. ...

...On our side, our ammunition supplies decreased day by day, we had to care for and evacuate our dead and wounded, and we were stuck in a tactically unfavorable position, so our combat strength was gradually being eroded. Meanwhile the political struggle spearhead, which was to have been launched by the students and the masses, still had not appeared. ...After sev-eral days of fighting, our units were forced to conduct a gradual withdrawal to the outskirts of the city.

As soon as we left the city we received orders to keep our forces in the outskirts to await orders for a second wave of attack against Saigon. We carried out these orders, but in our hearts we suffered some unavoidable anxiety: How could we continue to make attacks on the city?

...During this period I lost my teen-age son during a sweep operation on the outskirts of the city. My son's name was Khang. At the age of 14 he left home to join Muoi Xuong's unit. He was quick, well-spoken, and was always helpful to everyone, so all our people loved him. Because he was so young, they did not want to put him in a combat unit, so they sent him back to serve in the security detachment protecting the Province Party Committee so that I could care for and train him. Early on this particular morning the command group (including me and Chin Can)... encountered an American sweep operation. The Americans fired thousands of artillery rounds into the area. Khang found a bunker for me to hide in and took care of Chin Can, then went to a forward position to observe the enemy. He was killed by an American artillery barrage as American troops landed in an adjacent open field. I sat beside the body of my 17 year-old son with my heart breaking and spoke to him as if he was still alive,

"You joined the army at an early age," I said, "and you were killed in a big battle against an American sweep operation. Rest in peace, my son. You have done your duty for the revolution."

...In addition to our assigned mission of clinging to the outskirts of the city to prepare for another attack against Saigon, we also received the following guidance: "The General Offensive-General Insurrection is a process." We understood this phrase to mean that we would be expected to launch many more attacks against Saigon.

After three months of waiting we received orders to launch a second wave of attacks.[6] When we received our orders this time we were not so surprised that we complained to the heavens, as we had the first time, but we were concerned that the orders revealed no changes in our organization, equipment, and tactics for this new round of attacks. In fact, there were even some reductions—for instance, this time we would have no internal forces to launch attacks inside the city; this time we would have only artillery to make shelling attacks on the city from the outer perimeter. Our assigned mission, however, called for our forces to penetrate as deeply as possible into the very heart of the city—at that time this tactic was called "bringing the flames of war right into the enemy's own lair."

Anyone with even a basic understanding of military matters and anyone who had commanded troops during the first wave of attacks on Saigon could immediately see the difficult nature of our mission. First of all, we no longer had the element of surprise—neither strategic, campaign, nor tactical surprise—while the enemy had organized and prepared very tight defenses around Saigon. ...Under these conditions it would be difficult for us to get our forces through two separate enemy defense lines to reach the outer edge of the city, to say nothing of expecting our forces to actually be able to penetrate deep into the heart of the city itself.

The realities of combat during the first wave of attacks told us that, given the special characteristics of the terrain in and around the city, we could not infiltrate our units forward surreptitiously, especially when we were sending large units. We would be forced to launch assaults in order to move forward into the city. From a military standpoint the city provided many advantages to the defender, and the attacker would need extremely powerful weapons to be able to expel defenders from areas with large, well-constructed buildings. We, however, had only light infantry weapons, and we would be facing

[6] This refers to the second phase of the Tet Offensive, a follow-up wave of attacks in Saigon and elsewhere that took place in May 1968. Americans referred to this second phase as "mini-Tet."

tanks and armored vehicles stationed at the well-fortified enemy targets. The attacking force would also have to penetrate deep behind enemy lines. This requirement was very difficult to justify from a military standpoint.

...All these problems were raised and discussed very thoroughly within the Sub-Region Military Headquarters and the Sub-Region Party Committee. In the end we were all able to agree on only one point, which was that we must strictly carry out our combat orders, even if we had to sacrifice our local forces in support of the over-all strategic plan. In truth, we went into the second wave of the Tet offensive with the attitude of suicide troops. ...

...The fighting ...was extremely violent, but our troops could not penetrate any deeper than they had during the first offensive, and in places didn't even get as far as they had the first time. All the fighting was done in the streets because our forces were unable to reach and penetrate any enemy military or political targets. ...

... Even now, every time I recall these events, my mind is still filled with thoughts and confusion. First of all, with regards to the strategic policy, I still do not understand why we attacked the cities again, at a time when the balance of forces had tilted so heavily against us. ... [In the later years of the war] when we wanted to liberate a district capital like Loc Ninh, out in the mountain jungles along the border, we had to launch a full-fledged campaign using main force units, tanks, and mechanized equipment in order to overrun and capture such a position. ...So in 1968, why did we use only very lightly equipped local-force battalions supported by urban commandos to try to attack and seize strategic targets deep in the heart of Saigon?

...From a purely military standpoint, it would have been impossible to reach the decision to attack and seize control of Saigon with the tactics and forces that were actually employed without the military attack being coordinated with a General Uprising. But then why did the political part of the offensive never materialize? What were the conditions among the masses and the students in Saigon that led our people to the conclusion that millions of people were boiling over with revolutionary zeal and were prepared to sacrifice everything for the cause of independence and freedom?!! When we entered Saigon we found that this assessment was incorrect. The masses did hate the U.S. and puppet regime for strangling their livelihoods and stifling democracy, but this hatred had not reached the "boiling" point and the masses were not "prepared to sacrifice everything" by going out into the streets to struggle against enemy guns to overthrow the Saigon regime and establish a revolutionary government. The students were a force that had some organization, but they were not able to pull themselves together into organized ranks....

...For me, Tet 68 was the most anxious period in my entire career as a combat commander. My tension was not caused by the ferocity of the fighting, but was instead primarily the result of the impossible task of trying to resolve the contradictions between the requirements of the mission and the forces and methods that were to be used to accomplish the mission...

Tet 1968 was a time filled with memories and bloody experiences which none of us, the cadre and soldiers of Long An, can ever forget. The strategic Tet Offensive throughout the entire nation of South Vietnam won an enormous victory and helped to force the troops of the Americans and their allies to withdraw from our country. I believe, however, that if we had stopped after the first wave of attacks (those launched during the Tet New Year celebration) and instead pulled our forces back to hold onto our base areas and to defend the rural lowlands, we could have avoided the heavy losses we suffered and the resulting terrible consequences we had to endure during the years of 1969 and 1970.

Walter Cronkite, Remarks on the Tet Offensive (February 1968)[7]

In the United States and around the world, the Tet Offensive was big news. Print and broadcast journalists noted that the communists' ability to launch so many simultaneous attacks seemed to give the lie to the Johnson administration's recent claims of progress in the war. And while reporters noted the US military's claims to have inflicted massive casualties on the enemy, they also observed the rising number of American combat deaths, which exceeded 500 per week by mid-February 1968. Some critics would later accuse the media of allowing their antiwar biases to distort their coverage of the offensive. According to these critics, American journalists greatly exaggerated the enemy's achievements during Tet and downplayed his failures, thus turning a US and RVN military victory into a shattering psychological defeat.

Those who blame the US media for "losing" the Tet Offensive have often cited the remarks delivered by CBS news anchor Walter Cronkite during a broadcast in late February. The remarks came at the end of a half-hour special report on the offensive, based on Cronkite's own reporting in South Vietnam. Because Cronkite was by far the most admired and respected American newsman of his generation, some have argued that his comments effectively turned the US public against the war. However, as the actual substance of his remarks shows, Cronkite was careful to portray the offensive

[7] *Reporting Vietnam: American Journalism 1959–1975* (New York: Library of America, 1998), 1: 581–582.

not as an American defeat, but as evidence that the United States was "mired in stalemate."

Tonight, back in more familiar surroundings in New York, we'd like to sum up our findings in Vietnam, an analysis that must be speculative, personal, subjective. Who won and who lost in the great Tet offensive against the cities? I'm not sure. The Vietcong did not win by a knockout, but neither did we. The referees of history may make it a draw. Another standoff may be coming in the big battles expected south of the Demilitarized Zone. Khe Sanh could well fall, with a terrible loss in American lives, prestige and morale, and this is a tragedy of our stubbornness there; but the bastion no longer is a key to the rest of the northern regions, and it is doubtful that the American forces can be defeated across the breadth of the DMZ with any substantial loss of ground. Another standoff. On the political front, past performance gives no confidence that the Vietnamese government can cope with its problems, now compounded by the attack on the cities. It may not fall, it may hold on, but it probably won't show the dynamic qualities demanded of this young nation. Another standoff.

We have been too often disappointed by the optimism of the American leaders, both in Vietnam and Washington, to have faith any longer in the silver linings they find in the darkest clouds. They may be right, that Hanoi's winter-spring offensive has been forced by the Communist realization that they could not win the longer war of attrition, and that the Communists hope that any success in the offensive will improve their position for eventual negotiations. It would improve their position, and it would also require our realization, that we should have had all along, that any negotiations must be that – negotiations, not the dictation of peace terms. For it seems now more certain than ever that the bloody experience of Vietnam is to end in a stalemate. This summer's almost certain standoff will either end in real give-and-take negotiations or terrible escalation; and for every means we have to escalate, the enemy can match us, and that applies to invasion of the North, the use of nuclear weapons, or the mere commitment of one hundred, or two hundred, or three hundred thousand more American troops to the battle. And with each escalation, the world comes closer to the brink of cosmic disaster.

To say that we are closer to victory today is to believe, in the face of the evidence, the optimists who have been wrong in the past. To suggest we are on the edge of defeat is to yield to unreasonable pessimism. To say that we are mired in stalemate seems the only realistic, yet unsatisfactory, conclusion. On the off chance that military and political analysts are right, in the next few months we must test the enemy's intentions, in case this is indeed his last big gasp before negotiations. But it is increasingly clear to this reporter that the only rational way out then will be to negotiate, not as victors, but as an honorable people who lived up to their pledge to defend democracy, and did the best they could.

This is Walter Cronkite. Good night.

Lyndon B. Johnson, Address to the Nation Announcing Steps to Limit the War in Vietnam (March 31, 1968)[8]

By March 1968, US and RVN forces had regained control of almost all of the South Vietnamese cities, towns, and villages targeted in the first wave of the Tet Offensive. However, the political implications of the offensive had only just begun to unfold. On March 12, antiwar Senator Eugene McCarthy (D-Minnesota) came within a few hundred votes of defeating Lyndon Johnson in the New Hampshire presidential primary – an outcome widely viewed as an indicator of the deep dissatisfaction with Johnson's Vietnam policies. Four days later, Johnson's re-election hopes suffered another blow when Robert Kennedy, the charismatic brother of the slain John Kennedy, announced his own bid for the Democratic nomination. Meanwhile, confidence in the US government's ability to finance the hugely expensive war in Vietnam appeared to be plummeting, as investors began redeeming American dollars for gold at an alarming rate.

On March 31, exactly two months after the start of the offensive, Lyndon Johnson delivered the following address on national television. In it, he spoke of his desire to end the war. He also announced new measures to entice DRV leaders to enter into peace talks; these measures included a partial suspension of the Operation Rolling Thunder bombing campaign against North Vietnam. However, Johnson saved his most dramatic announcement for his closing lines.

Good evening, my fellow Americans:

Tonight I want to speak to you of peace in Vietnam and Southeast Asia.

No other question so preoccupies our people. No other dream so absorbs the 250 million human beings who live in that part of the world. No other goal motivates American policy in Southeast Asia.

[8] Lyndon B. Johnson: "The President's Address to the Nation Announcing Steps To Limit the War in Vietnam and Reporting His Decision Not To Seek Reelection," March 31, 1968. Online by Gerhard Peters and John T. Woolley, *The American Presidency Project.* http://www.presidency.ucsb.edu/ws/?pid=28772.

For years, representatives of our Government and others have traveled the world–seeking to find a basis for peace talks.

Since last September, they have carried the offer that I made public at San Antonio. That offer was this:

That the United States would stop its bombardment of North Vietnam when that would lead promptly to productive discussions–and that we would assume that North Vietnam would not take military advantage of our restraint.

Hanoi denounced this offer, both privately and publicly. Even while the search for peace was going on, North Vietnam rushed their preparations for a savage assault on the people, the government, and the allies of South Vietnam.

Their attack–during the Tet holidays–failed to achieve its principal objectives.

It did not collapse the elected government of South Vietnam or shatter its army–as the Communists had hoped.

It did not produce a "general uprising" among the people of the cities as they had predicted.

The Communists were unable to maintain control of any of the more than 30 cities that they attacked. And they took very heavy casualties.

But they did compel the South Vietnamese and their allies to move certain forces from the countryside into the cities.

They caused widespread disruption and suffering. Their attacks, and the battles that followed, made refugees of half a million human beings.

The Communists may renew their attack any day.

They are, it appears, trying to make 1968 the year of decision in South Vietnam–the year that brings, if not final victory or defeat, at least a turning point in the struggle.

This much is clear:

If they do mount another round of heavy attacks, they will not succeed in destroying the fighting power of South Vietnam and its allies.

But tragically, this is also clear: many men–on both sides of the struggle–will be lost. A nation that has already suffered 20 years of warfare will suffer once again. Armies on both sides will take new casualties. And the war will go on.

There is no need for this to be so.

There is no need to delay the talks that could bring an end to this long and this bloody war.

Tonight, I renew the offer I made last August–to stop the bombardment of North Vietnam. We ask that talks begin promptly, that they be serious talks on the substance of peace. We assume that during those talks Hanoi will not take advantage of our restraint.

We are prepared to move immediately toward peace through negotiations.

So, tonight, in the hope that this action will lead to early talks, I am taking the first step to deescalate the conflict. We are reducing–substantially reducing–the present level of hostilities.

And we are doing so unilaterally, and at once.

Tonight, I have ordered our aircraft and our naval vessels to make no attacks on North Vietnam, except in the area north of the demilitarized zone where the continuing enemy buildup directly threatens allied forward positions and where the movements of their troops and supplies are clearly related to that threat.

The area in which we are stopping our attacks includes almost 90 percent of North Vietnam's population, and most of its territory. Thus there will be no attacks around the principal populated areas, or in the food-producing areas of North Vietnam.

Even this very limited bombing of the North could come to an early end–if our restraint is matched by restraint in Hanoi. But I cannot in good conscience stop all bombing so long as to do so would immediately and directly endanger the lives of our men and our allies. Whether a complete bombing halt becomes possible in the future will be determined by events.

Our purpose in this action is to bring about a reduction in the level of violence that now exists.

It is to save the lives of brave men–and to save the lives of innocent women and children. It is to permit the contending forces to move closer to a political settlement.

And tonight, I call upon the United Kingdom and I call upon the Soviet Union–as cochairmen of the Geneva Conferences, and as permanent members of the United Nations Security Council–to do all they can to move from the unilateral act of deescalation that I have just announced toward genuine peace in Southeast Asia....

I call upon President Ho Chi Minh to respond positively, and favorably, to this new step toward peace.

But if peace does not come now through negotiations, it will come when Hanoi understands that our common resolve is unshakable, and our common strength is invincible.

Tonight, we and the other allied nations are contributing 600,000 fighting men to assist 700,000 South Vietnamese troops in defending their little country.

Our presence there has always rested on this basic belief: The main burden of preserving their freedom must be carried out by them–by the South Vietnamese themselves.

We and our allies can only help to provide a shield behind which the people of South Vietnam can survive and can grow and develop. On their efforts–on their determination and resourcefulness–the outcome will ultimately depend.

That small, beleaguered nation has suffered terrible punishment for more than 20 years.

I pay tribute once again tonight to the great courage and endurance of its people. South Vietnam supports armed forces tonight of almost 700,000 men–and I call your attention to the fact that this is the equivalent of more than 10 million in our own population. Its people maintain their firm determination to be free of domination by the North...

I cannot promise that the initiative that I have announced tonight will be completely successful in achieving peace any more than the 30 others that we have undertaken and agreed to in recent years.

But it is our fervent hope that North Vietnam, after years of fighting that have left the issue unresolved, will now cease its efforts to achieve a military victory and will join with us in moving toward the peace table.

And there may come a time when South Vietnamese–on both sides–are able to work out a way to settle their own differences by free political choice rather than by war.

As Hanoi considers its course, it should be in no doubt of our intentions. It must not miscalculate the pressures within our democracy in this election year.

We have no intention of widening this war.

But the United States will never accept a fake solution to this long and arduous struggle and call it peace.

No one can foretell the precise terms of an eventual settlement.

Our objective in South Vietnam has never been the annihilation of the enemy. It has been to bring about a recognition in Hanoi that its objective–taking over the South by force–could not be achieved.

We think that peace can be based on the Geneva Accords of 1954–under political conditions that permit the South Vietnamese–all the South Vietnamese–to chart their course free of any outside domination or interference, from us or from anyone else....

One day, my fellow citizens, there will be peace in Southeast Asia.

It will come because the people of Southeast Asia want it–those whose armies are at war tonight, and those who, though threatened, have thus far been spared.

Peace will come because Asians were willing to work for it–and to sacrifice for it–and to die by the thousands for it.

But let it never be forgotten: Peace will come also because America sent her sons to help secure it.

It has not been easy–far from it. During the past four-and-a-half years, it has been my fate and my responsibility to be Commander in Chief. I have lived—daily and nightly–with the cost of this war. I know the pain that it has inflicted. I know, perhaps better than anyone, the misgivings that it has aroused.

Throughout this entire, long period, I have been sustained by a single principle: that what we are doing now, in Vietnam, is vital not only to the security of Southeast Asia, but it is vital to the security of every American.

Surely we have treaties which we must respect. Surely we have commitments that we are going to keep. Resolutions of the Congress testify to the need to resist aggression in the world and in Southeast Asia.

But the heart of our involvement in South Vietnam–under three different presidents, three separate administrations–has always been America's own security.

And the larger purpose of our involvement has always been to help the nations of Southeast Asia become independent and stand alone, self-sustaining, as members of a great world community–at peace with themselves, and at peace with all others.

With such an Asia, our country–and the world–will be far more secure than it is tonight...

Finally, my fellow Americans, let me say this:

Of those to whom much is given, much is asked. I cannot say and no man could say that no more will be asked of us.

Yet, I believe that now, no less than when the decade began, this generation of Americans is willing to "pay any price, bear any burden, meet any hardship, support any friend, oppose any foe to assure the survival and the success of liberty."

Since those words were spoken by John F. Kennedy, the people of America have kept that compact with mankind's noblest cause.

And we shall continue to keep it.

Yet, I believe that we must always be mindful of this one thing, whatever the trials and the tests ahead. The ultimate strength of our country and our cause will lie not in powerful weapons or infinite resources or boundless wealth, but will lie in the unity of our people.

This I believe very deeply.

Throughout my entire public career I have followed the personal philosophy that I am a free man, an American, a public servant, and a member of my party, in that order always and only.

For 37 years in the service of our Nation, first as a Congressman, as a Senator, and as Vice President, and now as your President, I have put the unity of the people first. I have put it ahead of any divisive partisanship.

And in these times as in times before, it is true that a house divided against itself by the spirit of faction, of party, of region, of religion, of race, is a house that cannot stand.

There is division in the American house now. There is divisiveness among us all tonight. And holding the trust that is mine, as President of all the people, I cannot disregard the peril to the progress of the American people and the hope and the prospect of peace for all peoples.

So, I would ask all Americans, whatever their personal interests or concern, to guard against divisiveness and all its ugly consequences.

Fifty-two months and 10 days ago, in a moment of tragedy and trauma, the duties of this office fell upon me. I asked then for your help and God's, that we might continue America on its course, binding up our wounds, healing our history, moving forward in new unity, to clear the American agenda and to keep the American commitment for all of our people.

United we have kept that commitment. United we have enlarged that commitment.

Through all time to come, I think America will be a stronger nation, a more just society, and a land of greater opportunity and fulfillment because of what we have all done together in these years of unparalleled achievement.

Our reward will come in the life of freedom, peace, and hope that our children will enjoy through ages ahead.

What we won when all of our people united must not now be lost in suspicion, distrust, selfishness, and politics among any of our people.

Believing this as I do, I have concluded that I should not permit the Presidency to become involved in the partisan divisions that are developing in this political year.

With America's sons in the fields far away, with America's future under challenge right here at home, with our hopes and the world's hopes for peace in the balance every day, I do not believe that I should devote an hour or a day of my time to any personal partisan causes or to any duties other than the awesome duties of this office—the Presidency of your country.

Accordingly, I shall not seek, and I will not accept, the nomination of my party for another term as your President.

But let men everywhere know, however, that a strong, a confident, and a vigilant America stands ready tonight to seek an honorable peace–and stands ready tonight to defend an honored cause–whatever the price, whatever the burden, whatever the sacrifice that duty may require.

Thank you for listening.

Good night and God bless all of you.

Discussion questions

1. Compare the CIA's initial assessment of the Tet Offensive (produced less than 24 hours after the first attacks) with the goals of the offensive as outlined by senior VWP leaders in Resolution 14. What did US intelligence analysts get right about the main objectives of the offensive? On what points were they incorrect?
2. Did Eddie Adams' photograph of the execution of Nguyen Van Lem distort the political and military realities of the Vietnam War, as some critics (and Adams himself) would later argue? Was it wrong for American newspaper editors to publish the photograph? Why or why not?
3. Does Huynh Cong Than's later account of the Tet Offensive in Saigon confirm or undermine Walter Cronkite's view that the war was "mired in stalemate" in 1968? Explain.
4. Is it correct to portray the Tet Offensive as a victory for any of the armies that participated in it? If so, which armies? If not, why not?

Chapter 9   Home Fronts

Students for a Democratic Society, "Build, Not Burn" (1965)[1]

One of the best-known of the many groups that participated in the American movement against the Vietnam War was Students for a Democratic Society (SDS). Founded in 1960, SDS had dozens of affiliate organizations on American college campuses by the mid-1960s. It was viewed as the leading vehicle of the "New Student Left," a movement whose participants criticized mainstream American liberalism and who advocated an alternative political economy organized around "participatory democracy." In its first years of existence, SDS focused mainly on domestic issues such as poverty and civil rights. However, with the escalation of the Vietnam War in 1965, SDS members denounced the policies of the Johnson administration in Southeast Asia. In April 1965, just months after US warplanes began sustained bombing operations against North Vietnam, SDS helped organize the first major rally in Washington against the war.

[1] "Build, Not Burn," Students for a Democratic Society Press release, reprinted in Kirkpatrick Sale, *SDS: Ten Years Toward a Revolution* (New York: Random House, 1973), 233–234.

Original publication details: 9.2 Young Americans for Freedom, The New Guard, 1965. 9.6 McGovern. Congressional Record, p. 30682. 9.7 Ngo Cong Duc, 1970. 9.8 Wilson & Smith, 1971.

*By the fall of 1965, SDS was getting national news attention for its
antiwar activism – much of it negative. In October, on the eve of a new round
of protests organized by SDS chapters around the country, the syndicated
columnists Rowland Evans and Robert Novak announced that the
organization had prepared a "master plan" to "sabotage the war effort" in
Vietnam by encouraging young men to evade the draft. The US attorney
general subsequently stated in public that some of SDS's antidraft activities
were "begin[ning] to move in the direction of treason" and insinuated that
communists might be active in the organization. In fact, SDS had not yet
adopted any specific plan of draft resistance. However, SDS national leaders
believed it was important to answer the accusations that had been made
against them. The following statement was presented to the media at a press
conference in Washington in late October. As the text makes clear, SDS
emphasized that it advocated legal opposition to the draft by encouraging
American men of draft age to seek conscientious objector (CO) status.*

Students for a Democratic Society wishes to reiterate emphatically its intention to pursue its opposition to the war in Vietnam, undeterred by the diver-
sionary tactics of the administration.

We feel that the war is immoral at its root, that it is fought alongside a
regime with no claim to represent its people, and that *it is foreclosing the
hope of making America a decent and truly democratic society.*

The commitment of SDS, and of the whole generation we represent, is
clear: we are anxious to build villages; we refuse to burn them. We are
anxious to help and to change our country; we refuse to destroy someone
else's country. We are anxious to advance the cause of democracy; we do not
believe that cause can be advanced by torture and terror.

We are fully prepared to volunteer for service to our country and to democracy. We volunteer to go into Watts to work with the people of Watts to
rebuild that neighborhood to be the kind of place that the people of Watts
want it to be—and when we say "rebuild," we mean socially as well as phys-
ically. We volunteer to help the Peace Corps learn, as we have been learning
in the slums and in Mississippi, how to energize the hungry and desperate
and defeated of the world to make the big decisions. We volunteer to serve in
hospitals and schools in the slums, in the Job Corps and VISTA, in the new
Teachers Corps—and to do so in such a way as to strengthen democracy at
its grassroots. And in order to make our volunteering possible, we propose
to the President that all those Americans who seek so vigorously to build
instead of burn be given their chance to do so. We propose that he test the
young people of America: if they had a free choice, would they want to burn
and torture in Vietnam or to build a democracy at home and overseas? There

is only one way to make the choice real: let us see what happens if service to democracy is made grounds for exemption from the military draft. I predict that almost every member of my generation would choose to build, not to burn; to teach, not to torture; to help, not to kill. And I am sure that the overwhelming majority of our brothers and cousins in the army in Vietnam, would make the same choice if they could—to serve and build, not kill and destroy . . . .

Until the President agrees to our proposal, we have only one choice: we do in conscience object, utterly and wholeheartedly, to this war; and we will encourage every member of our generation to object, and to file his objection through the Form 150 provided by the law for conscientious objection.

Young Americans for Freedom, "Aid and Comfort to the Enemy" (1965)[2]

The emergence of a small but vocal Vietnam antiwar movement in 1965 provoked criticism from many quarters. While much of this criticism was voiced by Johnson administration officials, it was also expressed by certain conservative commentators and organizations. One such organization was Young Americans for Freedom (YAF), a conservative student group that had been founded in 1960 with the encouragement of William F. Buckley, editor of the National Review. *As an organization dedicated to libertarianism, free market ideology, and anticommunism, YAF was the conservative alternative to SDS on many American college campuses during the 1960s. In their monthly journal* The New Guard *and in other publications, YAF members staunchly defended the US intervention in the Vietnam War. They also accused SDS and other antiwar organizations of engaging in illegal activities designed to undermine the US war effort.*

The New Left does not merely dissent from the American commitment in Vietnam—it is actively engaged in sabotaging it. Under the doctrines of non-violence and direct action, leftist activists are attempting to halt troop trains, hamstring the movement of materiel, block ingress to the Oakland Army Terminal (a key embarkation point for Vietnam) and disrupt the selective service system by burning draft cards, demonstrating, and dissuading enlistees from serving.[3] In a time of formally-declared war such frenetic undermining of

[2] "Aid and Comfort to the Enemy," *The New Guard* 5 (October 1965), 6.
[3] This is apparently a reference to the actions of antiwar protestors in northern California who attempted to block military trains transporting US soldiers during the summer of 1965. It

American security would probably be treasonable. But the war in Vietnam is undeclared, and so these attempts to soften the muscle of the Republic are lightly punished.

The touchstone of the anti-war activity is not true pacifism—for that would involve stern condemnation of the Viet Cong invaders—but rather a hatred of Western, and especially American institutions, beliefs, and strategic security. It is not pacifism that induced University of California Professor Richard C. Strohman to throw a benefit wing-ding in behalf of the Viet Cong; not pacifism that induces young radicals to show Viet Cong propaganda films around the country; not pacifism that goads Yale's Professor Staughton Lynd to propose that LBJ be driven from office by nonviolent pressures. The thrust of the New Left's anti-Viet war activities is directed, ultimately, toward ourselves and our beliefs. They are not pacifists (though there are pacifists among them); they are a fifth column.

The sabotage program operates outside the realm of dialogue and philosophy. We cannot halt train-ins, draft-card incendiarism and the investment of military posts with rational argument. The New Left is radicalized; it is not susceptible to reason and discussion. It acts on the primitive supposition that our whole society is rotten, and from that base it moves to street politics reminiscent of early Nazism. For example, its recent effort to commandeer the House of Representatives was a fascistic physical thrust at the heart of ordered, parliamentary government.[4]

The only way to cope with such irreconcilables is through force—force sufficient to maintain the sovereignty and integrity of our institutions. This poses a dilemma for conservatives, who rightly distrust federal force. Even so, we must recognize that the cardinal duty of government is to maintain order. To the extent that the New Left violates existing law, it must be punished. Certain new laws, such as the recently-enacted one protecting draft cards, would also help.

But the best and most effective solution involves not so much the application of federal force as intelligent private opposition. In other words, curbing the New Left is the business of organizations like Young Americans for Freedom. The task is to isolate the New Left; to render it impotent. This

---

probably also refers to a 15 October 1965 demonstration in which 15,000 antiwar protestors, including many students, held a rally and march in Berkeley, CA. The protestors attempted to march to the nearby Oakland Army Depot but were stopped en route by Oakland police. Several of the male protestors then burned their draft cards.

4 This apparently refers to an August 1965 event in which antiwar activists organized an "Assembly of Unrepresented People" in Washington, DC. The participants attempted to march to the US Capitol with the declared intent of streaming into the House chambers and staging a vote in which they would declare peace in Vietnam.

involves damning its members with their own words and deeds, producing a sophisticated defense of a hard line in Vietnam, and perhaps maintaining a conservative presence at radical activities.

The whole anti-Viet movement is vulnerable because it is ignorant and irresponsible. Its apologies for the Viet Cong are specious and circumlocutionary. There is every reason to believe that YAF chapters can blunt the radical movement wherever it crops up.

Student Non-Violent Coordinating Committee, Statement Against the War in Vietnam (1966)[5]

In addition to garnering support from the New Left and peace groups, the emerging American antiwar movement also drew support from US civil rights activists. One of the first civil rights organizations to come out against the war was the Student Nonviolent Coordinating Committee (SNCC), an antisegregation group established by black college students in North Carolina in 1960. SNCC members emphasized grassroots forms of organizing aimed at working-class constituencies; they also drew on traditions of pacifism and Gandhian theories of nonviolent direct action.

In January 1966, SNCC chairman John Lewis – who would go on to a long and successful career as a member of the US House of Representatives – called a press conference at which he read this statement of opposition to the American war effort in Vietnam. Although Dr Martin Luther King and other prominent civil rights leaders had not yet publicly denounced the war, Lewis and other SNCC members felt compelled to take a stand, in part because African American men were being drafted to fight in Vietnam in disproportionately large numbers. The statement was also a direct response to the recent murder of Sammy Younge, a black SNCC volunteer and Navy veteran who was shot by a white man after he asked to use the "whites only" restroom at an Alabama gas station. For SNCC activists, Younge's violent murder presented disturbing parallels to the killings of innocent civilians in South Vietnam.

The Student Nonviolent Coordinating Committee has a right and a responsibility to dissent with United States foreign policy on any issue when it sees fit. The Student Nonviolent Coordinating Committee now states its opposition to the United States' involvement in Vietnam on these grounds:

We believe the United States government has been deceptive in its claims of concern for the freedom of the Vietnamese people, just as the government

[5] SNCC statement of January 6, 1966, printed in James Foreman, *The Making of Black Revolutionaries: A Personal Account* (New York: Macmillan, 1972), 445–446.

has been deceptive in claiming concern for the freedom of colored people in other countries such as the Dominican Republic, the Congo, South Africa, Rhodesia, and in the United States itself.

We, the Student Nonviolent Coordinating Committee, have been involved in the black peoples' struggle for liberation and self-determination in this country for the past five years. Our work, particularly in the South, has taught us that the United States government has never guaranteed the freedom of oppressed citizens, and is not yet truly determined to end the rule of terror and oppression within its own borders.

We ourselves have often been victims of violence and confinement executed by United States governmental officials. We recall the numerous persons who have been murdered in the South because of their efforts to secure their civil and human rights, and whose murderers have been allowed to escape penalty for their crimes.

The murder of Samuel Younge in Tuskegee, Alabama, is no different than the murder of peasants in Vietnam, for both Younge and the Vietnamese sought, and are seeking, to secure the rights guaranteed them by law. In each case, the United States government bears a great part of the responsibility for these deaths.

Samuel Younge was murdered because United States law is not being enforced. Vietnamese are murdered because the United States is pursuing an aggressive policy in violation of international law. The United States is no respecter of persons or law when such persons or laws run counter to its needs or desires.

We recall the indifference, suspicion and outright hostility with which our reports of violence have been met in the past by government officials.

We know that for the most part, elections in this country, in the North as well as the South, are not free. We have seen that the 1965 Voting Rights Act and the 1966 Civil Rights Act have not yet been implemented with full federal power and sincerity.

We question, then, the ability and even the desire of the United States government to guarantee free elections abroad. We maintain that our country's cry of "preserve freedom in the world" is a hypocritical mask, behind which it squashes liberation movements which are not bound, and refuse to be bound, by the expediencies of United States cold war policies.

We are in sympathy with, and support, the men in this country who are unwilling to respond to a military draft which would compel them to contribute their lives to United States aggression in Vietnam in the name of the "freedom" we find so false in this country.

We recoil with horror at the inconsistency of a supposedly "free" society where responsibility to freedom is equated with the responsibility to lend oneself to military aggression. We take note of the fact that 16% of the draftees from this country are Negroes called on to stifle the liberation of Vietnam, to preserve a "democracy" which does not exist for them at home.

We ask, where is the draft for the freedom fight in the United States?

We therefore encourage those Americans who prefer to use their energy in building democratic forms within this country. We believe that work in the civil rights movement and with other human relations organizations is a valid alternative to the draft. We urge all Americans to seek this alternative, knowing full well that it may cost them their lives—as painfully as in Vietnam.

Nicholas Garland, Cartoon of Lyndon Johnson (1966)[6]

As the American involvement in the Vietnam War escalated during the mid-1960s, US leaders came in for increasing criticism in the press, both in the United States and around the world. This cartoon, drawn by the British

[6] Originally published in *The Daily Telegraph*, April 12, 1966. http://www.cartoons. ac.uk/record/ng0019

artist Nicholas Garland and published in a London newspaper in 1966,
suggested that Lyndon Johnson had misjudged the situation in Vietnam.
Garland depicted an oversized and clumsy Johnson struggling to avoid
stepping on a squabbling array of South Vietnamese. In front of Johnson
stands Nguyen Cao Ky, the premier of the US-backed Saigon government,
who is fighting with a pair of Buddhist monks; behind Johnson are several
other angry South Vietnamese, who seem ready to join the brawl. Notably
absent from the frame are any depictions of the Vietnamese communists –
except for a smoldering ruin in the distance, which presumably represents the
ongoing US strategic bombing campaign against North Vietnam.

   Garland's drawing was a commentary on the latest crisis in South
Vietnam, in which Ky had sent his soldiers to Central Vietnam to put down a
Buddhist-backed rebellion led by a rival ARVN general. The cartoon
suggested that South Vietnam's noncommunist leaders and factions were
hopelessly divided – to the point that they preferred to fight each other, rather
than the communist-led NLF. Even America's formidable military might
could not conjure the political unity that would be necessary for success.

Pete Seeger, "Waist Deep in the Big Muddy" (1967)[7]

As the American antiwar movement gathered strength during the late 1960s,
expressions of opposition to the Vietnam War proliferated in US popular
culture. Some of the most memorable and impactful forms of protest were
musical. In 1967, folk singer Pete Seeger, who was known both for his music
and his civil rights and peace activism, wrote an allegorical song about a US
Army platoon that nearly drownsen masse when its commander orders his
men to ford a muddy river. Although the song was set in Louisiana in the
1940s and did not mention Vietnam, Seeger clearly intended it as a critique of
US policy in Southeast Asia – especially the optimistic predictions of victory
issued by Lyndon Johnson.

   In September 1967, Seeger performed "Waist Deep in the Big Muddy"
during a taping of an episode of The Smothers Brothers Comedy Hour on the
CBS television network. However, CBS executives, worried about the song's
critical tone, decided to cut it from the broadcast. The network relented only
after the hosts of the show complained to newspaper reporters about the
censorship. Seeger was invited to re-record the song, which was broadcast to
a national television audience on February 25, 1968, during the midst of the
Tet Offensive.

---

7 "Waist Deep in the Big Muddy," words and music by Pete Seeger. TRO: Copyright 1967 by
Melody Trails, Inc., New York, NY.

It was back in 1942.
I was a member of a good platoon.
We were on maneuvers in Lou'siana one night
By the light of the moon.
The Captain told us to ford a river.
That's how it all begun.
We were knee deep in the Big Muddy,
And the big fool said to push on.

The Sergeant said, "Sir, are you sure
This is the best way back to the base?"
"Sergeant, go on, I've forded this river
About a mile above this place.
It'll be a little soggy, but just keep sloggin'.
We'll soon be on dry ground."
We were waist deep in the Big Muddy,
And the big fool said to push on.

The Sergeant said, "Sir, with all this equipment,
No man will be able to swim."
"Sergeant, don't be a Nervous Nelly,"
The Captain said to him.
"All we need is a little determination.
Men, follow me. I'll lead on."
We were neck deep in the Big Muddy,
And the big fool said to push on.

All at once the moon clouded over.
We heard a gurglin' cry.
A few seconds later the Captain's helmet
Was all that floated by.
The Sergeant said, "Turn around, men.
I'm in charge from now on."
And we just made it out of the Big Muddy
With the Captain dead and gone.

We stripped and dived and found his body
Stuck in the old quicksand.
I guess he didn't know that the water was deeper
Then the place he'd once before been.
Another stream had joined the Big Muddy
About a half mile from where we'd gone.
We were lucky to escape from the Big Muddy
When the big fool said to push on.

Now I'm not going to point any moral —
I'll leave that for yourself.

Maybe you're still walking, you're still talking,
You'd like to keep your health.
But every time I read the papers, that old feeling comes on,
We're waist deep in the Big Muddy
And the big fool says to push on.

Waist deep in the Big Muddy,
The big fool says to push on.
Waist deep in the Big Muddy,
The big fool says to push on.
Waist deep, neck deep,
Soon even a tall man will be over his head.
We're waist deep in the Big Muddy,
And the big fool says to push on.

Senator George McGovern, Speech in Support of the McGovern–Hatfield Amendment to End the War in Indochina (1970)[8]

In the spring of 1970, US Senators George McGovern (D-South Dakota) and Mark Hatfield (R-Oregon) introduced legislation to end the American involvement in the Vietnam War. Their amendment proposed to end all funding for US military operations in South Vietnam by late 1970; it also required the withdrawal of all remaining US troops from Vietnam by mid-1971. The two legislators viewed the measure as an act of resistance to Richard Nixon's highly controversial decision to invade eastern Cambodia with US and South Vietnamese ground troops in April 1970. The debate over the McGovern–Hatfield amendment was also shaped by events at Kent State University in Ohio, where US National Guardsmen killed four students when they opened fire on a group of unarmed antiwar protestors.

Throughout the spring and summer of 1970, McGovern and Hatfield lobbied their Senate colleagues to endorse the amendment. They also launched a campaign to mobilize public support. Opinion polls taken during the late summer suggested that a majority of Americans favored the amendment. However, the Nixon administration and its supporters fought hard against the proposal, portraying it as defeatist and as a "declaration of surrender." When the measure was finally taken up by the Senate on September 1, 1970, it failed by a vote of 39 to 55.

---

[8] Congressional Record, p. 30682.

The speech below was delivered by McGovern just minutes before the voting began. By the time he rose to speak, everyone in the chamber knew that the measure did not have enough support to pass. But his fellow senators were still shocked by his speech, and especially by his searing remarks about their personal responsibility for the ongoing carnage in Vietnam. After McGovern had finished, one of his colleagues sought him out and angrily told him that he felt offended by McGovern's remarks. "That's what I meant to do," McGovern shot back.

Mr. President, the vote we are about to cast could be one of the most significant votes Senators will ever cast.

I have lived with this vote night and day since last April 30—the day before the Cambodian invasion—the day this amendment was first submitted.

I thank God this amendment was submitted when it was, because as every Senator knows, in the turbulent days following the invasion of Cambodia and the tragedy at Kent State University, this amendment gave a constructive rallying point to millions of anguished citizens across this war-weary land.

I believe that, along with the Cooper-Church amendment, the pending amendment helped to keep the Nation from exploding this summer. It was the lode-star that inspired more mail, more telegrams, more eager young visitors to our offices, more political action, and more contributions from doctors, lawyers, workers, and housewives than any other initiative of Congress in this summer of discontent.

Now this question is about to be resolved. What is the choice it presents us? It presents us with an opportunity to end a war we never should have entered. It presents us with an opportunity to revitalize constitutional government in America by restoring the war powers the Founding Fathers obliged the Congress to carry.

It gives us an opportunity to correct the drift toward one-man rule in the crucial areas of war and peace.

All my life, I have heard Republicans and conservative Democrats complaining about the growth of centralized power in the Federal executive.

Vietnam and Cambodia have convinced me that the conservatives were right. Do they really believe their own rhetoric? We have permitted the war power which the authors of the Constitution wisely gave to us as the people's representatives to slip out of our hands until it now resides behind closed doors at the State Department, the CIA, the Pentagon, and the basement of the White House. We have foolishly assumed that war was too complicated to be trusted to the people's forum—the Congress of the United States. The result has been the cruelest, the most barbaric, and the most stupid war in our national history.

Every Senator in this Chamber is partly responsible for sending 50,000 young Americans to an early grave. This Chamber reeks of blood.
Every Senator here is partly responsible for that human wreckage at Walter Reed and Bethesda Naval and all across our land—young men without legs, or arms, or genitals, or faces, or hopes.

There are not very many of those blasted and broken boys who think this war is a glorious venture.

Do not talk to them about bugging out, or national honor, or courage.

It does not take any courage at all for a Congressman or a Senator or a President to wrap himself in the flag and say we are staying in Vietnam, because it is not our blood that is being shed.

But we are responsible for those young men and their lives and their hopes.

And if we do not end this damnable war, those young men will some day curse us for our pitiful willingness to let the Executive carry the burden that the Constitution places on us.

So before we vote, let us ponder the admonition of Edmund Burke, the great parliamentarian of an earlier day:
"A conscientious man would be cautious how he dealt in blood."

Ngo Cong Duc, "Anti-Americanism: Common Cause in Vietnam" (1970)

During the latter half of the 1960s, as the movement against the Vietnam War gathered strength in the United States, antiwar sentiment was also growing in South Vietnam. A diverse range of South Vietnamese individuals and groups called for an end to the fighting and a negotiated settlement to the conflict between the RVN and DRVN. These included Buddhists and Catholics, urban professionals and workers, members of opposition political parties, and intellectuals. Participants in the movement often referred to it as the "Third Force" in South Vietnamese politics; this term underscored their separateness from both the US-backed Nguyen Van Thieu government and the communist-controlled NLF movement. (This use of the term "Third Force" was distinct from its meaning during the late 1940s and early 1950s, when it referred to those anticommunist Vietnamese who opposed French colonialism as well as the Viet Minh.)

The statement below was written and published in September 1970 by Ngo Cong Duc, a prominent Third Force figure. Duc was the editor of a Saigon newspaper (Tin Sang, or "Morning News") as well as an opposition deputy in the RVN National Assembly. He released his statement in Paris, where US, DRVN, RVN, and NLF representatives had been engaged in peace negotiations since 1968. While Duc did not claim to speak for all those who considered themselves part of the Third Force in South Vietnam, many of his views were widely shared in antiwar circles.

The South Vietnamese people aspire currently, more than ever, to peace, independence, and a life worthy of human beings. These aspirations are obvious, for at this moment the population of South Vietnam is caught up in one of the most atrocious of wars. Political, economic and cultural life is dominated by foreigners.

I. A Few Salient Points Concerning the Population of South Vietnam

1. The current war is destroying untold human and material resources in South Vietnam. Not including the forces of the NLF, the army of the Republic of Vietnam numbers one million men; to this figure must be added the forces of self-defense numbering one million men; and police forces numbering 100,000 men. In other words, two million young people, instead of pursuing their studies and engaging in productive work, are forced to take up arms in order to help American imperialism achieve its political aim in Southeast Asia.

    American forces and the forces of the allies of the Americans, numbering close to 500,000 men, are engaged in round-the-clock massacres of our innocent compatriots. Cases such as those of My Lai-Son My, which each time take 500-600 victims, are by no means isolated. The US has dropped more than ten million tons of bombs on our country, and scattered an untold quantity of toxic chemical products as well as nearly 100,000 tons of defoliants on our fields and rice plantations, which have resulted in the sterilization and destruction of all the harvests. Rich in rice, South Vietnam is now reduced to consuming American rice. As a result of the use of toxic products, South Vietnam is currently plagued with strange diseases: women are giving birth to monsters, and there is an ever growing number of women afflicted with psychic disorders.

2. On the political level, with the Vietnamization of the war, the United States seeks only to uphold the militarists and prolong the war.

The government of Mr. Nguyen Van Thieu is a dictatorial government which persecutes all those who struggle for peace and independence, and jails the innocent. In the single province of Vinh Binh, of which I am a deputy, more than 300 people were last year arbitrarily arrested and jailed. In 1969 the Americans stated that there were only 20,000 cadres in South Vietnam; at the end of 1969, however, the government arrested more than 70,000 people, and it appears that the number of Communist cadres has not diminished. These very figures condemn the repressive policies of the Saigon government.

At present the Nguyen Van Thieu government severely represses all opposition movements. Several hundred war victims are being held in jails; several hundred students were taken to military training camps; the president of the Student Union of Saigon-Hué is in prison. All are subjected to the most savage kinds of torture.

During the past six months of this bitter struggle, the opposition movements were not alone in being subjected to repression; the press met the same fate. The press was not only deprived of indispensable paper, but was confiscated more than 200 times; the daily *Tin Sang* ("Morning News") in particular was suspended eight times and confiscated seventy-five times during a six-month period.

The Vietnamization of the war is merely an extension of the American war. Although the US has agreed to the Paris Conference, it actually does not want peace at all and is compelling the Nguyen Van Thieu government to seek a military victory.

3. On the economic level, South Vietnam is in a catastrophic situation. The annual budget amounts to 210 billion piasters; income amounts to only seventy billion. Every year, in addition to American aid, inflation wipes out eighty billion piasters.

The chief purpose of American aid is to divide the Vietnamese among themselves. The US has transformed the South Vietnamese market into a one-way consumers' market. Contraband American foods are inundating the South Vietnamese markets. Of the seventeen million people currently living in South Vietnam, as many as two million families live on war profits by serving the interests of the United States. This is why the purpose of American aid is by no means to raise the standard of living of the population; on the contrary, it plunges the population into ever increasing misery. For instance, twenty years' salary of a South Vietnamese army officer with a wife and five children would not purchase a Peugeot 404 at current prices.

The experience of the past few years has led the South Vietnamese to this conclusion: the purpose of American aid to South Vietnam is to force the Vietnamese population to become totally dependent on the United States.

4. American political and economic aims have completely altered the nature of Vietnamese society. With their money the Americans are setting communities against one another, and are destroying all their traditional spiritual and moral values. The number of prostitutes increases daily. More than 400,000 Vietnamese women are currently engaged in this wretched and humiliating profession. The Americans also try to promote corruption so as to use their accomplices in pursuing their imperialist aims in South Vietnam.

On the cultural level, the US seeks to transform South Vietnam into an American-type society by sweeping away all the positive aspects of the Vietnamese heritage. Millions of young people are deprived of education, nine-and ten-year-old children do not go to school but tend buffaloes, work in rice fields, shine shoes, and sell newspapers. American policy in South Vietnam aims at Americanizing the Vietnamese people, transforming the Vietnamese into foreigners in their own country, into increasingly ignorant creatures stripped of all dignity.

II. The Upsurge of Opposition Movements Against the US and the Nguyen Van Thieu Government

Having become aware of the imperialist policies the US wants to impose in South Vietnam, and having also become aware of the dependence of Nguyen Van Thieu's government on the US, the South Vietnamese population is now rising in revolt.

The time has come when not only the NLF partisans but also the entire South Vietnamese people are revolting against the US and against Generals Nguyen Van Thieu and Nguyen Cao Ky. Living with the Americans, or in close proximity to the Americans, the South Vietnamese understand better than anyone how wicked American policies are. This wickedness is understood even by those who have collaborated, or are collaborating, with the Americans or with the government of Nguyen Van Thieu.

Let us cite a few examples: in Binh Tuy, last August 28, a group of American soldiers raped, thus provoking the deaths of an old woman and her daughter-in-law, who were on their way to work in their field. During their burial crowds turned the funeral into a street demonstration against the American presence. In Saigon, on August 22, a little shoe-shine boy lying on a street corner was run over and killed by a car driven by a GI. Over 200 other little shoe-shine boys pooled their meager earnings to buy him a coffin, displaying their solidarity with the tragedy of one of their own provoked by the cruelty of the Americans.

At present there is not a single newspaper which has not taken a position against the US, for this is the position of the entire South Vietnamese people.

With respect to the Nguyen Van Thieu government, the people are becoming increasingly aware that it is a puppet of the Americans: it has collaborated with the Americans in order to prolong the fratricidal war; it employs more than 100,000 military police agents to repress and savagely torture the adherents of the movements defending the right to life and demanding a return to peace.

The South Vietnamese people know that Mr. Nguyen Van Thieu supports the Lon Nol regime [in Cambodia] which has massacred more than 20,000 South Vietnamese citizens in Kampuchéa.

Faced with a government which is totally dependent on the Americans, and with neocolonialist policies, the popular forces have revolted against the Nguyen Van Thieu government and against the establishment of American imperialism. The movements most actively engaged in this struggle are the following:

- The Buddhist movement, which is demanding a return to peace and independence, led by the United Buddhist Church.
- The Movement of Struggle of the Students, which is inspired by the Student Union of Saigon and the big cities, and which is demanding independent universities, the abolition of compulsory military training, the abolition of forced recruitment into the army, and is opposing the policy of pursuing the war.
- The Movement of Women, which is demanding the right to life and a return to peace, and which is led by the Women's Action Committee for the Defense of the Right to Life.
- The Movement of War Victims, which is demanding food and housing, and which opposes the poor treatment these victims have received from the US and the Nguyen Van Thieu government.

In addition, there are youth and secondary school student movements, the movement of small landed proprietors opposed to the agrarian policy, and the movement opposed to the government's fiscal policies.

Although these movements are savagely repressed, we are convinced that nothing will prevent the growth of these opposition movements. The US and Mr. Nguyen Van Thieu seek to destroy them or, barring that, to buy them off. The power of the dollar, however, is no match for the spiritual and moral strength of the Vietnamese people.

The opposition movements are inspired neither by the Communists nor by the NLF. The entire population, conscious of its patriotic responsibilities, is preparing for struggle against the threat of extermination by war and against the danger of imperialism.

They serve neither the NLF nor any particular ideology. We must frankly admit that most South Vietnamese are firm in their resolve to struggle against the US and against the Nguyen Van Thieu government. Nevertheless, they are still fearful of an eventual "communization" of South Vietnam.

In conclusion, these are the deepest aspirations of the South Vietnamese people: (1) The immediate withdrawal of all American and foreign troops from South Vietnam. (2) An immediate end to the war, so that the Vietnamese may settle their affairs among themselves.

III. Proposals

Whereas

— this atrocious and endless Vietnam war is threatening Vietnamese society with total destruction,
— there can be no definitive military victory,
— peace is the deepest aspiration of the Vietnamese people and constitutes the basic condition for any social reform,
— a numerous popular force in South Vietnam demanding peace, independence, democracy, freedom and national reconcilation is not yet represented at the Paris Conference,
— an over-all solution to the Vietnam conflict cannot be realized unless it rests on the basic right of self-determination of the South Vietnamese people,
— the right of self-determination can be genuinely achieved only through truly free elections, with no pressure flowing from the presence of foreign troops and free from any intervention by any military or political force,

We solemnly propose:

I. A de-escalation of the war and a halt to all repression of the movements struggling for peace, independence, democracy, freedom, and national reconciliation through the following conditions:
   1. The Americans must withdraw from the territory of South Vietnam all their forces and war matériel, as well as the forces and war matériel of Thailand, New Zealand, Australia, and South Korea.

2. The Americans must cease encouraging and supporting the Nguyen Van Thieu government in its repression of the opposition movements struggling for peace, independence, democracy, freedom and national reconciliation.

3. The Nguyen Van Thieu government must put an end to its practice of torture, free all illegally held prisoners, stop all repression of Buddhists, university and secondary school students, women, those wounded and disabled by the war, workers and all progressive movements struggling for peace, independence, democracy, freedom and national reconciliation in South Vietnam.

4. All parties to the war must begin to de-escalate the war. The Americans must stop the bombings and stop using harmful chemical products on the territory of South Vietnam. The National Liberation. Front must halt all indiscriminate bombings by rockets or mortars, which victimize the innocent.

II. When the above-mentioned conditions have been fulfilled, the Paris Conference must be enlarged:

The Paris Conference on Vietnam currently consists of four parties: the American delegation, that of the Nguyen Van Thieu government, that of the National Liberation Front, and that of North Vietnam. But the overwhelming majority of the South Vietnamese population demanding peace, independence, democracy, freedom and national reconciliation are not represented.

This is why there must be a delegation representing the political and religious groups and forces struggling for peace, independence, democracy, freedom and national reconciliation, in order that it may join the other delegations in finding a concerted solution to the problem of Vietnam.

III. With the seating of the delegation of the forces struggling for peace, independence, democracy, freedom and national reconciliation, the Conference will be able to proceed:

1. To discuss the conditions for a cease-fire and for the withdrawal of the North Vietnamese forces from South Vietnam, and to solve the problem of the Army of the Republic of Vietnam and of the Army of the National Liberation Front.

2. To establish a neutral provisional government in South Vietnam.

3. This neutral provisional government will have the task
   – of implementing the conditions agreed upon at the Paris Conference,
   – of normalizing political, economic, cultural, and social activities in South Vietnam,

– of establishing relations with North Vietnam,
– of organizing free elections in South Vietnam.

Terry Nelson and C-Company, "The Battle Hymn of Lt Calley" (1971)[9]

Most Americans were shocked to learn the horrific details of the My Lai massacre when they first became public in 1969. However, as more information about the massacre became publicly available, different Americans drew divergent conclusions about the event. The courts martial of some of the soldiers and officers accused of committing atrocities at My Lai provoked a range of responses. The most polarizing case proved to be that of Lt. William Calley – who, in the end, was the only individual to be convicted and punished for participating in the massacre. At his trial, Calley acknowledged that he had ordered his men to kill any and all people that they encountered at My Lai, but insisted that he had just been following orders. In March 1971, he was sentenced to life in prison with hard labor; on appeal, however, his sentence was reduced first to 20 years of confinement and then to ten years. In the end, Calley served only three and a half years of house arrest in a military barracks before regaining his freedom.

Despite the fact that he was a convicted war criminal, Calley was viewed sympathetically by many Americans. Some of his supporters objected to the original sentence of life at hard labor on the grounds that it was excessively harsh; others believed that he had been made a scapegoat for his superiors. Several state legislatures passed resolutions asking for clemency for Calley. Among those who expressed their sympathy for Calley was Georgia Governor and future US President Jimmy Carter, who instituted "American Fighting Man's Day" as a gesture of support for the convict.

The song below was written prior to Calley's trial in 1970 by songwriters Julian Wilson and James M. Smith. An initial recording was made in late 1970, but only a few copies of it were sold. The song was then re-recorded in March of 1971 with vocals by Terry Nelson and music performed by the group C-Company. The song, which features a combination of sung and spoken-word vocals, was performed to the tune of "The Battle Hymn of the Republic." The 1971 release of the song – which came immediately after Calley's life sentence had been handed down – eventually sold nearly two million copies.

---

[9] "The Battle Hymn of Lt. Calley," performed by Terry Nelson and C-Company. From *Next Stop is Vietnam: The War on Record, 1961–2008*, Bear Family Records, 2010, Disk 14, No. 29.

Once upon a time there was a little boy who wanted to grow up
And be a soldier and serve his country in whatever way he could
He would parade around the house with a sauce pan on his head
For a helmet, a wooden sword in one hand and the American flag in the
other
As he grew up, he put away the things of a child but he never let go of the
flag

My name is William Calley, I'm a soldier of this land
I've tried to do my duty and to gain the upper hand
But they've made me out a villain they have stamped me with a brand
As we go marching on

I'm just another soldier from the shores of U.S.A.
Forgotten on a battle field then thousand miles away
While life goes on as usual from New York to Santa Fe
As we go marching on

I've seen my buddies ambushed on the left and on the right
And their youthful bodies riddled by the bullets of the night
Where all the rules are broken and the only law is might
As we go marching on

While we're fighting in the jungles they were marching in the street
While we're dying in the rice fields they were helping our defeat
While we're facing V.C. bullets they were sounding a retreat
As we go marching on
With our sweat we took the bunkers, with our tears we took the plain
With our blood we took the mountains and they gave it back again
Still all of us are soldiers, we're too busy to complain
As we go marching on

When I reach my final campground in that land beyond the sun
And the great commander asks me, "Did you fight or did you run?"
I'll stand both straight and tall, stripped of medals, rank and gun
And this is what I'll say:

Sir, I followed all my orders and I did the best I could
It's hard to judge the enemy and hard to tell the good
Yet there's not a man among us would not have understood

We took the jungle village exactly like they said
We responded to their rifle fire with everything we had
And when the smoke had cleared away a hundred souls lay dead

Sir, the soldier that's alive is the only one can fight
There's no other way to wage a war when the only one in sight
That you're sure is not a VC is your buddy on your right

When all the wars are over and the battle's finally won
Count me only as a soldier who never left his gun

With the right to serve my country as the only prize I've won

Glory, glory hallelujah glory, glory hallelujah (fade)

Daniel Ellsberg, "Murder and the Lying Machine" (2002)[10]

On June 13, 1971, the New York Times *began publishing excerpts of what it described as a secret "Pentagon Study" of US decisionmaking about Vietnam from the mid-1940s to 1968. The study, which had been commissioned by former US Defense Secretary Robert McNamara in 1967, was massive; it ran to over 7,000 pages and included extensive analysis of various US decisions as well as copies of hundreds of internal US government documents. The study contained many revelations about various aspects of US policy in Vietnam. Many antiwar critics declared that the evidence in the study proved that the US intervention in Vietnam was immoral and that US leaders had deceived the public about the reasons for their decisions. As the public debate over the study exploded, journalists and others began referring to it as "the Pentagon Papers."*

The central figure in the leaking of the Pentagon Papers was Daniel Ellsberg, a former Marine who had worked on various aspects of US policy in Vietnam since the mid-1960s. In 1967, Ellsberg was assigned to write and compile one portion of the secret study. After the Papers were finished, Ellsberg arranged to get access to them in his capacity as an employee of the RAND corporation, a think tank that provided consulting services to the US military. Although Ellsberg had previously supported the war, he was increasingly disillusioned with it. He began to wonder if releasing the Papers might serve to hasten the end of the conflict.

In this excerpt from his memoir, Ellsberg recalls making the decision to copy the Papers. He did so one morning in September 1969 as he read a newspaper article about some US soldiers in Vietnam who had escaped punishment for the murder of a Vietnamese man suspected of working for the communists. For Ellsberg, the "ladder of lies" revealed in the article led him to the conclusion that he had to take new steps to end what he now saw as a profoundly immoral war.

I lay in bed that Tuesday morning and thought: This is the system that I have been working for, the system I have been part of, for a dozen years—fifteen, including the Marine Corps. It's a system that lies automatically, at

[10] Daniel Ellsberg, *Secrets: A Memoir of Vietnam and the Pentagon Papers* (New York: Viking Penguin, 2002), 286–295.

every level from bottom to top—from sergeant to commander in chief—to conceal murder.

That described, as I had come to realize from my reading that month, what that system had been doing in Vietnam, on an infinitely larger scale, continuously for a third of a century. And it was still going on. I thought: I'm not going to be part of it anymore. I'm not going to be part of this lying machine, this cover-up, this murder, anymore.

It occurred to me that what I had in my safe at Rand was seven thousand pages of documentary evidence of lying, by four presidents and their administrations over twenty-three years, to conceal plans and actions of mass murder. I decided I would stop concealing that myself. I would get it out somehow.

It would have to be copied. I couldn't do that at Rand or at a copy shop. Maybe it was possible to lease a machine. I got out of bed and picked up the phone in my living room and called a close friend, my former Rand colleague Tony Russo. I said there was something I would like to discuss with him. I'd be over shortly....

Tony had been part of the Rand VC Prisoner and Defector Interrogation Study in Vietnam. I'd first met him briefly when I arrived in Saigon in 1965. When we were back together in Santa Monica in 1968, he had often disussed with me, in his office just down the hall from mine, what he'd learned from his interviews. He showed me a number of the transcripts, some of them sixty single-spaced pages. Many of those he had talked to, through interpreters, had impressed him very much by their patriotism and dedication, their conviction of the rightness of their cause. Even the defectors, nearly all of whom had left for personal reasons or because of the hardships of guerrilla life, had nothing negative to say about the cause or their national leaders....

Tony had a degree in aeronautical engineering and had worked for NASA before studying political science at Princeton. He had started out as a cold warrior like me, but meeting the North Vietnamese and Vietcong and hearing their stories had changed him: He had come not only to admire them as people but to believe they were right about the justice of their cause. I remained focused on the injustice of ours, as I had come to see it by mid-1969. I hadn't had his face-to-face experience—I never knowingly encountered an actual member of the NLF—and I remained skeptical that their hopes would be fulfilled if their well-justified nationalist struggle led to a Stalinist regime, as I thought likely....

After Tony left Rand, I started seeing him after work. I came to like him more and more. He was funny, and he had a very original and creative mind, and not just about the war. We became close friends. He had begun reading radical analyses that presented our Vietnam policy not as an aberration or misadventure but as being in line with unacknowledged U.S. objectives and covert activities elsewhere in the third world. Again, I wasn't there yet; I hadn't done that reading (and didn't get to it till after the war). But on September 30 I didn't have any doubt that this was one friend, the only one, I could tell what I wanted to do.

As I got dressed, I was thinking about what was in the minds of the people I'd just read about, the ones who'd done the lying and helped the killing. So many of them had lied (and some of them may have helped kill) for no other reason than that they'd been told to. They were ordered to lie, or kill, by a boss. They were told it was for the good of the service, or the war, or the administration, or the Special Forces, or their bosses, or to keep their jobs. That was good enough for them; it was all they needed to know. I understood that. I'd been there, and I'd worked in those same offices. But they'd been mistaken to have acted like that, just as I'd often been. Too long, no longer.

A thought came into my head in the form of a rule: No one is ever going to tell me again that I have to lie, that I have a duty to lie, that it's all right just because someone's telling me to do it. No one is going to say that and have me believe him, or think I have to obey him. I'm not going to listen to that anymore. It no longer has any authority for me.

Lying to the public, about anything, but above all on issues of life and death, war and peace, was a serious matter; it wasn't something that you could shift responsibility for. I wasn't going to do it anymore. It came to me that the same thing applied to violence. No one else was going to tell me ever again that I (or anyone else) "had" to kill someone, that I had no choice, that I had a right or a duty to do it that someone else had decided for me....

...as I drove over to Tony's house, I was thinking how this would fit in with what I was trying to do this month. Sickened, at last, as I was by the lying machine, the simple act of exposing it wasn't an urgent priority. My concern was what the current lies (like the old ones, in this history) were about: what they were concealing, what they were facilitating. It was bad that they indicated past killings to have been murder, but I personally had no interest in putting anyone on trial or behind bars. I certainly wouldn't have courted trial or a life behind bars myself to accomplish retribution or just to set straight the historical record of Vietnam. My interest was in stopping the ongoing killing, preventing murders in the months and years ahead.

At first it wasn't obvious that revealing the McNamara study to the public would contribute to that at all, however educational it might be for the longer run. But from the moment that morning I had decided to do it anyway, I had begun to have new thoughts that suggested that it might be useful even in the short run.

It was that the study didn't prove what needed to be exposed about Nixon's secret strategy: what Halperin had told me, what I'd passed on to my Rand colleagues and to the establishment figures I had written recently. But at the same time, it did strengthen the case for it, more than a little. It showed that what I was claiming Nixon was doing was essentially what his predecessor had done. When I claimed he was prepared to mislead Congress and the American people on what he was doing, what he was ready to do, and what his real aims were, the study demonstrated that four of his predecessors had done exactly that...

Simply revealing the McNamara study would not end the war or come close to it. But it could help, and in my present mood that was justification enough. If I could get this out—ideally, if there were hearings in Congress based on it, with witnesses under subpoena and oath, or if it could be published otherwise—Nixon would have to worry that his secret policy couldn't be protected from debate and skeptical challenge....

....When I got to Tony's apartment, I said to him, "You know the study I told you about a couple of weeks ago? I've got it at Rand, in my safe, and I'm going to put it out." As I expected, Tony didn't need to be asked to help. He said, "Great! Let's do it." He didn't wait to hear the reasoning I'd just come through on the way over. I'm not sure I ever did discuss it with him; it wasn't necessary. I told him the study was very long and would take a lot of work to copy. I wanted to give a copy to the Senate or maybe the newspapers. Did he happen to know where we could get hold of a Xerox machine? He said he did. He had a girlfriend, Lynda Sinay, who owned a small advertising company. He called her while I was there, and she said it would be fine for us to use her machine after hours. We could start the next night.

Discussion questions

1. On what grounds did the Young Americans for Freedom accuse the New Left of "treasonable" activity in 1965? Were these accusations justified? Why or why not?
2. What connections did John Lewis draw between the war in Vietnam and conditions within the United States in 1966? Was his opposition to the war justified, in your view?
3. Pete Seeger's "Waist Deep in the Big Muddy" was praised by some commentators as an "even-handed" antiwar song. Do you agree with this assessment? Explain.
4. Was Nicholas Garland's caricature of Lyndon Johnson supposed to make viewers feel sympathy towards the president? How do you know?

5. If you had been in the US Senate in 1970, would you have voted for the McGovern–Hatfield Amendment? Why or why not?
6. What did Ngo Cong Duc see as the root cause of the Vietnam War? How did he propose to end the conflict? Were his proposals realistic?
7. Was "The Battle Hymn of Lt. Calley" a prowar song? Explain.
8. Why did Daniel Ellsberg decide to leak the Pentagon Papers? Do you think his decision was justified? Why or why not?

Chapter 10   Pacification, Vietnamization, and "Fighting While Negotiating"

William Westmoreland, "The Refugee Problem" (1968)[1]

Throughout the Vietnam War, US and South Vietnamese forces made numerous attempts to undercut the power of the NLF by conducting counterinsurgency operations in rural areas. These operations, known officially as "pacification," included both persuasion and coercion. US and RVN leaders often spoke of the need to win the "hearts and minds" of ordinary South Vietnamese. Yet they insisted that they needed to use military force to maintain security and to eliminate the tens of thousands of communist cadres who were operating covertly in villages and hamlets —even if such tactics sometimes caused civilian casualties, social upheaval, and feelings of resentment against US forces and the RVN state.

Between 1964 and 1968, the commander with overall responsibility for pacification in South Vietnam was US Army General William Westmoreland. During and after his tenure, Westmoreland was accused of relying too heavily on firepower-intensive tactics; according to many critics, the general was indifferent to the suffering of the civilian population and concentrated only

[1] Document 23, Folder 1, File 28, Box 15, William C. Westmoreland Papers, Lyndon Baines Johnson Presidential Library.

Original publication details: 10.1 Westmoreland, 1968. 10.5 Kissinger, 1971 in Luu Van Loi and Nguyen Anh Vu, 1996. 10.6 Nixon & Kissinger, 1972.

on killing as many insurgents as possible. However, Westmoreland insisted
that he had devised his strategy and tactics specifically to protect civilians. In
this memorandum, written just prior to the Tet Offensive, Westmoreland
reflected on one of the most controversial tactics used in pacification: the
forced relocation of entire hamlets and villages to government-run refugee
camps. In Westmoreland's view, the security gains that resulted from this
harsh practice sometimes outweighed the heavy costs it imposed on the
civilians who lost their homes and livelihoods.

4 January 1968

Recently, public interest has been generated in the refugee problem in South Vietnam. Although there have been refugees in all wars, the refugee situation in Vietnam is unique—as are many aspects of this war. A word of explanation of what creates refugees should assist in an understanding of the problem.

The success of the communist insurgency campaign is dependent upon control of the people, and all doctrine has been devised toward that end. Roads are cut by cratering, mining, or the disruption of bridging in order to isolate the people from the government and outside influence and make them captive to the communists' desires. Once the people are under enemy control, they are exploited in order to assist the Viet Cong in achieving their ends. They are required to fortify their hamlets and to produce rice and other substance to support guerrillas, local forces, main forces, and units of the North Vietnamese Army. They provide a force of labor and recruits for the enemy's ranks, and the people become completely captive to their propaganda.

In order to thwart the communists' designs, it is necessary to eliminate the "fish" from the "water," or to dry up the "water" so that the "fish" cannot survive.[2] Therefore, only two options are available in a practical sense: either the communists and their political control must be driven from the populated areas and security provided to keep them out, or the people must be relocated into areas that will facilitate security and prevent [the] communist control apparatus from re-entering the community.

---

[2] Westmoreland here is referring to Chinese Communist leader Mao Zedong's famous metaphor about the use of guerrilla tactics in insurgency warfare: "The guerrilla must move among the people as the fish swims in the sea."

The first course of action is time-consuming and expensive in terms of troops. Cadres have to be trained and installed in the community, and troops in adequate numbers have to be provided to drive out the communist apparatus and to protect the people from retaliation by terror or attack. From experience, we know that this procedure produces problems, not only for large numbers of troops but also [with respect to] casualties among the people and damage to their homes. In addition, this is a long, time-consuming process. On the other hand, it is a more palatable action from the viewpoint of the people and the government, primarily because it does not remove them from their land and the graves of their ancestors and therefore does not create an obligation by the government to resettle and support them.

The second course of action can be carried out relatively quickly and is not as expensive in security troops as the first course of action. Although the military situation does not always permit, it is desirable to prepare well in advance for the relocation of the population. However, expediences may have to be resorted to as a military necessity. Once the people have been relocated to secure areas, they are not subject to being recruited for the VC military ranks, to being drafted as porters, or to producing subsistence for the enemy. Although refugee camps are frequently subject to enemy harassment, since these are contrary to the enemy's interests, they are relatively more secure and safe than would be the case if the people remained dispersed in isolated or remote areas. On the other hand, the Vietnamese people dislike leaving the land they have tilled and where their ancestors are buried.

In summary, there are two basic ways of eliminating communist influence: one, by tediously catching the "fish" (the VC) and letting the "water" (the people) remain in place; two, by draining off the "water" and recapturing it at another location and allowing the "fish" to strangle. Discrimination must be exercised in choosing the method to be employed. The relocation of the population should not in all practicability be disallowed, since it can save lives, destruction, and time. However, the refugee care must be anticipated and sympathetically planned.

W. C. WESTMORELAND

General, United States Army

Commanding

Robert Komer, "The Phoenix Program and the Attack on the Viet Cong Infrastructure" (1969)[3]

In 1967, the task of coordinating all US and RVN pacification operations in Vietnam was assigned to a newly created organization known as Civil Operations and Revolutionary Development Support (CORDS). Under the leadership of Robert Komer, its first director, CORDS implemented many activities and programs that were supposed to win the sympathies of ordinary South Vietnamese rural dwellers. Yet Komer – a famously abrasive bureaucrat whose nickname was "Blowtorch Bob" – also emphasized the importance of using force to establish security in South Vietnamese villages and hamlets. He was especially interested in exposing and eliminating what he and other Americans referred to as the "Viet Cong Infrastructure" (VCI) – the tens of thousands of communist cadres who worked undercover among the population.

In this excerpt from an interview conducted in 1969 after his return from Vietnam, Komer discussed the Phoenix (Phung Hoang) program, the most controversial counterinsurgency initiative developed by CORDS. Under Phoenix, joint US–South Vietnamese units known as Provincial Reconnaissance Units were deployed in rural districts, where they sought to identify and "neutralize" (kill or capture) suspected members of the VCI. Many critics argued that Phoenix was really just a torture and assassination program, and that the US and South Vietnamese soldiers who served in it could violate the human rights of suspects with impunity. In this interview, Komer defended Phoenix as a valuable tool in the fight against the insurgency, but also admitted that the program did not always operate in the way that he hoped it would.

KOMER: Few pacification sub-programs have become more con-
                troversial than the U.S.-supported GVN effort to do
                something at long last about neutralizing the clandestine
                VC political and administrative structure that was one
                of the secrets of VC success. It directed the village and
                terror war; logistically supported it, and gave it political
                direction, conscripting or proselyting recruits, enforcing
                VC taxation; made anti-GVN propaganda, and the like.
                If Vietnam was a "people's war" as Hanoi called it, a polit-
                ical and revolutionary as much as a military conflict, then

[3] Excerpted from Robert Komer, *Organization and Management of the New Model Pacification Program: 1966–1969*. RAND Corporation Publication D-20104-ARPA (Washington, DC: RAND, 1970), 158–167.

rooting out this network of perhaps 100,000 to 150,000 hard core cadre at its peak was one of the most critical tasks we faced. Without it, no matter what our purely military achievements, their lasting impact would be in doubt.

It is a sad commentary on the overly conventional nature of the U.S./GVN approach to insurgency war that not until mid-1967 did we even begin to mount a major concerted attack on the VC clandestine political structure – its shadow government at all levels down to hamlet. Our failure was <u>not</u> because we didn't recognize the problem – you can find studies going all the way back to the mid-fifties that correctly identified the key VCI [Viet Cong Infrastructure] role. It was largely because nobody tackled it as an operational and management problem – it was everybody's business and nobody's. It fell between the cracks. The reason I began zeroing in on it in late 1966 was because I saw that winning over the farmers would require not just providing territorial security against the enemy main and local forces but also rooting out the clandestine political and terror apparatus. So I made it an integral part of pacification.

The GVN at all levels grasped its importance from the outset, but for various reasons it was slow to get off the ground and even today suffers from numerous weaknesses that impair its effectiveness. Ideally it should be a professionally executed police-type program, conducted according to well-known legal procedures, backed by an effective system of trial courts, and ending with imprisonment in adequate facilities for political rehabilitation. All this was done in Malaya. But in Vietnam by 1967-1968 these institutions had largely to be rebuilt from scratch. Some have criticized Phung Hoang for being a counter-terror program, which it wasn't; others have claimed it has been used for other political purposes than rooting out the VCI, which I doubt. Indeed, the greatest criticism of Phoenix has been its sloppy and feeble GVN execution, despite U.S. advisory help. So many thousands of arrested VCI have been let go again promptly as to raise questions as to why they were apprehended in the first place or whether they bribed their way out.

	Yet even if the claims of 12,000 VCI neutralized in 1968 and 19,500 in 1969 are quite exaggerated and included mostly low-level VCI, it is hard to avoid the conclusion that we are putting a serious dent in the VC cadre structure... Moreover, the simple fact that they know the GVN is after them in a big way probably has a destabilizing and deterrent impact on VCI ability to do their jobs. Hopefully, Phung Hoang will yet get the priority and resources it deserves. It could be worth more than three ARVN divisions...
INTERVIEWER:	Were you satisfied with the methods of elimination employed against the infrastructure and also the GVN's disposition of apprehended infrastructure persons?
KOMER:	No. We placed great emphasis on capture rather than kill. Obviously we wanted to interrogate these guys and find out more. This is standard. As a matter of fact, in every stage of the program there have been far more captures than kills. Increasingly it's been rallying. But we were not satisfied. I got CIA to put the PRUs in support of Phoenix. They were very effective, but sometimes they were more inclined to knock these guys off than to bother to bring them in. By and large, statistics show that the emphasis was on capture and interrogation.

There were many problems and flaws in the Phoenix Program, mostly problems of execution – inertia, slowness – rather than problems of concept. For example, we did not accept the inflated Vietnamese figures as to the infrastructure they brought in. The Phoenix record and reporting systems that we developed and sold to the GVN finally, were the first large-scale professional attempt at this. We plugged blacklists and lists of "most-wanted." We set up our own evaluation staff to screen every one of these cases by name, and we generally accepted only about two-thirds of the names the Vietnamese brought in. So we worked hard on measurement programs, etc... The disposition of captured VCI was a constant thorn. In the first place, the procedures for handling [detainees] were not very good. A lot of them were let go. We were constantly working on this....

...We stressed the rifle shot [approach]. Target the individual. Identify him through careful police work. Then go out and pick up that guy. Don't surround a hamlet and herd together 5000 people and then go through them. You can't do a good job that way. The 1st Air Cav up in Binh Dinh Province was running these "Dragnet" operations and claiming a thousand VCI a month. Their figures were ridiculous. What they were bringing in was everybody – farmers, cooks, bakers, candlestick makers, etc. – and calling them VCI. We were sure that this was not sensible. I am not an admirer of "County Fair" and "Dragnet" type operations. They generally were very loose sieves. They gathered up hundreds of people. They did not have an effective mechanism for screening. They didn't know whom they were looking for.

INTERVIEWER: In April 1969 I found in IV Corps, for example, they were doing a lot of searching the village and bringing everybody into the square. At least that gave them an opportunity to fingerprint everybody, and they turned up a lot of deserters and draft dodgers and this sort of thing over and above VCI. This was the "Dragnet" concept, I think.

KOMER: Only partly. This was also the National ID Card Program conceived by CORDS Public Safety Division. The old GVN ID cards were sloppy and could be easily forged. The U.S. sold the GVN on a program to issue revised, tamperproof identification cards to every Vietnamese man and woman over age 15. This key program had been moving very slowly under USAID, and when CORDS took it over I regarded it as crucial to population control in a counter-insurgency war. It was potentially invaluable to identification and tracking of VCI, catching draft dodgers, and the like. I took it personally under my wing, and made several major changes, but it still moved all too slowly, even though I kept pushing it personally...

...AID got good FBI experts to design the system. We set up a great big national fingerprint center in the police compound in downtown Saigon. We trained hundreds of little Vietnamese girls at the technique of collating and filing fingerprints, and we worked out every detail of the program so that we could, over a period of three years, give a new ID card and fingerprint everybody in the country. I kept emphasizing: "Let's fingerprint the VCI. We've got to have a central file. We capture a guy in Vinh Dinh. We interrogate him; we identify him; we fingerprint him; and then some guy releases him. He may show up the next time down in Lam Dong. How can you trace him?"

...To sum up, Phoenix/Phung Hoang was one of those relatively low efficiency GVN programs that take a long time to get up steam. It was very hard to raise to real efficiency. What the British did in Malaya was to develop this sort of thing over a period of 25 years. We started really in June 1967. The fact that by the end of 1968 it was going somewhere, because again it was a Vietnamese program, is impressive. Eighteen months was pretty fast in one sense, and Phung Hoang was outstandingly cost-effective from the standpoint of very modest resources invested. Cumulative results were beginning to show at the end of 1969. However inefficient Phung Hoang is, I believe that it is cumulatively eroding the VCI, which is critically important.

A Communist Cadre Describes Pacification in My Tho Province During 1969–1970[4]

In the wake of the Tet Offensive, the US and South Vietnamese pacification efforts appeared to gain momentum. Because of the heavy losses that the NLF had sustained during the offensive, its forces were forced to pull back from many areas that they had previously controlled. In this account, an insurgent commander from the Mekong Delta province of My Tho describes the difficulties that the revolutionaries faced in the post-1968 period. Since this cadre's words were recorded while he was being interrogated by South Vietnamese security forces, the reader cannot rule out the possibility that he may have exaggerated or otherwise distorted the true circumstances of the situation. Nevertheless, his account seems to fit well with other sources that describe the 1969–1970 period as the darkest hour for the revolution in the south.

From 1969 to 1970, the GVN [the South Vietnamese government] launched the pacification program, which had a major impact [in My Tho]. I must say that there is no question that the pacification campaign had a powerful negative impact on the morale of the cadres and the rural people. During the Tet Offensive, the plan was to seize land and expand out from it like an oilspot. Unexpectedly, the pacification program shrank these areas bit by bit,

[4] Translation of an interview with a captured communist cadre, in David Elliott, *The Vietnamese War: Revolution and Social Change in the Mekong Delta, 1930–1975* (Armonk, NY: M. E. Sharpe, 2003), 2: 1178.

like a piece of meat drying in the sun. That idea of expanding the liberated areas after the Tet Offensive was gradually defeated, and then land was lost and there were no more people. Both cadres and people lost their confidence gradually, until it finally collapsed altogether. At the time the [communist party] infrastructure and the armed units tried continuously but didn't succeed. The cadres and units fled from one place to another, but there were no safe havens.

It was the same for me. I was at the time deputy commander of the province unit in charge of Route 20. I used the [NLF's] 514th Battalion to hit continuously along the road, with the aim of blocking pacification going deep into the liberated areas. Lt. Col. Hap, the GVN district chief, and I clashed all the time. [At first,] Lt. Col. Hap couldn't ever get across Route 20 or pacify that area. I tried hard to hold on to that area but gradually it shrank, though not rapidly as in other places...

At that time, the situation in the areas to the east...had deteriorated alarmingly, just like soap bubbles exposed to the sunlight. The cadres there took refuge but had no place to hide. The province Party committee had to send me to northern Chau Thanh district to destroy pacification. I restored Front control [in that area] for a time, but then Route 20 was lost. This time a direct order [from my superiors] sent me back to Route 20. It was not a routine order from just the province Party committee. This was because Route 20 in northern Cai Be was the key area of the region...This was the key gateway for the region to send cadres and material from [the regional headquarters] down here. I returned to Route 20 and [shortly thereafter] northern Chau Thanh had all its villages cleared and the cadres all ran like hell and hid.

I felt really let down. My life was miserable and my struggle was really worthless. I couldn't hold the territory and I myself had to be exiled like a sacrificial beast. I saw clearly that I couldn't do anything under those circumstances....

I returned to Route 20 and sent Ba Kieu, the deputy unit commander, to Tan Phu to block pacification. A few days later he was shot and killed.

Le Duc Tho and Chinese Foreign Minister Chen Yi Discuss the Paris Peace Talks (1968)[5]

Although the Tet Offensive of 1968 did not lead to the military breakthrough that Vietnamese communist leaders had hoped to achieve, it had a profound

5 Document No. 38, Transcript of a conversation between Chen Yi and Le Duc Tho, 17 Oct 1968, printed in Odd Arne Westad *et al.*, eds., *77 Conversations between Chinese and Foreign Leaders on the Wars in Indochina, 1964–1977*, Cold War International History Project Working Paper No. 22 (Washington, DC: CWIHP, May 1998), 136–137.

impact on the war and especially on the diplomatic strategies pursued by all the governments involved in it. In early April 1968, in response to the partial suspension of Operation Rolling Thunder announced by Lyndon Johnson in his March 31 speech, DRV leaders consented to meet with US representatives in Paris. In October, after several months of wrangling, negotiators agreed on a framework for peace talks involving four parties: the United States, the governments of North and South Vietnam, and the National Liberation Front.

Hanoi's participation in the four-party talks in Paris was supported by the Soviet Union, which had been pressing DRV leaders for years to seek a negotiated settlement with Washington. However, the DRV decision was criticized by Chinese communist leaders, who warned their Vietnamese counterparts that it was a mistake to begin peace talks before they had gained the upper hand on the battlefield. The growing tension between Hanoi and Beijing was apparent during an October 1968 secret meeting between Chinese Foreign Minister Chen Yi and Le Duc Tho, a senior North Vietnamese official. As this transcript of their conversation reveals, Chen Yi was worried that North Vietnam was seeking to exploit China's intensifying rivalry with the Soviet Union (the "Sino-Soviet split" that had emerged during the early 1960s). In response to Chen's criticisms, Le Duc Tho indicated that Hanoi intended to keep its own counsel. He also pointedly reminded Chen Yi that the Chinese had given bad advice to DRV leaders in the past.

Beijing, 17 October 1968

CHEN YI: Since last April, when you accepted the U.S. partial cessation of bombing and held peace talks with [the Americans], you have lost the initiative in the negotiations to them. Now, you accept quadripartite negotiations. You lost to them once more. Therefore, this will cause more losses for the Vietnamese people, especially the people in the South.

At present, Washington and Saigon are publicizing the negotiations, showing the fact that you have accepted the conditions put forward by the United States. Your returning home for party instruction all the more proves it to the world's people. With your acceptance of the quadripartite negotiations, you handed the puppet government legal recognition, thus eliminating the National Liberation Front's status as the unique legal representative of the people in the South. So, the Americans have helped their puppet regime to gain legal status while you have made the Front lose its own prestige. This makes us wonder whether you have strengthened the enemy's position while weakening ours. You are acting in contradiction to the teachings of President Ho, the great leader of the Vietnamese people, thus destroying President Ho's prestige among the Vietnamese people.

This time, your acceptance of quadripartite negotiations will help Johnson and [U.S. Vice President and Democratic Party presidential candidate Hubert H.] Humphrey win their elections, thus letting the people in the South remain under the rule of the US imperialists and their puppets. You do not liberate the people in the South but cause them more losses. We do not want you to make another mistake. We believe that the people in the South of Vietnam do not want to surrender and they will win the war. But now the cause is more difficult and the price [for victory] more expensive.

In our opinion, in a very short time, you have accepted the compromising and capitulationist proposals put forward by the Soviet revisionists. So, between our two parties and the two governments of Vietnam and China, there is nothing more to talk about. Nevertheless, as President Ho has said, our relationship is one of both comrades and brothers; we will therefore consider the changes of the situation in November and will have more comments.

LE DUC THO: On this matter, we will wait and see. And the reality will give us the answer. We have gained experience over the past 15 years. Let reality justify.

CHEN YI: We signed the Geneva accords in 1954 when the U.S. did not agree to do so. We withdrew our armed forces from the South to the North, thus letting the people in the South be killed. We at that time made a mistake in which we [Chinese] shared a part.

LE DUC THO: Because we listened to your advice.

CHEN YI: You just mentioned that in the Geneva Conference, you made a mistake because you followed our advice. But this time, you will make another mistake if you do not take our words into account.

Henry Kissinger Negotiates with Le Duc Tho (1971)[6]

In 1969, the newly installed Nixon administration proposed to hold secret peace talks with North Vietnam. (These secret talks were to take place in parallel with the four-party negotiations, which had been publicly announced

---

[6] Luu Van Loi and Nguyen Anh Vu, eds., *Le Duc Tho–Kissinger Negotiations in Paris* (Thế Giới Publishers, Hanoi 1996), 194–201.

*in Paris the previous year.) DRV leaders accepted Nixon's proposal, and US
National Security Advisor Henry Kissinger held the first in a series of
meetings with high-level North Vietnamese officials at a safe house in Paris in
early 1970. Kissinger's counterpart during many of these sessions was Le Duc
Tho, who was widely known as a close ally of Le Duan.*

*Kissinger hoped that the secret talks would lead in short order to a peace
agreement, but he soon discovered that the North Vietnamese were
formidable negotiators. In this excerpt from the records of a meeting held in
July 1971, the participants discussed one of the points on which Le Duc Tho
and his comrades were most unyeilding their insistence that South
Vietnamese President Nguyen Van Thieu would have to be removed from
office before any peace agreement could be implemented.*

The 26 July meeting began with the statement of Xuan Thuy[7], and a series
of questions about almost all issues, concentrating on two major questions:
the deadline for the withdrawal of US forces and the question of the Saigon
administration [of RVN President Nguyen Van Thieu]. Xuan Thuy urged
clarifications of the vague answers of Kissinger. At one point Kissinger commented, "No point can escape the minister's attention."

Regarding the troop withdrawal, Xuan Thuy repeated that the US was
not ready to set a definite date, though it had been agreed upon in principle,
thus prolonging the negotiation and not hastening it. He queried Kissinger:
"Is it true that you refuse to replace the Saigon administration headed by
the Nguyen Van Thieu group?" He remarked that, "In the US proposal, the
question of the Saigon administration is not laid down as a separate point.
It is clear that without solving both military and political issues in SVN we
cannot settle the problem."

Regarding the questions that the US side had agreed to in principle or
would rewrite or complete, Xuan Thuy said that the Vietnamese side would
study them. There was no great difficulty, not even in Kissinger's statement
about grant aid.

In conclusion, Xuan Thuy said "We have made some progress by taking
our 9 points and your 7 points as subjects of discussions, but there remain
two key points that you have said nothing about: the time limit for troop
withdrawal linked with the release of prisoners of war and the administration in [South Vietnam]. We have clearly said that you should replace the
Nguyen Van Thieu group. Your point 7 makes no mention of this question

---

[7] Xuan Thuy: Foreign Minister of the DRV from 1963 to 1965 and Chief of the DRV negotiating team at the four-party talks in Paris during 1968–1973. He often attended and participated
in the secret talks with Kissinger.

and you have not said anything about it. You said that we should agree on a framework but this key point is the spinal column of the framework. If you do not refer to it, how can the framework take shape?"

Le Duc Tho added: "A framework without a spinal column."

Kissinger said: "Mr. Special Adviser is again engaging in creative writing."

Le Duc Tho continued: "A framework without a backbone will collapse."

[Le Duc Tho] went on: "I would like to make a general review of your views regarding the solution of the Vietnam problem and your approach to the solution on of the problems of Indochina.

"You have gone too deep into the war in Vietnam and in Indochina. In the process, you have met with many failures and now you are facing many difficulties in finding a way to settle the war. We have also realized that you want to disengage from the Vietnam war and the Indochina war, but you are calculating and trying to get the greatest advantage for your side. Therefore you imagine withdrawing in ways: negotiation and Vietnamization. You think that these two ways will complement each other. Vietnamization will help maintain in [South Vietnam] a strong administration and a strong army as instruments for the implementation of your neocolonialist schemes. If negotiation is unsuccessful, active Vietnamization will facilitate the achievement of your intention of turning SVN into a new-type colony.

"Your negotiating tactics are aimed at that objective. Therefore you always separate the military issues from the political issues. You try to elude the political issues and only pay attention to the military issues. Moreover, to solve the military issues, your intention is to withdraw slowly so that no matter whether a negotiated solution is possible or not, you will always be able to maintain the Nguyen Van Thieu administration.

"For that reason you are unwilling to set a definite date for complete troop withdrawal, but you attach conditions to the withdrawal. Studying your framework we clearly see the points you agree to are all in your interest. This is also true for the points to which you demand amendments. But there are two points which are the backbone of the framework, as minister Xuan Thuy said, and you put them outside of the framework.

"In brief, the points you agree to or to which you propose amendments are subsidiary points. As for the principal ones, your approach is different from ours. The principal alleged concessions and points are that you will give up demanding that we release prisoners of war before the completion of troop withdrawal. Last time we said these were points of progress, but very tiny ones as compared to the points we have proposed and you have agreed to. You say you want a rapid solution, but your desire is contradictory to your objective."

Le Duc Tho stressed: "We agree to the framework and from there we should go into concrete discussions. The general framework is acceptable to both sides, but first of all we should agree on the two major questions: point 1 (time limit for troop withdrawal) and point 3 (the administration in Saigon)."

In conclusion, Le Duc Tho added: "Over the past few years, you have gone here and there to seek a way out. I wonder whether you have drawn from your experience. In fact, your efforts are futile and they make things more complicated."

Le Duc Tho said slowly and explicitly: "There is no miraculous way to settle the Vietnam problem other than seriously negotiating with us at the Paris conference on the basis of our proposals and yours. In a chess match, the winner and the loser must be the players themselves, there is no other way. We are independent in solving our problem."

Kissinger welcomed the views expressed by Le Duc Tho and Xuan Thuy; almost all of them were positive and constructive [he said]. Then, he also raised many questions about the influence Le Duc Tho and Xuan Thuy might have on their allies in SVN, about Vietnam's consent to keeping its forces within its borders, particularly about the replacement of Thieu, the difference between the new government and that of the Thieu administration, the change of persons or of both persons and policies, about what the future government in Saigon looks like, etc.

He also said that Le Duc Tho's analysis of the US strategy was correct and intelligent, then he commented on Vietnamese strategy:

"If I understand you correctly, your strategy is aimed at securing two results: that our forces be withdrawn as soon as possible and after the completion of withdrawal, you will overthrow the existing political structure in SVN. Your demand is not a concession but a requirement that we offer to Hanoi the opportunity to reach your objectives. If you can secure them by yourselves, we shall respect the results, but probably you will not succeed in obtaining them at these negotiations. Of course, neither of us will sign an agreement to offer to the other side all the objectives it has set."

Kissinger continued his statement on three major issues: "Regarding US aid. After the signing of an agreement of principle, President Nixon will recommend to the Congress the approval of a five-year economic aid program for the Indochinese countries . . . which may amount to 7. 5 billion dollars, of which 2 to 3. 5 billion dollars will be allocated to North Vietnam. The reimbursement of the aid is not a problem. Over 2 / 3 will be grant aid, 1/3 as a very long-term loan with very low interest . . . with no conditions attached."

Regarding the time limit for troop withdrawal, Kissinger said, "We are prepared to fix a date for the completion of the withdrawal of our forces and those of our allies within nine months of the signing of the agreement."

Regarding the political issues in SVN, Kissinger recognized that they were the key subject for Vietnam. He saw that Vietnam wanted to achieve its fighting aims through US actions. Vietnam could not demand from the US both a rapid withdrawal and the settlement of all internal political problems. He further [observed] that the withdrawal of US forces would have a political effect before its completion . . . The US acceptance of the point on neutrality, out of Madame Binh's 5 points, would already have an important political impact in SVN and the US announcement of the limitation of aid to Saigon or its neutrality in the coming election would also have a strong political influence in Saigon.[8] He reiterated that the US [does not want] to upset the political situation in Saigon but it was prepared to assume an active role in finding a solution. However, after the US withdrawal and the success of Vietnamization, the US would no longer have the power to influence politics in SVN. He stressed that in the future, the US would not be a threat to the independence of Vietnam but that other countries nearer Vietnam might be better candidates for this.

Answering Le Duc Tho's allusion to his trip to China, Kissinger said: "We know that the solution to the Vietnam war should be found in Paris. We respect and admire the spirit of independence that you have always shown . . . We do not want to find a solution anywhere other than here."

Finally he proposed that the two parties should agree on a statement of principle as instructions for the negotiating delegations at Kléber to move into detailed discussions.

Xuan Thuy raised questions again regarding the deadline for troop withdrawal within 9 months, the start of the withdrawal, the retaining of technical personnel, the solution of the Indochina problems, the international conference, etc.

He remarked that if a definite date were not set for the beginning of the withdrawal it would be like the announcement "meals are offered free tomorrow here!"

However the most debated question was always the issue of administration in Saigon. Xuan Thuy said:

---

[8] "Madame Binh" was Madame Nguyen Thi Binh, the Foreign Minister of the NLF's Provisional Revolutionary Government. Binh represented the NLF at the four-party peace talks in Paris during 1968–1973. The reference here is apparently to her earlier negotiating proposal, which contained a ban on the formation of military alliances between any Indochinese government and any outside power, as well as a ban on foreign military bases in Indochina.

"If you persist in maintaining Thieu, your honor will be smeared. On the contrary, if you replace Thieu the people in the US and in SVN will welcome you. Moreover, we do not request that you make a public announcement. Go ahead and take action! You don't have to announce it."

Kissinger said: "That is obvious!"

Xuan Thuy replied: "How can it be obvious, no one knows it but you and us? Otherwise, you would prove to want to keep Thieu. The questions of the date of troop withdrawal and the replacement of Thieu, if not solved, will prolong the negotiations despite the fact that we want to progress rapidly."

Le Duc Tho said: "It can be said that today we have not discussed the political issues at all. You still keep your intention to settle the military issues only. No war can be ended through the solution of military questions only, while ignoring the political questions. You are advancing very slowly in negotiations."

Kissinger replied: "You are putting forward demands and criticizing our answers as if you were examining a student at an oral examination. We cannot come to an agreement in this way."

He disagreed with Le Duc Tho that there had been no discussion of political issues. He repeated that what the US could not do was secretly agree with Vietnam on replacing the leader of a country allied to the US. Should the US take such actions, Thieu would already be in a disadvantageous position and another candidate to the liking of Vietnam might win the election.

The discussions became tense. Le Duc Tho said: "Not any Vietnamese who has been struggling for years fails to know what the political results will be in SVN. If you just make a vague statement about standing neutral in the election, that will not do!"

Kissinger corrected him: "What I mean is a statement of non-commitment and not a statement of neutrality. Any government in SVN should pursue a foreign policy of neutrality, should accept a limitation of military aid from other countries, and should agree to a number of the 7 points proposed by Madame Binh. This is a statement of non-commitment by both sides."

Le Duc Tho replied: "But if the key question remains unsolved, how can the framework take shape?"

The meeting came to an end. Le Duc Tho said that both sides should study each other's views. "If you feel it necessary to meet again, we shall meet."

Kissinger said: "In 1954, J. F. Dulles wanted to have military bases, now you are negotiating with an administration that is not interested in military bases in SVN.[9] For the US, Vietnam is no longer a key problem. We know that you still have a great deal of suspicion. That is the tragedy!"

---

[9] Kissinger is contrasting the Nixon administration's position in 1971 with that of the Eisenhower administration in 1954. At that time, Secretary of State John Foster Dulles spearheaded

Both sides agreed that another meeting should be held. Xuan Thuy urged that at the next meeting, the US should present something concrete and substantial.

Kissinger told him: "It will be difficult to persuade Mr. Nixon to let me come here once again but I hope I will succeed." He proposed that the next meeting should take place on Saturday, August 7.

Xuan Thuy said: "To give you enough time to persuade Mr. Nixon, we should fix a later date, for instance during the second half of August."

Finally it was agreed that the parties would meet again on August 16.

Richard Nixon and Henry Kissinger Discuss the Fate of South Vietnam (August 1972)[10]

In late March of 1972, North Vietnamese forces in South Vietnam launched a massive new offensive to try to win the Vietnam War – their first such attempt since the Tet attacks of 1968. During the first few weeks of the offensive, PAVN troops won several victories and appeared close to a major breakthrough. However, stronger-than-expected resistance from ARVN units and a massive US tactical bombing campaign (codenamed Operation Linebacker) eventually halted the North Vietnamese advance. In the late summer, as it became clear that the offensive had failed, both US and DRV leaders refocused on the negotiations in Paris. This would lead eventually to the signing of the Paris Peace Agreement of January 1973, in which the US agreed to withdraw its remaining combat forces from Vietnam and the DRV agreed to return hundreds of American prisoners of war.

Why did Richard Nixon and Henry Kissinger endorse the Paris Agreement? Both men would later insist that the accords offered a genuine chance to achieve "peace with honor" in Vietnam. However, many historians insist that the two leaders knew all along that the agreement was a sham, since it did not require Hanoi to withdraw the hundreds of thousands of PAVN troops that had been infiltrated into South Vietnam. In an Oval Office conversation recorded by Nixon in early August 1972, the president and Kissinger discussed the future of South Vietnam and its leader, Nguyen Van Thieu. As their comments show, Nixon's and Kissinger's thoughts about the prospective peace agreement were shaped not only by geopolitical concerns but also by US domestic politics – and especially by the fact that Nixon was due to stand for re-election in November 1972.

---

the creation of the Southeast Asian Treaty Organization (SEATO), an organization specifically designed to facilitate foreign intervention in South Vietnam in the event of a communist invasion.

[10] Conversation 760-6, Richard Nixon Presidential Materials Project, National Archives and Research Administration.

PRESIDENT NIXON: Let's be perfectly cold-blooded about it. If you look at it from the standpoint of our game with the Soviets and the Chinese, from the standpoint of running this country, I think we could take, in my view, almost anything, frankly, that we can force on Thieu. Almost anything. I just come down to that. You know what I mean? Because I have a feeling we would not be doing, like I feel about the Israelis, I feel that in the long run we're probably not doing them an in—uh, a disfavor due to the fact that I feel that the North Vietnamese are so badly hurt that the South Vietnamese are probably gonna do fairly well [unclear—overlapping voices]. Also due to the fact—because I look at the tide of history out there, South Vietnam probably can never even survive anyway. I'm just being perfectly candid—I—

HENRY KISSINGER: In the pull-out area—

NIXON: [Unclear] got to [unclear] that we can get certain guarantees so that they aren't, uh, as you know, looking at the foreign policy process, though, I mean, you've got to be—we also have to realize, Henry, that winning an election is important.

It's terribly important this year. But can we have a viable foreign policy if a year from now or two years from now, North Vietnam gobbles up South Vietnam? That's the real question.

KISSINGER: If a year or two years from now North Vietnam gobbles up South Vietnam, we can have a viable foreign policy if it looks as if it's the result of South Vietnamese incompetence. If we now sell out in such a way that, say, within a three- to four-month period, we have pushed [South Vietnamese President Nguyen Van] Thieu over the brink—we ourselves—I think, there is going to be—even the Chinese won't like that. I mean, they'll pay verbal—verbally, they'll like it—

NIXON: But it'll worry them.

KISSINGER: But it will worry everybody. And domestically in the long run it won't help us all that much because our opponents will say we should've done it three years ago.

NIXON: I know.

KISSINGER: So we've got to find some formula that holds the thing together a year or two, after which—after a year, Mr. President, Vietnam will be a backwater. If we settle it, say, this October, by January '74, no one will give a damn.

Discussion questions

1. Based on William Westmoreland's memorandum on refugees and Robert Komer's interview about the Phoenix Program, do you agree with the arguments of critics who said that US pacification tactics in Vietnam were counterproductive to the goal of winning the "hearts and minds" of villagers? Why or why not?

2. Does the account by the captured communist cadre from My Tho support the contention of some historians that the United States and South Vietnam were winning the war in the countryside by 1970? Explain.

3. Based on the documents in this chapter, why did North Vietnam agree to participate in peace talks with the United States after the 1968 Tet Offensive?

4. What were Richard Nixon's and Henry Kissinger's ultimate objectives in Vietnam? Did they betray America's South Vietnamese allies, as some critics have alleged?

Chapter 11   Victory and Defeat

Jacques Leslie, A Visit to Viet Cong Territory (1995)[1]

The Paris Agreement of January 1973 did not bring peace to Vietnam. Even before the last US combat units had left the country in March, the tenuous ceasefire that the agreement was supposed to establish in South Vietnam had begun to break down. By the summer of 1973, the so-called "war of the flags" was under way in the south, as both North and South Vietnamese forces sought to grab territory controlled by the other side.

Jacques Leslie, an American reporter for the Los Angeles Times, travelled to a part of the Mekong Delta that was under communist control in early 1973 – perhaps the first US journalist to do so. In his 1995 memoir, Leslie recounted how he, a French colleague, and their Vietnamese interpreter nervously crossed into NLF territory, unsure of the reception they would receive. While Leslie found the local population's enthusiasm for the revolution hard to gauge, his account shows that the communists' power in the countryside was far from spent.

As we glided down the canal, word spread that we were journalists, and people greeted us by waving Viet Cong flags: I felt like a passenger on a Rose Bowl float. Once Véronique told me to look towards the canal bank, and I turned quickly, for I could hear excitement in her voice: two Viet Cong soldiers stood there, coolly regarding us. With their black pajamas and AK-47s, they looked like the Platonic ideal of VC soldiers. I took pictures. We had arrived.

[1] Jacques Leslie, *The Mark: A War Correspondent's Memoir of Vietnam and Cambodia* (New York: Four Walls Eight Windows, 1995), 139–145.

A few minutes later other soldiers waved and called us ashore, and guided us along a path. All the friendliness was eerie, and it took me a while to see why: we never took anyone by surprise. Word of our presence always preceded us; in this zone without telephones, communication triumphed. More and more villagers followed us, looking pleased, like fishermen with an unexpected catch. At last we were delivered to the village chief, who stood on the trail, quietly watching us. In my mind the idea of a Communist village chief conjured up a steely build, chiseled cheekbones, and a hero's pose, and this man looked stamped out of the mold. Just one feature was discordant, and it only added to his mystique: he was missing a thumb. He was dressed just like the villagers: his flashlight and radio were what set him apart.

He said his name was Le Hoang Oanh, and asked for our business cards, of all things. Perhaps he intended the gesture to convey formality, but it struck us as innocent – compared to the net of South Vietnamese visas and press cards in which we were constantly entangled, a request for a mere business card was practically amusing. My card all but announced that I was an American, but if Oanh understood that, it didn't show. All he did was pronounce, in an even, understated tone, "We are happy to welcome foreign correspondents to visit our liberation area. This is the first time the press has come here." To him "here" perhaps meant the village, but to us it encompassed all Communist territory in South Vietnam. We felt flushed with triumph, one far more astounding to us than Oanh or the other villagers understood. The people around us cheered, and Oanh smiled. A woman handed glasses of iced tea to the three of us. It tasted like ambrosia.

We had reached the quiet center. The Viet Cong soldiers looked us over and didn't shoot; the village chief welcomed us. We were in the forbidden dark zone, and found that the sun indeed shone here, seemingly more brightly than in Saigon. The people around us didn't look murderous; on the contrary, they displayed more warmth than I'd seen in 13 months in government-controlled areas. My heart opened, swelled with the notion that Véronique and I were explorers, not just of Viet Cong terrain but of the humanly possible, and that what sustained our journey was not so much our courage as our trust.

"Be sure to provide double protection for our guests," Oanh told the village security cadre. He instructed three messengers to report on our presence to the Viet Cong district secretary, the chairman of the village revolutionary committee, and ordinary villagers respectively. The orders were carried out immediately, a fact which distinguished the messengers from their languid Saigon counterparts. Discipline in the village was impressive, perhaps overly so: when the village chief asked us to cease taking notes, as we'd been doing since we entered the village, we considered it prudent to accede.

Oanh proposed an afternoon tour beginning with an inspection of war damage he said was caused by ARVN ceasefire violations. As we walked to the first site, we were escorted by a barefoot soldier and a few children whom Oanh had instructed to carry Viet Cong flags on long bamboo poles. A festive mood pervaded our entourage, which constantly grew larger. Children giggled. I was handed a conical straw hat to shield my head from the sun; when I put it on, the people pointed and laughed good-naturedly. One boy pointed to a Viet Cong banner and said to us in awkward English, "My flag." I surmised that he'd spent time in ARVN territory, as probably most of the other villagers had; some of them may have crossed back and forth between the two zones daily.

As we walked, Oanh answered our questions about the village. We were in Binh Phu, a 100-percent Viet Cong-controlled village seven square miles and 6,800 people. We were amazed that the Viet Cong occupied territory so close to the main road through the Delta — from where we stood at one point, we could see cars plying it. I'd driven that stretch many times without suspecting the Viet Cong were so close.

Considering that we could see battle smoke twisting upwards in the distance, I thought Oanh's claims of ARVN ceasefire violations in the village were plausible, but the evidence he showed us undercut his assertion. We saw bomb craters, splintered rooftops, houses burnt to their foundations, but the damage almost certainly was done months or years earlier, not in the previous two and a half days. A bomb crater filled with murky water obviously had been there a long time. So Oanh was prepared to lie to us.

Continuing on our tour, we were confronted by surprising evidence of the thoroughness of the village's ceasefire preparations, as several peasants greeted us with harangues and angry gestures. Véronique and I were momentarily puzzled, but since we couldn't understand what they were saying, our attention was soon diverted. Later on, when Long told us what the villagers said, we realized they'd mistaken us for members of the peace-supervisory force, and were demanding payment for war damage. It was a planned performance, delivered before the wrong audience, which unexpectedly revealed that the Communists had high expectations for the ceasefire. The peace-supervisory force, for instance, never came close to playing a significant role, and combat hardly paused in some areas, yet all the ceasefire preparations in Binh Phu suggested that the Communists expected a peaceful struggle at least for a time after the ceasefire began. No wonder Binh Phu's residents greeted us so enthusiastically: taking their cues from Viet Cong preparations, they probably believed the ceasefire would hold. To them we were harbingers of peace.

Oanh led us inside a pagoda partially destroyed by explosives, another example of alleged American and ARVN-wrought damage. With 50 people gathered around us inside that shattered shell, the setting appeared sufficiently theatrical for a formal announcement, which was what Oanh had in mind. Implicitly acknowledging for the first time that he wasn't entirely sanguine about our presence, he announced, "The people are happy to receive all journalists, including those who work for the rebel government of Saigon, but on the sole condition that they do their job fairly." A man behind Oanh whispered in his ear, and then Oanh announced that we could take notes. Grateful to be relieved of the burden of trying to memorize everything we saw and heard, we took out our notebooks, and Oanh invited us to ask questions. We began gingerly, first asking what his job as village chief entailed. "My function is to command politically and militarily with the goal of conquering the American aggressors," he said. We asked how many villagers were members of the National Liberation Front, the umbrella Communist political apparatus. "Because this is a question of defense, I can't say how many people there are, but I can say that the Front represents the whole population of the village, all religions, and also men who work for the Saigon government."

It was another rhetorical reply, more evidence of Oanh's suspicions about us, but I wasn't bothered. It was enough for us to know that our lives weren't in danger, that we faced no threat of punishment, that we were free to leave the Viet Cong zone when we wished. Oanh's evasions were the least of what we had to fear, and were understandable considering that the United States had ceased being his archenemy only two days earlier. I was more struck by his decorousness and restraint than his unwillingness to give us accurate information. My job was to check his assertions against the physical evidence, to distinguish the truth from his rhetoric.

In the midst of our questioning a messenger handed Oanh a pink slip of paper. It had obviously come from his superiors. He read it, then announced, "The members of this village are very happy to invite you two journalists to spend the night here to celebrate together a ceremony of peace." Véronique and I exchanged glances, recognizing the elation in each other's eyes; the journey was surpassing our expectations. Our only worry was that some other journalist might have duplicated our feat in another Communist zone and would report on it that night, but we'd happily take the gamble. When we accepted, Oanh applauded, and the surrounding villagers joined in....

Oanh gave another formal statement, in which we were told to write "what our consciences dictate" — he was again revealing his distrust. Then we were led out of the pagoda, and immediately more villagers hailed us.

We were football heroes; they were cheerleaders. They shouted, "Welcome the correspondents! Welcome peace! We support peace! Welcome!" Long told us the next day that Oanh had instructed villagers to make the chants, but at the time we were more mindful of the villagers' apparent enthusiasm than their lack of spontaneity. Wherever we walked for the next hour, people hailed us on a cue from a cadre with "Welcome!" Youths appeared to carry our packs and help us across the gangplank-like bamboo crossings.

As we walked to a villager's house where we would have dinner, Oanh, more relaxed now, explained a bit of his background to Long. Forty-three years old, he had been an N.L.F. member for many years. He said he was arrested by government troops in 1969, then paid a bribe for the substantial sum of $125; as a result, he was released from prison three months later. He said villagers donated the money; I imagine that "villagers" was a euphemism for the N.L.F. Despite Oanh's revolutionary rhetoric, he didn't give the impression of being a one-dimensional zealot. He had his bourgeois habits, such as chain-smoking, and he wore, of all things, a Seiko watch, set on Hanoi time.

The conversation between Oanh and Long had an unquestioned potential for volatility. On the one hand, Oanh's flashlight, radio, and lighter had all been taken off the bodies of American soldiers, and he had lost his thumb fighting against the U.S. Ninth Infantry Division in 1969...

The sun had set by the time we reached the house where we'd have dinner. At first Oanh, Véronique, Long, about fifteen villagers, and I crowded inside the tiny earthen-floored house, uniquely situated in the middle of the rice field. We were offered a sweet candy, our appetizer, and then the four of us had a chat. Still preoccupied with our trustworthiness, Oanh asked if we intended to write the truth. "You came here unexpectedly," he said. "We have nothing to hide. We hope that what you see is the truth." Then he asked if we believed what we had seen so far. Searching for the right word, I said I'd been impressed. Oanh asked Véronique what the flag of the French Communist Party looked like, and after hearing the answer, asked us what parties we belonged to. I said, "As a journalist I don't belong to any party." Véronique later told me she was appalled by this un-Marxist comment, while Gibson, when he found out about it, was so pleased he cited it in the *Times* newsletter as evidence of my objectivity. I disagreed with both of them: I meant the remark to reflect not objectivity, which I considered an illusory standard of journalism, but independence.

Bui Tin, An Account of the Surrender of South Vietnam (1981)[2]

The end of the Vietnam War came remarkably quickly. In early 1975, after nearly two years of stalemate, PAVN units broke through ARVN defenses in the central highlands. By March, most of central Vietnam was under PAVN control, and North Vietnamese forces were moving closer to Saigon. In mid-April, the communist advance was temporarily halted by the ARVN 18th Infantry Division, which put up fierce resistance at the town of Xuan Loc. However, Xuan Loc fell on April 21, leaving the South Vietnamese capital virtually undefended. RVN President Nguyen Van Thieu resigned that day and fled into foreign exile. Thieu's successors tried to negotiate a ceasefire with the advancing enemy, but to no avail. By April 28, Saigon had been encircled by North Vietnamese troops and US leaders acknowledged that both the city and the war were lost.

On the morning of April 30, North Vietnamese infantry and armor units entered Saigon and quickly took control of the city. Independence Palace, the official seat of the South Vietnamese government, was captured around 11:30am, after a North Vietnamese tank crashed through its front gate. Among the South Vietnamese officials taken into custody at the palace was Acting President Duong Van Minh – the former ARVN general who had led the coup against Ngo Dinh Diem in 1963, and who had been sworn in just two days earlier.

The fall of the South Vietnamese capital had come so quickly that there was no flag-rank North Vietnamese officer on the scene to accept the South Vietnamese surrender. The task of officially ending the war thus fell to Bui Tin, a North Vietnamese Army Colonel and journalist who worked for the PAVN's official newspaper. Although Bui Tin would later become a prominent critic of the Vietnamese Communist Party and its policies, at the time he was overjoyed and relieved that the war had ended in victory for the party and its allies. In this 1981 interview, he recalled the dramatic events of April 30 and the feelings they inspired.

Regarding the 1975 Offensive, we knew after the fall of Da Nang things would progress very quickly. We therefore headed for Ban Me Thuot. When we arrived in Ban Me Thuot we went to the Command Headquarters of the Liberation Army at Dau Tieng. We learned then that the General Offensive was about to begin; and so we headed for Bien Hoa, arriving on the night of the 29th.

[2] Interview conducted with Colonel Bui Tin, 2 February 1981, for *Vietnam: A Television History*, WBGH Media Library and Archives. Transcript at http://openvault. wgbh.org/catalog/vietnam-f729b0-interview-with-bui-tin-2-1981 [accessed 19 July 2012].

The advance from Bien Hoa to Saigon was very speedy, making everyone feel that the war was soon coming to an end. The soldiers were all very tired, but they were all happy to take part in an historic day. As we advanced with our tanks to the Saigon Bridge, a battle took place. Their F-5s attacked us from the air and their artillery shells came from the other side of the river. We had to charge across the river with many of our tanks.

After we reached the other side of the Saigon Bridge we went straight down Hong Thap Tu Avenue, turned to Thong Nhat, or Norodom, Avenue, and then headed straight for the Independence Palace. When we arrived at the Palace, I walked up to the second floor where members of the puppet administration were already gathering there. There were President Duong Van Minh, Prime Minister Vu Van Mau, Deputy Prime Minister Vu Van Huyen, and many ministers sitting in a large room there.

One of our officers went into the room and declared that a high officer of the Liberation Army was about to meet with them. I was then introduced into the room. As I entered, everybody stood up. Duong Van Minh then stepped out of the crowd and said: "I've been waiting for you since early this morning in order to turn over the government to you." To which I replied at once: "There is no need to talk of transferring the government to us. Your entire administration has collapsed. People cannot turn over what they don't have in their own hands. Your only choice is to surrender."

At that time all the people in the room bowed their heads in total dejection. Immediately after that there was artillery fire outside the Palace, causing all its windows and door to vibrate violently. The people in the room were frightened, and some cowered along the walls. I told them not to worry, saying that it was only the soldiers celebrating outside and that they were all safe where they were. When I saw that fear persisted on their faces, I said to Duong Van Minh, Vu Van Mau and their ministers who were sitting there that, "Although the war ends today, all Vietnamese are victors. Only the American imperialists are the vanquished. If you still have any feeling for the nation and the people, you can consider today your happy day." Their faces brightened up at this.

I would like to add that, as far as the advance on Saigon was concerned, we had five main targets. The first main target was the Independence Palace, the second was the Tan Son Nhut airport, the third was the ARVN Command Headquarters, the fourth was the Command Headquarters for Saigon, and the fifth was the National Police Headquarters.

As far as the American Embassy was concerned, we had orders that we should not attack and destroy it. It was alright to capture Americans. But the main thing was to allow the Americans to flee, thereby securing our victory. The American Embassy was never a target because we knew that the Americans had been fleeing from there and that the Embassy was not defended. If they had resisted us with arms, then we would have had to attack the place. But the important thing was to get them to surrender or to flee...

...I felt very happy although I was very tired that day, having had to sit in the tank all day without eating anything. I had only gulped down some water now and then from my canteen. But I felt very happy because I knew complete victory was at hand and that I was one of the participants of the historic event, an eyewitness as well as a person who helped in that historic event. That night, when I sprawled on the lawn of the Independence Palace with members of a communication unit, we all agreed that it was the happiest day of our lives because it was a day of complete victory for the nation, because the war ended.

Nguyen Thi Hoa, "Mom, I'm leaving now. I will make you very proud of me."[3]

In the weeks and days leading up to the fall of Saigon on April 30, 1975, huge numbers of South Vietnamese sought to flee the country. Many feared that they might be targeted by the advancing communist forces because they had served in the South Vietnamese government or military. Others simply did not want to live under communist rule. In the end, about 125,000 Vietnamese escaped. Most left the country by boat; others were flown to an offshore flotilla of US Navy ships in the largest helicopter airlift in history. But as the city's defenses crumbled, thousands more Vietnamese – including many whom US officials had promised to evacuate—were left behind.

Nguyen Thi Hoa was one of the Saigon residents who escaped. In this oral history, recorded in the late 1980s, she explains her last-minute decision to depart, as well as the wrenching turn of events that caused her to leave her sister and the rest of her family behind.

I grew up in Saigon. My dad and mom ran a small cafeteria near Tan Son Nhut that served the Americans. But when the Americans left in 1973, my dad lost the cafeteria. Not enough business. He also said that many of the Americans had left without paying him. He let them pay bills on a monthly basis. And many of them just left the country without paying their bills, and my dad lost his little business. After that he was bitter and he did not like the Americans any more. My dad and mom had to take other jobs and we didn't live very well after that.

[3] Larry Engelmann, *Tears Before the Rain: An Oral History of the Fall of South Vietnam* (New York: Oxford University Press, 1990), 273–275.

In the spring of 1975 my friends and I were very afraid that the Communists would come into Saigon and take over. There were stories that they would kill everybody, like they did in Hue in 1968. In Hue, during Tet, they killed 3,000 people for no reason at all. They tied their hands behind them and then shot them in the head. So we were very afraid.

But my father was not afraid. He said that those were just stories. He said that when the Communists took over nothing would change. But I didn't think so. I wanted to leave the country, and so did my younger sister. But my father said, "No. Nobody is going to leave. Nobody is going to die. Don't you believe what people are saying. The Communists are not going to hurt you."

I decided to go anyway. At first, I planned to go with my brother. But then he changed his mind and decided to stay. Then I decided to go with my sister. I was sixteen. My sister's name is Nguyen Thi Thiet Nghia. She is two years younger than me.

First, we had to find a way to get out. Of course, we did not have any money. But I found that one of my friends, Nguyen Thi Xuan, had parents whose friends owned a boat. And she said that if my sister and I wanted to leave on that boat we could. We would not need any money. So I said that we wanted to go on the boat and she said she would call when it was ready to go.

She called on the morning of April 29. She told us to go to a certain corner and a car would pick us up and take us to the Saigon River. My sister and I each took one bag of clothes. We had to sneak out of the house because my father did not want us to leave. So I did not say goodbye to my father. But we went to the restaurant where my mother was working. She didn't know that we would be going on that day. I said to her, "Mom, I'm leaving now. I will make you very proud of me." She kissed me and she kissed my sister and she said, "Okay. Good luck." She was very strong at that moment. She did not cry. She just said goodbye. If she had cried my sister and I would have stayed. I think she knew that. And she wanted us to go. Her name is Thanh Thi Tran. She made me strong enough to leave.

My sister and I went to the corner where the car was supposed to meet us. We waited, and the car never came. So my sister said, "I'll go back and call them and see when they are coming." She left her bag with me and went to a telephone. While she was gone the car came. It was full of people already. I told the driver that we had to wait for my sister and he said there was no way to do that. "We cannot wait," he said. "If we wait we cannot get out." So I got in the car. I left my sister's bag there on the curb. I was very nervous now and very frightened without my sister.

When we got to the river we had to hurry to get on the boat, and in the confusion I lost my bag. So I left the country without anything but the clothes on my back.

The name of the boat was the Tan Nam Viet. It was a big boat and it carried about five or six hundred people. I thought maybe my sister would arrive before the boat left. But she didn't.

I was very scared as we went down the river. Some of the people on the boat stayed on the deck to get a last look at Vietnam. The last thing they saw was the beach at Vung Tau. But I did not look back. I was so sad. I was leaving everything behind. And I didn't know where I was going or what would happen to me.

Later I learned that my sister tried to get out and she got caught. She was sent to jail. When she got out of jail she tried to leave Vietnam again. And again she was caught and put in a special camp. She is still in Vietnam.

Discussion questions

1. Does Jacques Leslie's account of his visit to NLF-controlled territory in the Mekong Delta show that the revolution had gained the upper hand in the struggle for control of the South Vietnamese countryside by 1973? Why or why not?

2. Based on the documents in this and earlier chapters, do you think that the defeat of South Vietnam in the Vietnam War was inevitable? Why or why not?

Chapter 12 Memories and Legacies

The POW/MIA Flag

Figure 12.1 POW/MIA Flag.
Source: http://en.wikipedia.org/wiki/POW/MIA_flag#mediaviewer/File:United_States_POW-MIA_flag.svg. Public Domain.

Original publication details: 12.3 OH0380, Kara Dixon Vuic Collection, The Vietnam Center and Archive, Texas Tech University. 12.5 Bush, New York Times, 2007. 12.6 Vo Van Kiet, 2005.

Except for the US national flag, the banner depicted above may be the most widely displayed flag in the United States today. The POW/MIA flag was designed in the early 1970s by the National League of Families of American Prisoners and Missing in Southeast Asia, an advocacy group that aimed to increase public sympathy for US servicemen who were being held as prisoners in Indochina. ("POW" stands for "prisoner of war" and "MIA" stands for "missing in action.") In light of the unpopularity of the war in the US at the time, the League's lobbying efforts were remarkably successful. The 591 American prisoners released by North Vietnam under the terms of the 1973 Paris Agreement were hailed as heroes upon their return to the United States – a stark contrast to the treatment of American prisoners who had returned home after the Korean War and other conflicts.

The controversy over American POWs and MIAs in Vietnam did not end in 1973. Some League supporters became convinced that Hanoi had lied about the total number of prisoners it had been holding. They concluded that some of the Americans listed as MIAs were still alive and languishing in Vietnamese prison camps. During the late 1970s, the myth of Americans "left behind" in Indochina gained broad currency in the United States, despite a lack of credible evidence to support it.

In the 1980s, when the popularity of this myth was at its peak, the POW/MIA flag became an American cultural icon. In 1988, the banner flew over the White House; it remains the only flag other than the American flag ever raised over the presidential residence. Congress subsequently ordered that the flag be installed in the rotunda of the US Capitol, and that it be flown over major government and military facilities on six national holidays. The POW/MIA flag also appears regularly over many post offices, local government buildings, and veterans' memorials across the country. Some critics see the enduring popularity of the black-and-white banner as evidence of a kind of national neurosis about Vietnam. But others – even some who do not believe in the "left behind" myth – continue to embrace the flag as a way to remember and honor the Americans who served in the war, including the hundreds still listed as missing.

Excerpt from Quang X. Pham, *A Sense of Duty: Our Journey from Vietnam to America* (2005)[1]

After the fall of South Vietnam in 1975, many Americans seemed determined to forget about the Vietnam War. However, the consequences of such a long

[1] Quang X. Pham, *A Sense of Duty: Our Journey from Vietnam to America* (New York: Presidio Press, 2005), 109–118.

and agonizing war could not be so easily ignored. This was particularly true for Vietnamese Americans, whose collective and individual fates were transformed at war's end. Although only about 15,000 Vietnamese emigrated to the US before 1975, hundreds of thousands more arrived in the US during the decade after the war. Many were "boat people," who had left Vietnam illegally by sea and who often endured harrowing voyages before reaching America. Like countless immigrants before them, Vietnamese Americans often found life in in their new country difficult; they experienced language barriers, poverty, unemployment, and racism. However, they also achieved many personal and collective successes, especially in the thriving local communities they built. Today, there are more than two million people of Vietnamese descent living in the United States, and Vietnamese is the seventh most-spoken language in the country.

Ten-year-old Quang Pham was among the first wave of Vietnamese refugees that arrived in the United States in the spring of 1975. Along with his mother and three sisters, Pham settled in the working-class town of Oxnard, CA. Pham's father, a Lt Colonel in the South Vietnamese Air Force, remained behind in Vietnam and survived 17 years in communist "re-education camps" before he finally rejoined his family in 1992. In this excerpt from his 2005 memoir, Pham recalled the challenges of growing up in a new country. Among other things, Pham inherited his father's interest in military aviation – an interest that would eventually lead him to a successful career as a fighter pilot in the US Marines.

It was three years after coming to the United States before I finally felt comfortable speaking and writing English. Reading comprehension would take a little longer. I had achieved a 3.8 grade-point average by the end of my freshman year in high school, receiving A's in college preparatory classes, including Spanish. I guess my Vietnamese didn't meet the college entrance requirement for a foreign language.

My mother worked several jobs during the day while completing her associate degree in accounting at night. I remember hardly seeing her during those years except on the weekends. After she got her degree, she accepted a new position working in the back room of a small bank. My older sister also found a part-time job at the local shopping mall. I worked various part-time jobs, from a clerk at a local state government office typing forms to a janitor cleaning toilets and picking up trash at a local accounting company. With the income we were now all bringing in, my family was able to move to a nicer part of town on the north end of Oxnard.

Finally gone were the days of having to use food stamps and receiving welfare checks. Although grateful for these services, I was embarrassed every time I went to the grocery store clutching food stamps. Even the federally subsidized school-lunch program didn't feel comfortable. I would use the allowance my mother gave me to pay for "discounted" lunches (20 cents), which I hoped would make me appear to other children (paying the full 50 cents) as if I weren't poor. *For Christ's sake, I was the son of Lt. Col. Pham Van Hoa.* I can't describe that feeling of low self-esteem and shame but I was glad public assistance was there: without it our family would not have been able to make it here. My mother worked overtime so our family could jettison that stigma of poverty even though, in reality, we hovered right above the line.

My family made friends with only one other Vietnamese family (although there were several Vietnamese at my schools) during our first several years here. I played with one of the boys, who was a few years younger. We visited each other's house only once a month, and after a while we went our separate ways. Since the nearby navy bases brought Filipino sailors and veterans to the area, we went to school with many of their children, but only to toil in their shadow. The Filipino kids were called "Flips," while we garnered an acronym that pretty much marked us in the minds of the other kids.

"FOB" was short for "fresh off the boat." FOBs often didn't speak proper English (choppy, incomplete sentences lacking action verbs, and with no "s" in plurals); looked as if they were still traumatized (as if many Asians displayed much emotion anyway); and wore mismatched clothes from Goodwill stores or the Salvation Army. Most of all, FOB boys had the same haircut, the supposedly universal Asian "bowl cut." For my sisters, they dreaded the "à la garçon" bob. For me, becoming a Marine would not be the first time I had had a bad haircut.

There were other Asian-American students at my school: several Chinese and *sansei* kids, third-generation children of Japanese-American farmers and ranch owners (the Mexicans picking strawberries and other crops from the formers' fields). I made friends with some although I overheard some of the *sansei* boys refer to us Vietnamese as "those fucking FOBs" on many occasions...

...Another jeer I often heard was, "Go back to Vietnam!" I wanted to yell my comeback, "I can't!" but I never did. Nobody would understand anyway. That's the difference between a refugee and an immigrant...

In my spare time I continued my fascination with the military and aviation. With money from washing neighbors' cars and selling raffle tickets, I bought model airplane kits even though I wasn't very adept at putting the plastic parts together. My planes always ended up with extra glue, visible on their fuselages; their insignia were slightly crooked, and the propellers often didn't spin because parts were broken or somehow lost during assembly. Still, I could rattle off the types of airplanes that were flown in World War II by U.S., British, German, and Japanese pilots.

The only planes I knew my father had flown were the C-130 and C-123 transports. My mother kept a photo of my father's Air Commando training class, taken in the United States in 1966, along with pictures of him in Texas. I also had one headshot of him smiling and wearing a flight helmet with U.S. Air Force inscription. I knew transport pilots didn't wear helmets; I also knew bomber pilots didn't wear helmets because I had seen *Twelve O'Clock High*.

I rode my bike to the annual Point Mugu airshow featuring the Blue Angels, the U.S. Navy's flight demonstration team. I watched in awe their display of aviation precision, those beautiful blue jets soaring so close to each other. Other planes participated in the show, including vintage aircraft and modern fighters reenacting dogfights and strafing runs. Then, one time, a blue-gray aircraft appeared, a sleek, dual rudder, twin-engine fighters, with a short probe on its nose and "MARINES" panted on its fuselage. The plane looked like a space-age aircraft in contrast to the other jets at the show, even the A-4 Skyhawks flown by the Blue Angels. The crowd of mostly aviation enthusiasts were mesmerized, and so was I...

I would occasionally pull out my father's B-25 flight school yearbook from Class 1959-E at Reese Air Force Base in Texas. Along with his photos and records, the book was in one of the bags he gave us the night we left Saigon. My mother stored most of his documents in her bedroom closet but I kept the yearbook. It was the only item I could understand because it was like our high school yearbook. But I couldn't comprehend why my father had been training in the United States or why he was wearing the flight helmet. There were several pages of crumpled VNAF documents with short Vietnamese phrases and abbreviation typed on onion paper. I had no clue what they meant, nor was I interested in asking my mother....

Back then, never once did I think I could do what my father did, achieving pilot's wings in a foreign country. Nor did I ever envision myself as a U.S. pilot even after I had attended the military airshows and seen the war movies and TV shows. FOBs couldn't possibly become fighter pilots, although I was really a FOP or "fresh off the plane." It also didn't occur to me until much later that all the U.S. military pilots I saw were white—at the airshows, in the aviation books, and in films...

In the Fall of 1981, just before my senior year, my mother bought our first home with help from my Uncle An and Aunt Ly. It was a small four-bedroom house on Doris Avenue two miles from the high school. The mortgage took most of her salary, so we basically lived on Thi's part-time wages and my monthly newspaper delivery check of some $400. My mother had incredibly achieved the American Dream of home ownership after just six years, after starting with nothing.

I still remember waking up with my mom every day at 4 a.m. to deliver the Los Angeles Times. Afterward, she would go to work at her bank and I would go to school, often nodding off by the early afternoon....We delivered newspapers to about 200 customers—she'd crisscross the streets in the wee hours, while I sat in the passenger seat throwing the rolled-up papers with my right hand. (The other "paperboys" were grown men in their forties and fifties, holding another job to make ends meet.) For those few months, I spent more time with my mother than I had since we left Vietnam, but I don't remember much of our conversations though since we were hardly awake those mornings.

As the only boy I had my own bedroom, while two of my sisters shared one and my youngest slept with my mother. That special treatment would not go unnoticed by my sisters, especially Thi. My mother had also imposed different standards on us—Thi had to come home by 10 p.m. while I could stay out until 11, which she greatly resented. We occasionally crossed paths at high school parties but she was the one who had to leave first. (She also got grounded when she came home with cigarette smoke on her breath.) Thi added another nickname to my long list, "Mama's Boy"...

On one occasion, I came home with alcohol on my breath after driving back from a party. I could taste it so I figured my mother would be able to easily smell it. That was *the* rule I could not break. I was hoping my mother had gone to sleep so I could sneak in through the garage as I had done before.

My mother stood like a madwoman in the living room when I staggered through the front door. She had been wide awake, her hair all mussed, her eyes already red from crying. Without saying a word she slapped me so hard that I saw stars. I could barely see my sisters in the background and their blurry faces. Nobody had ever struck me that hard, even after all those street fights with the other boys. She hit me again. Tears welled up in my eyes as I became angry. My chest tightened in angry response and my fists were clenched.

My mother must have seen the look on my face and my tensed body. She backed off. I could see my sisters looking down from the stairwell, their faces smiling at "Mama's Boy" crying again. My mother began to weep, covering her face. "If your father was here, you would not get away with this. God, in Vietnam, I would not have to put up with you undisciplined children. You uneducated and disrespectful imbeciles. Please send me back to Vietnam, god." That's when my sisters began to cry as well.

We children had heard her cries many times, but a reference to my father would bring a stop to every argument, his presence felt from

some jungle camp 12,000 miles away. We all quietly retreated to our
bedrooms...

I don't know how my mother ever did it, coming to the United States
by herself and raising four kids. But it also never occurred to me that we
were a single-parent household. Unlike the other kids with single parents
in my neighborhood and in school, my father hadn't left us, we'd left him.
As the years went by, though, my hopes of seeing my father again began to
vanish, leaving room for me to go on with my life. My Vietnamese cultural
knowledge and language were slowly slipping away.

A US Army Nurse Remembers Vietnam (2004)[2]

*Although the vast majority of Americans who served in the American
military in Vietnam were men, several thousand women also served in all
branches of the US armed forces. Almost all of them were volunteers, and
most worked as nurses in field hospitals or other medical facilities. While
nursing was officially considered a noncombat assignment, the women who
worked as nurses frequently found themselves on or near the front lines; they
also witnessed the awful toll that the war took on the bodies and psyches of
both soldiers and civilians. After returning to the United States, many female
veterans struggled to come to terms with their painful memories of the war.
They also encountered the same expressions of criticism and disdain that
were frequently directed against male veterans by some of their fellow
Americans.*

*Diane Carlson Evans was a Minnesota native who worked as a US Army
nurse in Vietnam during 1968–1969. A self-described "country girl" who
grew up on a dairy farm, Evans was stationed first at a hospital in the coastal
city of Vung Tau then volunteered to go to Pleiku in the Central Highlands.
In this oral history, recorded in 2004, Evans recalls her experiences in
Vietnam and the ways in which the service of American women in the war
has often been overlooked or forgotten. She also explains why she helped
organize support for the Vietnam Women's Memorial, a sculpture that
commemorates the service of American women in the war. Thanks in part to
Evans' activism, the Women's Memorial became part of the Vietnam Veterans
Memorial in 1993.*

I graduated in 1967 from Saint Barnabas Hospital and I was in a wonderful place. It was a wonderful school of nursing and we did our academic

[2] Interview with Diane C. Evans, 1 May 2004, Kara Dixon Vuic Collection, The
Vietnam Center and Archive, Texas Tech University, http://www.vietnam.ttu.edu/
virtualarchive/items.php?item=OH0380

work at the University of Minnesota. So I had very good professors and very good teachers... when I decided to go to Vietnam, thank goodness the hospital that I was at was just starting intensive care. Think about it. You think intensive care has been around forever, but it was just beginning in the '60s. So in intensive care, I was caring for really seriously ill patients and they let me start IVs [intravenous drips]. So, I was getting some good experience.

I decided to do my two internships at a VA [Veterans Affairs] hospital and Hennepin County General Hospital, which was the worst hospital in Minneapolis... back then it was where the poor people went because they couldn't afford the other hospitals. So they got the Saturday night specials, which were the murders and wounds and knife stabbings and gunshots. The emergency room was an absolute nightmare, but I wanted to be in that emergency room because by this time I've decided I want to join the Army and I want to go to Vietnam...

In my nurses training, in our building, it was all women. We didn't have any male nurses.... There was one television for forty-five students within the Student Nurse Lounge. I was the only student who went down there at six o'clock every night to watch the Vietnam news. I was glued to it. I wanted to know what was happening in Vietnam. I was hearing about the casualties, and I was seeing the casualties...

I would've remembered if there was an image of a woman, but when I watched the six o'clock news, there were no images of women in Vietnam, not a single image. They didn't show a nurse, a Red Cross woman. I saw images of helicopter pilots. I saw images of body bags out in the field. They were always referred to as men. Men, you know, scrambling around and men in tanks and men running and men with weapons and the horrible images of men wounded, which were very graphic at the time, and no images of women. So it was like, "Well, gee, I wonder if there are any women there, but there must be some nurses there." Of course, the nurse recruiter said there was. I wondered, "Why aren't we seeing the women?"

I didn't tell my parents this, but what I had done was I had a picture taken of me in my uniform so I could give that to them before I left. It was a really nice picture in my dress blues uniform so that if something happened to me, they'd have this last picture of me. So I was already thinking, "I might not come home." I went to a lawyer in town and drew up a will. I mean, now, at twenty-one, what did I have to give away? Not much, but there would be something. I didn't tell my parents that. I took it to the bank and put it in a lock box in my parents box and then I left a note with the bank that if anything happens to me, contact my parents and give them the key to this box...

There was another woman on the airplane with me to Vietnam, so we sat together. We're in these God-awful uniforms that they force us to sit in, you know, with the girdle and the nylons and the pointed toe shoes and the short skirts, 'cause our skirts had to be the knee. They had to be perfectly hemmed, but we didn't get issued the jungle fatigues and combat boots until we got in-country. So we're sitting on a plane for two days feeling really uncomfortable and really out of place in these dressy uniforms when we're going on to Vietnam. But that's—we were just supposed to look military and look pretty and look the part, you know. We were advised, of course, at basic training on good grooming and that kind of thing because we were supposed to look feminine…

I was at Vung Tau for five months and working on a busy surgical ward as a staff nurse. Then I got transferred to the burn unit. The burn unit was really tough because it was the napalm, white phosphorous, any kind of burn. Grenade burns, anything that caused a fire and caused somebody to be burned was on our unit.

Some of these burns were just horrendous. A lot of them were children because the villages had been bombed and they brought the kids in. Working in a burn unit is just painful to see their pain and that you can't do anything for their pain because sometimes, especially for the children, we couldn't really give them much pain medication because it's not absorbed the way it's normally absorbed because of the nature of the burns. A lot of it is tactile because you had to touch the burns. You had to touch the wound because you had to debride it. When you debride it, you're taking off the necrotic dead tissue. So you're actually, you know, with your instruments, taking off dead skin. Every time you do that, they cry out in pain, but it has to be done 'cause you have to get the dead skin away so the new overgrowth, the new skin can come. Then you're smearing sulfamyalon all over that burn and it burns. The sulfamyalon stings. So everything you do to these patients hurts them…

From January of '69 to July of '69, when I was at Pleiku, was sort of like we had our Tet…When we referred to Tet, it was the Tet of '69 [not the Tet Offensive of 1968]. We had times when we would get—there was a time we got in two Chinook helicopters and had eighty-four casualties come in at once. That was the night that my telephone rang…The phone was ringing in the middle of night and I go answer it and the supervisor is saying, "Lieutenant, I want you to go open the spare ward immediately. Mass casualties are coming in."…So I called one of the corpsman and we got it set up and had an IV at every single bed…

We couldn't turn the lights on because if the hospital was lit up, we were a target. So it's pitch black in there and he had a flashlight. So my corpsman held a flashlight while I started these IVs. I could hardly get the IV started because they were so dehydrated, their IVs were gone. But by this time, we were—nurses who started IVs in Vietnam were extremely proficient because we started hundreds and thousands of them. So I'd really gotten good at finding the vein or thinking the vein was there and getting the IV in. So we got all the IVs started.

After I got out of the military and got a job at North Memorial Hospital in Minneapolis on the surgical unit, the order said, "IV," so I went and started the IV. Well, somebody saw that there was an IV started and the extern hadn't started it. I had never heard of an extern. So one of the chief nurses or nursing supervisors comes down the hall and takes me aside and says, "Ms. Carlson, did you start that IV?"

"Well, of course. The doctor's orders said IV."

She said, "I told you when you had your orientation that only externs start the IVs, or interns... You have to be supervised three times before you can start an IV."

I looked at her and you know what? I couldn't even tell her. I could not even tell her that I had started thousands of IVs in Vietnam. It was like, I wanted to almost slap her and say, "You don't know anything. You have not given me any credit for my service. You don't even care that I was in Vietnam." Nobody had even asked me, "Well, what did you do in Vietnam?"...

You know, I think about Vietnam the year I was there...How did we do that? How did we get through that? But we did. We did a good job. When I got out in '69, nobody thanked us. Nobody told us we did a good job. There was hostility. There was humiliating remarks made to us. If we said we were in Vietnam, it's like we set ourselves up for some sarcastic remark about, "What'd you go there for in the first place?"

So I just shut down. Didn't talk about it and I was very unhappy at North Memorial Hospital where I was told I couldn't start IVs. I couldn't do this. I couldn't do that. So I quit after three weeks and went back in the military and was in the military until 1972. I went to Fort Sam Houston, Texas, was surgical head nurse in the intensive care unit there. I was—that saved my life.

I know it saved my life, because I had emotionally shut down. I think I was still in shock. I was so hyper-vigilant I couldn't even take my clothes off at night. I would just sleep in my clothes on top of my bed. Then that way if I heard anything in the middle of the night I could get up and get out of there and wouldn't be naked or in my nightgown. So I slept in my clothes so if I had to run, I could get out the door to be safe....

In 1972, I was pregnant with our first child. So I stayed in the military until the last minute. That was the year women who were pregnant could stay in. Then we had another child and I got out of the service and decided if I was going to have children, I didn't want to be in the military. There wasn't good daycare and that kind of thing. So then I went into my ten-year mode of being a mom and raising the family. Stay-at-home mom except working part-time three days a week at a hospital.

Then there was an incident at the hospital where I had a flashback. It scared me to death and I didn't know what a flashback was. I was not an operating room nurse. I was working in the recovery room. The supervisor came and said I needed to go into the OR. I said, "No, I'm not an OR nurse. I'm an ICU-recovery (intensive care unit) nurse." She said, "Mrs. Evans"—by that time I was married, I had these children—"you have to go. I'm ordering you to go into the OR. This child is having an operation. They thought it was an appendectomy. There's some hemorrhaging. The surgeon needs somebody to count the sponges." I hadn't counted sponges since I was in nurses' training, but she ordered me to go.

So I'm standing in the operating room and the surgeon is throwing sponges at me. I could have counted them. It's not so hard... When the surgeon was throwing sponges at me, all of a sudden I froze because I smelled the blood. I saw the blood, I smelled the blood. All of a sudden I wasn't in the operating room, I was in Vietnam, and I froze. I literally froze. I stood there and I couldn't do anything. The surgeon was screaming bloody murder at me, "Get those sponges counted!" Just screaming at me. All of a sudden I heard this screaming, and I didn't know where I was. Then the circulating nurse came over and I looked at her and I said, "I have to leave. I have to leave." She looked at me like, "What kind of nurse are you?"

You know, I was a good nurse. I was a good nurse. I felt so incompetent. I felt so humiliated. It was terrifying. I just said, "I'm not well. I have to leave. I'm sorry, but you'll have to pull in another nurse now. I am not well." I knew I wasn't well. I did not know what was going on, I thought I was going crazy and that was scary, too. But the scariest thing was that I wasn't—I didn't feel like a competent, practicing, professional nurse. That's the first time that ever happened to me, that I couldn't perform. So the next day, I went to the nursing, the human resources and resigned. I didn't tell [my husband] why I resigned. I didn't tell anybody...

Later when I talked to the vet center counselor, he said, "You know, this was because of Vietnam. This was a flashback. It's post-traumatic stress disorder. You were not incompetent. You were suffering a consequence of your experience in Vietnam." I was so mortified and embarrassed and humiliated by all this, I couldn't tell anybody else...

In 1982, I learned that there was going to be the dedication of a memorial to honor the men serving in Vietnam... I could only remember one patient that I cared for whom I knew. I just prayed his name wouldn't be on The Wall. He was from Minnesota where I was from. I had struck up a conversation with him and I had remembered his name because he was from Minnesota and he was one of my first patients.

So when I got to The Wall, first I told my husband, "I went to Vietnam alone, and I'm going to The Wall alone. I don't want you with me." Which he told me later hurt his feelings, but I had to do this alone. I went to the '68-'69 plates and I looked up and I went, "Oh, my God." The plates from '69 and '68 were the tallest and the longest. Those were the years I was there. First I found Eddie's name. When I touched Eddie's name, I had no idea what was going to happen out there. I was afraid that if I ever started to cry, I would never stop. That's what happened. I touched Eddie's name. I burst into tears, and just sobbed and sobbed and sobbed.

It was like, you know, in Vietnam we never had a funeral. We never had a wake...We were never allowed to grieve over anything. We didn't grieve over their deaths. We didn't grieve over their suffering. We tried to shut down after Vietnam to survive, to get on with our lives. Then we felt all this guilt, this horrendous guilt about, "I could have done more. I should have done more." Or this guilt about, "Why have I forgotten these wonderful people? Why have I forgotten my patients? They were so wonderful and I can't even remember their names." So all this guilt and then not grieving. So I guess for me, going to the memorial in 1982 was a wake and a funeral all at the same time.

My vision is that women served and contributed immensely. They did it with courage and compassion and they were strong. They too suffered and they too need to heal like our brother veterans. They haven't even begun their healing. If a memorial in Washington, DC, can do that for them, plus teach America that women were also there... Approximately three hundred and fifty thousand men and women were wounded in Vietnam. A lot of those came through our hospitals. Some came through just aid stations, of course, and were treated by medics and docs. But we were there for them and [for] thousands of the names on The Wall, we were holding their hand when they left this world. That counted. That makes a difference. That cannot be omitted from history...

To me, the [Vietnam Women's] memorial just makes the Vietnam memorial more complete and whole and make it more powerful... We proved in Vietnam as women proved in Korea and World War II and World War I and the Spanish War and the Civil War, that we're not shrinking violets. I mean, shrinking violets aren't women who work twelve, fourteen hours a day with the wounded, three hundred-sixty-five days a year and don't give up. Not one of us. Did I—it never occurred to me, you know, to go home. "I don't like this anymore. I'll just leave." That ever occurred to me or most of us. That matters.

A Letter Left at the Vietnam Veterans Memorial[3]

In 1980, a nonprofit organization known as the Vietnam Veterans Memorial Fund announced a competition to design a memorial to honor American veterans of the Vietnam War. The US Congress agreed that the memorial could be located on three acres of land near the Lincoln Memorial in Washington DC; however, the construction of the memorial was paid for entirely by private donors, and the selection of the design was left up to the organizers of the Memorial Fund. More than 1,400 plans for the memorial were submitted and evaluated anonymously in the spring of 1981. The winner of the competition was a 21-year-old undergraduate architecture student at Yale University named Maya Lin.

Lin's design – a long, low wall of reflective black granite, etched with the names of all the members of the US armed forces who died in service during the war or who remained unaccounted for – was controversial. Some critics were upset that Lin had avoided the triumphalist tone usually associated with war memorials; one opponent denounced her design as a "black gash of shame." However, since its dedication in 1982, the Vietnam Veterans Memorial has been extraordinarily popular with veterans and the general public alike, attracting millions of visitors each year. By inviting visitors to walk along "The Wall" and touch the engraved names of individuals who died, the memorial provides a profoundly personal space for reflection and remembrance. Many of those who visit leave mementos: flowers, letters, photographs, medals, cigarette lighters, jewelry, and many other objects. All of the nonperishable items left at the memorial are collected and preserved by the US National Park Service.

The letter below was left at the memorial during the mid-1980s. Its author's identity is unknown, but he was apparently a veteran who served in an Army Airborne Unit. He seems to have intended his letter to be an act of both commemoration and communication with his fallen comrades, as well as an important part of a personal healing process.

Airborne

My Dear Friends,

It is good to touch your names, your memory, and to visit with you.

[3] Undated letter reproduced in Laura Palmer, *Shrapnel in the Heart: Letters and Remembrances from the Vietnam Veterans Memorial* (New York: Random House, 1987), 33.

I've struggled in your absence. I've been so angry that you left me. I miss you so much!

I've looked for you for so long. I worked for so long to try to figure out some way to save you. I've been afraid to rest, knowing that I had to find and save you, that to rest, to stop looking for you would make your deaths a certainty.

How angry I was to find you here—though I knew that you would be. I've wished so hard that I could have saved you. I would give my life if somehow it would bring you back.

It is only now on my second trip to the monument that I can admit that you, my friends, are gone forever—that I can say your names, call you my friends and speak of your deaths.

I've cried for you so many times. I've been dead for so long trying to keep you alive. If only I could have gotten there first—if only you had waited. I know I could have saved you.

I've carried the anguish of your deaths for so long, but I think I can stop looking for you now. I think I can start living without letting you die.

I will never forget you! You will always be a part of me—part of you lives in me. I will carry your memory forever and I will make people confront that memory—the memory of what was done to us. If I could, I would lead each person in hand past this monument and make them read each name and imagine each life that was cut short.

I promise you, my friends, I will never let them forget the price you paid.

"Singer"

George W. Bush, Speech at a Veterans of Foreign Wars Convention (2007)[4]

For Americans, one of the enduring legacies of the Vietnam War is the ongoing debate over the historical "lessons" that should be drawn from the conflict. Since the end of the war in 1975, many Americans have invoked the US defeat in Vietnam in arguments against the use of military power overseas. However, other commentators have cited the history and memory of the Vietnam War to argue in favor of American military interventions in foreign countries.

Since 2001, references to the lessons of Vietnam have figured prominently in debates over America's "war on terror" and especially in discussions of the US-led invasions of Afghanistan in 2001 and Iraq in 2003. As the president who launched the war on terror, George W. Bush knew that many Americans

4 *New York Times*, 22 August 2007.

criticized him for failing to apply the lessons of Vietnam in Afghanistan and Iraq. In this 2007 speech to American veterans, delivered as the violence in Iraq was peaking and his approval ratings were sliding toward near-record lows, Bush responded to these critics by drawing his own lessons from the histories of past American wars, including the war in Vietnam.

I stand before you as a wartime President. I wish I didn't have to say that, but an enemy that attacked us on September the 11th, 2001, declared war on the United States of America. And war is what we're engaged in. The struggle has been called a clash of civilizations. In truth, it's a struggle for civilization. We fight for a free way of life against a new barbarism – an ideology whose followers have killed thousands on American soil, and seek to kill again on even a greater scale.

We fight for the possibility that decent men and women across the broader Middle East can realize their destiny – and raise up societies based on freedom and justice and personal dignity. And as long as I'm Commander-in-Chief we will fight to win…

…Now, I know some people doubt the universal appeal of liberty, or worry that the Middle East isn't ready for it. Others believe that America's presence is destabilizing, and that if the United States would just leave a place like Iraq those who kill our troops or target civilians would no longer threaten us. Today I'm going to address these arguments. I'm going to describe why helping the young democracies of the Middle East stand up to violent Islamic extremists is the only realistic path to a safer world for the American people. I'm going to try to provide some historical perspective to show there is a precedent for the hard and necessary work we're doing, and why I have such confidence in the fact we'll be successful…

There are many differences between the wars we fought in the Far East and the war on terror we're fighting today. But one important similarity is at their core they're ideological struggles. The militarists of Japan and the communists in Korea and Vietnam were driven by a merciless vision for the proper ordering of humanity. They killed Americans because we stood in the way of their attempt to force their ideology on others.

Today, the names and places have changed, but the fundamental character of the struggle has not changed. Like our enemies in the past, the terrorists who wage war in Iraq and Afghanistan and other places seek to spread a political vision of their own – a harsh plan for life that crushes freedom, tolerance, and dissent.

Like our enemies in the past, they kill Americans because we stand in their way of imposing this ideology across a vital region of the world.

This enemy is dangerous; this enemy is determined; and this enemy will be defeated.

We're still in the early hours of the current ideological struggle, but we do know how the others ended – and that knowledge helps guide our efforts today...

... A democratic Japan has brought peace and prosperity to its people. Its foreign trade and investment have helped jump-start the economies of others in the region. The alliance between our two nations is the lynchpin for freedom and stability throughout the Pacific. And I want you to listen carefully to this final point: Japan has transformed from America's enemy in the ideological struggle of the 20th century to one of America's strongest allies in the ideological struggle of the 21st century.

Critics also complained when America intervened to save South Korea from communist invasion. Then as now, the critics argued that the war was futile, that we should never have sent our troops in, or they argued that America's intervention was divisive here at home...

Finally, there's Vietnam. This is a complex and painful subject for many Americans. The tragedy of Vietnam is too large to be contained in one speech. So I'm going to limit myself to one argument that has particular significance today. Then as now, people argued the real problem was America's presence and that if we would just withdraw, the killing would end...

In 1972, one antiwar senator put it this way: "What earthly difference does it make to nomadic tribes or uneducated subsistence farmers in Vietnam or Cambodia or Laos, whether they have a military dictator, a royal prince or a socialist commissar in some distant capital that they've never seen and may never heard of?" A columnist for The New York Times wrote in a similar vein in 1975, just as Cambodia and Vietnam were falling to the communists: "It's difficult to imagine," he said, "how their lives could be anything but better with the Americans gone." A headline on that story, dateline Phnom Penh, summed up the argument: "Indochina without Americans: For Most a Better Life."

The world would learn just how costly these misimpressions would be. In Cambodia, the Khmer Rouge began a murderous rule in which hundreds of thousands of Cambodians died by starvation and torture and execution. In Vietnam, former allies of the United States and government workers and intellectuals and businessmen were sent off to prison camps, where tens of thousands perished. Hundreds of thousands more fled the country on rickety boats, many of them going to their graves in the South China Sea.

Three decades later, there is a legitimate debate about how we got into the Vietnam War and how we left. There's no debate in my mind that the veterans from Vietnam deserve the high praise of the United States of

America. Whatever your position is on that debate, one unmistakable legacy of Vietnam is that the price of America's withdrawal was paid by millions of innocent citizens whose agonies would add to our vocabulary new terms like "boat people," "re-education camps," and "killing fields."

There was another price to our withdrawal from Vietnam, and we can hear it in the words of the enemy we face in today's struggle – those who came to our soil and killed thousands of citizens on September the 11th, 2001. In an interview with a Pakistani newspaper after the 9/11 attacks, Osama bin Laden declared that "the American people had risen against their government's war in Vietnam. And they must do the same today."

His number two man, Zawahiri, has also invoked Vietnam. In a letter to al Qaeda's chief of operations in Iraq, Zawahiri pointed to "the aftermath of the collapse of the American power in Vietnam and how they ran and left their agents."... Here at home, some can argue our withdrawal from Vietnam carried no price to American credibility – but the terrorists see it differently.

We must remember the words of the enemy. We must listen to what they say. Bin Laden has declared that "the war [in Iraq] is for you or us to win. If we win it, it means your disgrace and defeat forever." Iraq is one of several fronts in the war on terror – but it's the central front – it's the central front for the enemy that attacked us and wants to attack us again. And it's the central front for the United States and to withdraw without getting the job done would be devastating.

If we were to abandon the Iraqi people, the terrorists would be emboldened, and use their victory to gain new recruits. As we saw on September the 11th, a terrorist safe haven on the other side of the world can bring death and destruction to the streets of our own cities. Unlike in Vietnam, if we withdraw before the job is done, this enemy will follow us home. And that is why, for the security of the United States of America, we must defeat them overseas so we do not face them in the United States of America....

I recognize that history cannot predict the future with absolute certainty. I understand that. But history does remind us that there are lessons applicable to our time. And we can learn something from history. In Asia, we saw freedom triumph over violent ideologies after the sacrifice of tens of thousands of American lives – and that freedom has yielded peace for generations...

...The greatest weapon in the arsenal of democracy is the desire for liberty written into the human heart by our Creator. So long as we remain true to our ideals, we will defeat the extremists in Iraq and Afghanistan. We will help those countries' peoples stand up functioning democracies in the heart of the broader Middle East. And when that hard work is done and the critics of today recede from memory, the cause of freedom will be stronger, a vital region will be brighter, and the American people will be safer.

Thank you, and God bless.

Vo Van Kiet, "Healing the Wound" (2005)[5]

For the people of Vietnam, the decade following the end of the Vietnam War in 1975 was a period of continued upheaval and war. Communist leaders' initial attempts to normalize Vietnam's relations with the United States – a key objective of Hanoi's postwar diplomacy – were derailed by the start of the Third Indochina War, a conflict that pitted Hanoi against the Khmer Rouge government of Cambodia and the communist government of China. In its domestic policies, the Vietnamese Communist Party undertook what turned out to be a disastrous attempt to transform Vietnam into a fully socialized economy based on state ownership of industry and the collectivization of agriculture. Many Vietnamese would later remember the late 1970s and the early 1980s as the "subsidy" era – a time of rationing, scarcity, and hardship.

One of the leaders who helped to reverse the policies of the subsidy period was Vo Van Kiet (1922–2008). Although he was a dedicated communist who had helped lead the fight against the Americans in the south during the war, Kiet became a critic of the economic and social policies adopted by the party after 1975. He has been hailed as an early champion of the "renovation"(đổi mới) movement that began during the mid-1980s; he and like-minded party leaders called for reforms to encourage foreign investment in Vietnam and help integrate the country into the global economy. However, Kiet's agenda involved more than just economic changes. In this remarkably frank 2005 interview, published by a Vietnamese newspaper shortly before the 30th anniversary of the end of the Vietnam War, Kiet reflected on the legacies of war, the party's postwar mistakes, and the prospects for reconciliation among Vietnamese.

Q: Almost 30 years have elapsed since the initial days of our takeover of former Saigon. As a senior leader having served in the resistance war, what are your feelings on the historic event?

KIET: I simply think of what we have to do so that we won't have any more leaders who had to grow up in a war like we did. War ended in Vietnam 30 years ago and we handed over the leadership of the country to the next generation.

[5] Translated from "Những đòi hỏi mới của thời cuộc: Nguyên Thủ tướng Võ Văn Kiệt" ["The new requirements of the present times: Former Prime Minister Vo Van Kiet"], *Tuần Báo Quốc Tế*, 31 March 2005.

It means that I wish for the war to really be a part of the past. It's a past for which we want to have closure.

Q: Having closure is something that is not so easy to achieve, Mr. Kiet?

KIET: Nothing is impossible. Friendliness and clemency are traditional virtues of the Vietnamese people.

Vietnamese people stand up to resist when there is an outside enemy. Thirty years have elapsed since the end of the war. I think that when there is no longer military interference from an outside enemy, all Vietnamese [who were separated into different parties because of the war] can once again stand side by side and join hands in building the country.

And our country will be more developed when all Vietnamese people, regardless of wherever they are, can live in harmony with one another.

Q: Have we made a lot of effort to have closure, sir?

KIET: For this, we should look at the results of what we did, instead of the efforts we have made. Personally, I think we've still got mountains of work to get through.

Q: What do you think are some things we need to do next?

KIET: Our victory 30 years ago was great; however, we've had to pay a high price in pain and loss for our victory. History had placed many families in the southern region in intricate situations where they had, at the same time, relatives on both sides before 1975. This was the situation for my relatives.

Thus, any war-related event can cause millions of people to feel happy, and at the same time, cause millions of others to feel sad when they remember the event.

That is the same painful wound of our people and nation, thus, the wound needs to continue healing instead of seeping more blood.

Q: For the wound to continue to heal, it needs the contributions of all Vietnamese people?

KIET: This is a major task. We now rule the country, and therefore, we should prove ourselves sincerely merciful and work towards harmony in our affairs so that all Vietnamese people can join hands to heal and build the country.

After Liberation Day on April 30th, 1975, our comrade Le Duan – when stepping down the stairs of an aircraft in former Saigon – gave a raised-fist salute saying, "This is a victory of the whole nation, not of any individuals."

Thirty years after that statement, I still feel like it's not easy to make all Vietnamese people comprehend this idea.

Q: Where does the difficulty come from, sir?

KIET: President Ho Chi Minh had a wish to visit friendly countries to thank them for their contributions to help Vietnam during the resistance. After 1975, our senior leaders Le Duan and Pham Van Dong made those visits on behalf of our late president.

Showing appreciation for and thanking others are actions that suit our moral standards and traditions.

But as for home affairs, now is the time to admit the contributions and credit the Vietnamese patriots who lived under the former regime and are now living abroad or in Vietnam.

When other officials and I were assigned to take over Saigon in 1975 – a city which was not devastated after the war – I cannot help but think of the service and roles of members of the former cabinet of President Duong Van Minh as well as other political forces who were opposed to the regime of former President Nguyen Van Thieu and the American invaders.

Q: Former President Duong Van Minh who proclaimed the South's surrender?

KIET: Top-ranking general Duong Van Minh took office on April 28, 1975, which was a date on which a high-level military general like him could already forecast and anticipate the fall of the Saigon regime.

If Mr. Minh had ordered his generals and military forces to defend Saigon at any price, we would have still gained victory, but Saigon would have been much more devastated from the military attacks, and we would have suffered more losses of people in the city.

On the morning of April 30th, 1975, Mai Chi Tho, who was then leader of the city's Party Committee, and I let out sighs of relief when we heard on the radio Mr. Minh calling on his soldiers to lay down their arms and to wait for power to be transferred to the revolutionary forces.

You could have only known and felt the importance of Mr. Minh's decision if you'd been on the battlefield at that moment.

Q: Why do you think former President Minh made such a decision?

KIET: It was impossible to stop our momentum for victory. However, the decision of Mr. Minh was not only based on the fighting situation, but also on his previous political moves.

President Minh was the one who attempted a coup to overthrow the regime of former President Ngo Dinh Diem. And it was Mr. Minh who later refused to obey aggressive American leaders, so he was then toppled by General Nguyen Khanh following the green-light signal from the Americans.

Q: Was there any other force that influenced Mr. Minh's decision?

KIET: The re-appearance of President Duong Van Minh on the political scene in southern Vietnam at the time was really the result of positive contributions from a 'third force.' This is the force which joined in the struggle against Nguyen Van Thieu's regime inside of Saigon.

What I mean is that all Vietnamese patriots joined hands and contributed to the common cause of national liberation in their different ways.

Those Vietnamese patriots have the right to be proud of themselves.

Q: Do you feel pleased with what we have achieved in the past 30 years?

KIET: We are all happy to have national liberation, to see the country united, to have the determination to overcome poverty and we are keen on integrating into the world.

But I feel regret when I take a look back in our history since the end of the war.

We would not have suffered such a difficult period from 1975 to 1985 if we had adopted our renovation policy earlier.

Q: What are the lessons we learned from that period?

KIET: We must go on with further renovation and keep away from complacent attitudes.

In the past, we were successful in achieving good growth in our economy and society.

But, I want note that a growth rate of six or seven per cent for a country with gross domestic product of about 40 billion USD a year is not sufficient to meet the requirements for development and integration.

Q: What should we do in the next stage of our foreign policy?

KIET: To a certain extent, our foreign policy has helped tackle many social and economic difficulties.

After 20 years of innovation, we are ready to be reliable friends and partners of the international community.

In the next few years, how we define and set our role and position in the world to be will be a major and important task, especially in a world that is advancing and changing every day.

Following Sept. 11 in the U.S., upheavals in the Middle East, positive political renovation in ASEAN countries and the tsunami disaster in Southeast Asia—these have all shown that we cannot work alone if we want to succeed. The world is becoming closer.

Vietnam's must excel in its diplomatic tasks going forward. Foreign affairs should help the whole country to overcome challenges, sieze opportunities and meet the requirements of the present time.

Discussion questions

1. Why did so many people in the United States believe in the myth of American prisoners "left behind" in Vietnam after 1973?

2. What do the personal accounts of Quang X. Pham and Diane Evans reveal about changing American attitudes about military service after the end of the Vietnam War? Have these attitudes changed for the better, in your view?

3. What aspects of Vietnam War history does the Vietnam Veterans' Memorial in Washington, DC commemorate? What aspects does it not address? Given the unpopularity of the war in the United States prior to 1975, what accounts for the popularity of the memorial?

4. What lessons did George W. Bush draw from the history of the Vietnam War in his 2007 speech? Do you agree with his conclusions? Explain.

5. Compare Vo Van Kiet's 2005 recollections of the fall of Saigon with the version of events provided by Bui Tin in Chapter 11. What accounts for the differences between these two versions? How does Kiet's account reflect the particular lessons he draws from the history of the war?

Index

The Vietnam War, Edited by Edward Miller. Editorial material and organization.
© 2016 John Wiley & Sons, Ltd. Published 2016 by John Wiley & Sons, Ltd.

pacifism, 175, 177
Paris Conference, 185, 188, 189
  Paris Accords, xxviii
  Paris Agreement, 216, 227
Paris Peace Talks, 205–07, 213
Patti, Archimedes, 11
Peace Corps, 173
peace with honor, xxv, xxvi, xxviii, 213
peasants, classification of, 56–57
Pentagon, 103, 183
Pentagon Papers, 192–95, 196
People's Army of Vietnam (PAVN),
    xxiii, xxv, xxvii, 31, 124–25,
    126–127, 128, 143, 198
  and end of Vietnam war, 221–23
  March 1972 advance, 213
  purges, 58
  Tet Offensive, 152
People's Council for Denunciation of
    Communism, 70
People's Liberation Army (PLA), 23,
    222
Pham Van Dong, 245
Pham Van Hoa, Lt. Col., 229
Pham, Quang X., 228–32, 247
Phan Boi Chau, xviii, 5–6
Phan Huy Quat, 87
Phan Khac Suu, 87
Phan Van Phai, 18–19
Philippine presence in Vietnam, 44
Phoenix (Phung Hoang) program,
    200–04
Plain of Reeds, Mekong Delta, 116,
    119
Poland, 23, 24
Prisoners of War (POWs), 135, 139–41,
    209
  POW/MIA flag, 226–27
  POWs "left behind," 227, 247
President of Vietnam, 46, 49
Presidential Palace, xxviii, 42, 44, 92
Progressive Party, USA, 24
proletariat, 10, 23, 56, 57
psychological warfare, 39, 40, 43, 188

Quang Tri City, 127
Quiet American, The, 29

Raborn, Admiral William, 110, 111
Radford, Admiral Arthur, 32
Radio Saigon, 158
RAND corporation, 193, 194, 195
Rand VC Prisoner and Defector
    Interrogation Study, 193
Red Army (USSR), 23
Red River Delta, 33
refugee problem, 197–99
"renovation" (đổi mới) movement,
    243, 246
Republican Youth (South Vietnam), 70
Resolution Nine (Central Committee
    of the Vietnam Workers' Party),
    97–100, 114
Resolution 14, 171
revolutionary movement, nature of 66
Roosevelt, President Franklin D., 24n
Route 9, 126
Route 20, 205
Rowan, Carl, 101, 110, 112
Rusk, Secretary Dean, 110, 112, 113
Russo, Tony, 193–94, 195
RVN, see Vietnam, Republic of

Saigon Military Mission (SMM), 37,
    38–45
  and Geneva agreement, 43
  history, 39
Saigon, xvii, xxii, xxiii, xxv, xxvi, 20,
    29, 33, 37, 39, 41, 45, 52, 81, 90,
    112, 129, 185, 188, 203
  fall of, xxviii, 162, 221, 222, 243,
    244, 245, 247
  Forward Headquarters for the
    Southern Sector of Saigon, 159
  "revolving door" period, 96
  Tet Offensive, 152, 159–60, 161,
    171
search and destroy, xxiv, 107, 149
Second International, 8